Bosnia

Bosnia

Faking Democracy After Dayton

Second Edition

David Chandler

Pluto Press

LONDON • STERLING, VIRGINIA

First published 1999 by Pluto Press
345 Archway Road, London N6 5AA
and 22883 Quicksilver Drive, Sterling, VA 20166–2012, USA

Second edition 2000

British Library Cataloguing in Publication Data
A catalogue record for this book is available from the British Library

ISBN 0 7453 1690 5 hbk

Library of Congress Cataloging in Publication Data applied for

Produced for Pluto Press by
Chase Production Services, Chadlington, OX7 3LN
Printed in the European Union by TJ International, Padstow

Contents

For my parents, Michael and Eva.

List of Tables

List of Abbreviations

ARRC	Allied Rapid Reaction Corps
BBC	British Broadcasting Corporation
CAP	Citizens Alternative Parliament
CEEC	Central and East European countries
CFR	Coalition for Return
CoM	Council of Ministers
CSCE	Conference on Security and Co-operation in Europe
DPA	Dayton Peace Agreement
EASC	Election Appeals Sub-Commission
EBRD	European Bank for Reconstruction and Development
ECMM	European Community Monitoring Mission
EU	European Union
EUAM	European Union Administration Mostar
FERN	Free Elections Radio Network
FIC	Federation Implementation Council
FRY	Federal Republic of Yugoslavia
GFA	General Framework Agreement for Peace in Bosnia and Herzegovina
HCA	Helsinki Citizens Association
HDZ	Croatian Democratic Union
HRCC	Human Rights Co-ordination Centre
HTV	Hrvatska (Croatian) Television and Radio
ICFY	International Conference on the Former Yugoslavia
ICG	International Crisis Group
ICRC	International Committee of the Red Cross
ICTY	International Criminal Tribunal for the Former Yugoslavia
IEBL	Inter-Entity Boundary Line
IFOR	NATO Implementation Force
IMF	International Monetary Fund
IMSLC	Intermediate Media Standards and Licensing Commission
IOM	International Organisation for Migration
IPTF	UN International Police Task Force
JCC	Joint Civilian Commission

JCCS	Joint Civilian Commission Sarajevo
JIC	Joint Interim Commission
LEC	Local Election Commission
LNGO	Local Non-Governmental Organisation
MBO	Muslim Bosniak Organisation
MEC	Media Experts Commission
MIA	Main Implementation Agencies
MSAG	Media Support and Advisory Group
NATO	North Atlantic Treaty Organisation
NGO	Non-Governmental Organisation
OBN	Open Broadcast Network
ODIHR	OSCE Office for Democratic Institutions and Human Rights
OHR	Office of the UN High Representative
OSCE	Organisation for Security and Co-operation in Europe
PEC	Provisional Election Commission
PIC	Peace Implementation Council
QSP	Quick Start Package
RS	Republika Srpska
SDA	Party of Democratic Action
SDS	Serb Democratic Party
SFOR	NATO Stabilisation Force
SHAPE	Supreme Headquarters Allied Powers Europe
SNS	Serbian People s Alliance
SPD	Serbian Socialist Party
SRS	Serbian Radical Party
SRT	Serb Radio and Television
UBSD	Union of Bosnia and Herzegovina Social Democrats
UN	United Nations
UNESCO	United Nations Educational, Scientific and Cultural Organisation
UNHCR	United Nations High Commissioner for Refugees
UNMiBH	United Nations Mission in Bosnia and Herzegovina
UNPROFOR	United Nations Protection Force
UNTAES	United Nations Transitional Administration for Eastern Slavonia
US	United States
VOPP	Vance-Owen Peace Plan

Acknowledgements

This book would not have been possible without the support of the International Social Policy Research Unit (ISPRU) at Leeds Metropolitan University which provided both funding and research facilities, and I am especially thankful to my colleagues Bob Deacon, Gordon Johnston and Paul Stubbs for their suggestions and advice. Research in Bosnia was facilitated by officers from various institutions of the OSCE, in particular: Adam Bedkowski, Human Rights Co-ordinator for Bosnia-Herzegovina, OSCE Office for Democratic Institutions and Human Rights; Virginia Canil, Director General for Democratisation, OSCE Mission to Bosnia-Herzegovina and Betty Dawson, Press and Public Relations Officer, OSCE Mission to Bosnia-Herzegovina. I would also like to acknowledge the support of friends and associates, who have translated material, trawled cyberspace for information, and made comments and suggestions on draft material, especially journalism researcher William Woodger, with the London International Research Exchange, Adam Burgess, James Heartfield, Bernd-Uwe Herrmann, Matthew Kershaw, Michael Savage and my partner and inspiration Bonnie Chandler.

Introduction

The Dayton Peace Agreement, initialled on 21 November 1995, by the governments of Bosnia, Croatia and rump-Yugoslavia, brought the three-and-a-half-year Bosnian war to an end. The agreement, overseen by the institutions of the international community, at the Wright-Patterson Air Force base in Dayton, Ohio, not only established international control over military forces on the ground but also put into practice a new, post-Cold War, international agenda for long-term peace-building. This agenda has extended the sphere of international involvement in post-conflict situations from keeping warring sides apart to taking the lead in developing long-term political solutions; this new role for international institutions is increasingly described as democratisation .

As the UN Secretary-General has noted, democratisation is predominantly a new area for the UN, nevertheless it is already seen as a key component of peace-building addressing the economic, social, cultural, humanitarian and political roots of conflict (UN, 1996, pars 13 and 14). Democratisation is broadly defined by the UN to constitute a comprehensive approach covering the broad range of new peace-building priorities, top-down international regulation of elections, institutional development and economic management, and also bottom-up assistance to develop a democratic political culture through civil society-building (UN, 1996, par. 124).

Under Dayton, the framework of the Bosnian state was to be highly dependent on international supervision. There was to be a one-year transitional international administration, in place until the first state-level elections in September 1996. After this, the formal powers given to the central state authorities were to be uniquely minimalist , even to the extent of excluding central control over the armed forces, while wide-ranging powers over government institutions were to be given to international organisations and externally appointed individuals for between five and six years. These new powers of international involvement were written into the Bosnian Constitution, and the process of democratisation was to be overseen directly by outside administrators appointed by international bodies such as the United Nations, the Council of Europe, the Organisation of Security and Co-operation in Europe and the International Monetary Fund.

Three years on from Dayton, the one-year transitional administration has been indefinitely extended and the democratisation process in Bosnia has become a major international experiment in political engineering . Executive and legislative power today lies with the UN s High Representative who has the power to directly impose legislation, to veto political candidates and dismiss unco-operative elected members of Bosnian governing bodies. The mandates of the leading international institutions have been regularly extended and the role of international non-governmental organisations has continued to grow apace. As Simon Jenkins notes in *The Times,* Bosnia has become the world capital of interventionism (Jenkins, 1997). Internationally-run elections are held on a regular basis but remain, in these circumstances, little more than glorified opinion polls (UN, 1998). With all this international assistance there is little role for Bosnian people, or their elected representatives, in policy development or implementation. As the *Wall Street Journal* noted, in August 1998:

> In all, there are perhaps 10,000 foreign nation-builders in [the capital city] Sarajevo alone; at least 40,000 others are scattered across Bosnia, including 35,000 soldiers from around the globe. A New Zealander sits as chief of the central bank. An ex-cop from Los Angeles is deputy chief of Bosnia s international police force. Mr Klein, a French-born American, serves as deputy in Sarajevo s Office of the High Representative, or OHR, the closest thing Bosnia has to an executive branch. (King, 1998)

Three years of intensive involvement by the world s most powerful states, including the Contact Group of the US, Britain, France, Germany, Italy and Russia, and leading international institutions, including the International Monetary Fund, World Bank, United Nations, OSCE and NATO, has done little to create viable institutions of self-government in the state. This growing imbalance of power between international institutions and Bosnian representatives raises questions over the extensive external regulation of the state and the lack of local involvement and responsibility in the process of peace-building and conflict resolution. This book addresses these questions and suggests, first, that there are limits beyond which the regulatory intervention of international community bodies and NGOs becomes counterproductive and, second, that these limits have been greatly exceeded due to factors largely external to Bosnia itself.

The contradictory nature of such extensive external regulation, under the guise of democratisation, has been noted by those involved in implementing international policy within Bosnia itself.

It is now becoming apparent to some observers that the trend towards giving greater decision-making powers to international administrators can produce unintended results, undermining Bosnian institutions and creating relations of dependency rather than a basis for stable democratic self-government. A foreign official cited in the *New York Times* stated: It troubles me that the less democratically we act, the more success we have I mean, here we are with 32,000 foreign soldiers demanding that a country do what we want (O Connor, 1998c). The article goes on to question the enduring nature of changes that have been imposed from outside instead of democratically decided. Christian Clages, from the Office of the High Representative s political department, has stated similar concerns: We have an unprecedented amount of control on the legislative and executive branches of government. We do not know, however, how we will exit, how we will not perpetuate Bosnia s culture of dependency (Hedges, 1998). Long-term observers in Sarajevo have raised concerns in the *Wall Street Journal* that: Every day, more foreigners pour in to do every conceivable task, and the more they do, the less the Bosnians do for themselves (King, 1998). Similarly the *Economist* has raised worries that the protectorate seems to know no limits , citing one of the UN High Representative s aides saying that we do not know what we can t do and concluding that Bosnians may forget how to rule themselves (*Economist*, 1998a).

This book seeks, first, to highlight the dubious premises upon which international policies of democratisation are based, and to question the assumption that democracy can be taught or imposed by international bodies on the basis that some cultures are not rational or civil enough to govern themselves. This divisive moral framework of the nineteenth-century White Man s Burden today appears recast in the liberal language of ethical foreign policy, rights protection and civil society . Second, the book seeks to analyse how democratisation policies operate in practice, drawing out the regulatory and disempowering content behind the language of rights protection, multi-ethnic governance, open media and civil society-building. The more rights and freedoms granted to the Bosnian people by their international administrators the less freedom they have to reach negotiated compromises over disputed issues, as every aspect of Bosnian society from media content to housing policy is imposed by external regulators. Third, the book seeks to uncover why, despite its lack of success on the ground, democratisation in Bosnia has been such an attractive focus for international institutions and why the small state has been at the forefront of the international foreign policy agenda for the past three years.

Chapter 1 highlights the core assumptions behind democratisation approaches, exploring the shifting understanding of both the goals and agency of democratisation. Progress in democratisation is no longer measured by free elections and constitutional frameworks, but on the basis of alleged cultural distinctions or ill-defined assessments of civil society . This has led to the increasingly qualified acceptance of liberal democracy in states outside the West. The agency of democratisation is no longer held to be the demos or people, through the growth of political freedoms and liberties, self-government and sovereignty, but the international regulatory bodies which are now overseeing the political process in the new democracies . These changing assumptions are drawn together in the media portrayal of the Bosnian conflict and the demand for international involvement to ensure a democratic political framework in the new state.

In Chapter 2, the Dayton Peace Agreement is analysed along with the mandates of the international institutions involved in the democratisation process. The proposals for international institutional regulation prior to and during the Bosnian conflict are considered as well as developments since Dayton. The relationship between the powers of international appointees and Bosnian state institutions are highlighted to provide a contextual framework in which to situate the specific democratisation strategies, considered in the following four chapters.

Chapter 3 considers the democratisation strategy of institutionalising power-sharing authorities through multi-ethnic administrations. Power-sharing approaches are discussed at state, entity, city and municipal levels, contrasting the success of these policies on paper against their limited impact in breaking down ethnic divisions at the various levels. This strategy raises the question of whether removing majority rule and institutionalising international involvement in complex power-sharing measures has actually empowered minorities or made governing institutions more accountable to them.

International policy to institutionalise respect for human rights is the subject of Chapter 4. The Dayton Agreement imposed the highest levels of human rights protections on the Bosnian authorities. The formalisation of these norms and the impact that this has had on democratic life is looked at through the impact of signing up to international treaties and agreements, the monitoring of human rights by the international community, the prosecution of war criminals and the return of refugees and displaced persons. This chapter questions whether the international regulation of human rights issues has had a positive impact on Bosnian society or contributed to overcoming fears and insecurities.

Chapter 5 analyses international policy to challenge the political domination of mono-ethnic national parties. The central strategy has been to encourage the emergence of alternative political viewpoints through closely regulating the nature of political campaigning and ensuring that the media is open to other perspectives and avoids damaging nationalist rhetoric. The gradual accumulation of powers of intervention in the political and media realms are charted along with their application in successive elections. The analysis considers the contradictions raised for democratic life once international regulation excludes candidates and restricts media discussion to achieve democratic aims.

International strategy for civil society-building is considered in Chapter 6, which studies the development of policy designed to build civil society institutions such as NGOs and citizens groups. The limited success of this policy and the anti-democratic impulse behind promoting unelected civic groups over elected bodies is discussed. The difference in approach between democratisation policies which focus on institutions, the top-down approach, and those which focus on building civil society, the bottom-up approach, is considered and the nature of the relationship between these two apparently contrasting strategies.

In Chapter 7 the assessments of the leading international bodies and the international critics are analysed and, despite the range of perspectives, areas of consensus highlighted, returning to the themes of the democratisation approach set out in Chapter 1. The chapter concludes with a discussion of the contradictions within the international institutional view that the three-year external administration has been successful enough to justify the resources of the leading international bodies but not successful enough even to allow limited self-government, as promised by Dayton, in the foreseeable future.

Chapter 8 develops some of the central themes of the previous chapter to ask whether the extended nature of the democratisation process can be explained by factors external to Bosnia itself. The debate within the US foreign policy-making establishment over the extension of US involvement in Bosnia is used to highlight how concerns over new, post-Cold War, international institutional arrangements have been central to international policy in Bosnia. It seems possible that it is this external dynamic which has resulted in the extension of regulation to new areas of Bosnian political life rather than the success or failure of international practices on the ground.

Chapter 9 concludes the work with a consideration of whether extending the democratisation process has meant denying Bosnian institutions the capacity to play a cohering or aggregating role. This raises the question of whether the removal of sites of power and policy-making from popular accountability has institutionalised the fragmentation of Bosnian society and the relevance of ethnic identification. If so, current policy initiatives may institutionalise insecurities rather than help to overcome them, creating potential problems for international withdrawal. It also considers whether any further extension of international regulation is likely to address this underlying problem and whether the granting of greater political autonomy might allow cross-ethnic political forces to emerge which could consolidate the legitimacy of the new state.

1 Democratisation

This chapter provides an overview of the dominant ideas that have shaped international institutional intervention in Bosnia – the framework of democratisation. It will be argued that, although the language of democratisation appears universal, its content today is a highly ideological one that qualifies liberal democracy in the states of Eastern Europe and justifies the interference of Western institutions in their domestic affairs.

There are two key components of the current approach to democratisation that are interlinked and mutually reinforcing: first, the shifting definition of democracy itself, with less focus on the institutional level of elections and government process and more on the imputed values and culture of a society, and second, the internationalisation of questions of democratic consolidation, where the problems of democratisation are held to necessitate international institutional guidance and support. These two elements form the bulk of this overview, which concludes with the application of this approach to the context of Bosnia.

FROM DEMOCRACY TO DEMOCRATISATION

Until the early 1990s, 'democratisation' was the loose term for describing the process of establishing liberal or constitutional democracies along the lines of Western European or US models. This process has been analysed in the field of political science by commentators such as Samuel Huntington, most notably in *The Third Wave: Democratization in the late Twentieth Century* (1991a; see also O'Donnell et al., 1986 and Diamond et al., 1989). During this period, the 'transition to democracy' or the 'democratisation process' was seen as a global process in successive waves. The first wave occurred from the 1820s to the inter-war revival of authoritarianism in the 1920s, the second wave from 1945 to the early 1960s; the changes that swept Eastern Europe in 1989 are often referred to as part of the 'third wave', from 1974 to 1990 (Huntington, 1991b, p. 12; Schmitter and Karl, 1991, p. 75).

Liberal or constitutional democracy was understood to involve a certain number of institutional mechanisms, central to which was electoral competition, Schumpeter's classic definition of democracy being 'that institutional arrangement for arriving at political decisions in which individuals acquire the power to decide by means of a competitive struggle for the people's vote' (1943, p. 269). Robert Dahl defined seven attributes in his concept of 'polyarchy': elected officials, free and fair elections, inclusive suffrage, the right to run for office, freedom of expression, alternative information and associational autonomy (1989, p. 221). Elections were considered to be the key tests of democratic institutionalisation. If they were carried out when legally scheduled, organised in an inclusive, fair and competitive way, with voters registered and free from coercion, the votes counted fairly, and the winners allowed to take office without their terms being arbitrarily terminated, then the institutionalisation of democracy was considered to be fairly advanced (see, for example, O'Donnell, 1996a, p. 37).

As Lincoln Allison has highlighted, the positive view of the international expansion of democracy, held by the democratisation theorists up to the early 1990s, contrasted sharply with the increasingly negative view of democracy *per se* by the 'normative' democracy theorists, concerned with liberal democracy within the established democracies of the West (1994, p. 8). It is the contention of this chapter that this division has now been superseded through the focus on democratic 'consolidation'. Since the early 1990s, democratisation theorists have highlighted the weakness of the 'third wave' and the problems of consensus-building in liberal democratic systems along similar lines to the normative democracy theorists (see, for example, Huntington, 1991b; Diamond, 1994; Schmitter, 1994; and Fukuyama, 1995).

Today, democratisation involves deeper concerns that relate to the sustainability of democratic institutions rather than their establishment and operation. For this the new concept of 'consolidation' has been deployed: 'For our purposes, "democratisation" is seen as the overall process of regime change from beginning to end, including both stages of what are generally called in the comparative literature "transition" to a liberal democracy and its subsequent "consolidation"' (Pridham and Vanhanen, 1994, p. 2). Gunther and others argue that 'merely creating democratic institutions and holding elections captures only part of the process through which stable, viable democratic systems come into being' (Gunther et al., 1996, p. 155). Karen Dawisha, a leading authority in the field, goes further to argue that, for the purposes of her research project, 'democratisation is said to begin when the first set of free and fair elections for national-level office takes place' (1997, p. 42).

One international sphere where this discourse has been particularly influential has been in international strategy towards the reintegration of the newly independent states of Eastern Europe. Their need for international recognition and financial assistance, and their desire to enter Western institutions, such as the Council of Europe, the United Nations, NATO, and the European Union, established a focus for international community judgements of democratic standards. This focus on democratic standards soon shifted away from the formal political process to the nature of East European society itself. Geoffrey Pridham and Paul Lewis, two leading commentators on democratic transitions, argue that:

> New democracies are by definition 'fragile democracies' ... The political cultures of the countries in question do not necessarily provide a reasonable basis for system support. Initial transition may be an occasion for euphoria, but the overall process is usually the source of considerable disorientation at elite and mass levels ... But even without any immediate or direct threat from anti-democratic forces ... [new democracies may be] vulnerable to collapse or at least involve a lengthy and complicated process of transition. (Pridham and Lewis, 1996, p. 1)

Culture as key

The discussion on the problems of the new democracies normally takes the form of counterposing asserted Western cultural values, embedded in civil society, to merely having democratic institutions. Claus Offe, for example, argues that: 'Copied and transplanted institutions that lack the moral and cultural infrastructure on which the "original" can rely, are likely to yield very different and often counter-intentional results' (cited in Sztompka, 1996, p. 125). Pridham and Lewis stress:

> What happened in 1989 was only the beginning of a long and complicated process. Within little more than a year, it was noted that 'the East Europeans are discovering that there is a large, dangerous chasm between grabbing freedom and establishing democracy; there is no natural progression'. (Pridham and Lewis, 1996, p. 2)

Marcin Krol writes that those who saw the victory of liberal democracy internationally as straightforward were looking at the facade, not the real content:

> many of the world's new democracies are currently situated somewhere between real democracy and sham democracy. There is little doubt that if we restricted ourselves to the survey of institutional forms or democratic facades, we should perceive a still rising wave of democratisation. (1995, p. 37)

Without the cultural preconditions of civil society, the institutions of liberal democracy are seen to be little more than window-dressing. Electoral competition, the traditional focal point of institutional studies of democratic legitimacy, is often held to be less important in assessments of the new democracies:

> Without the mediating institutions of a vibrant civil society, popular influence over politics is going to be limited to election day, and elections in post-communist Europe all too often revolve around feelings and resentments rather than issues. For exactly these reasons, ex-communists came to power in Lithuania, Poland, and Hungary in 1993–94. (Krol, 1995, p. 39)

In fact, as the above quote indicates, elections are often seen in highly negative terms. Krol argues that without regulation 'venomous invective, accusatory rhetoric, *ad hominen* argumentation and the like' can get out of control, and that uncivil political discord can then influence the electorate and produce poor outcomes (1995, p. 39). Tom Gallagher fears that unrestrained political debate could be too much for East Europeans to handle: 'Agreement about the management of political competition is essential if nascent democracies are not to be tested beyond endurance by heavily adversarial parties' (1995, p. 353).

Today, as the capacity of the electorate in the 'new democracies' is openly questioned, it is Tocqueville, not Schumpeter, who serves as an inspiration for theorists of democratisation. His view that citizens needed to be educated in the values of democracy through voluntary associations, which served 'as large free schools, where all the members of the community go to learn the general theory of association', is much quoted (Tocqueville, 1945, vol. 2, p. 124). Bruce Parrott, for example, writes that: 'Without key components of civil society, government structures that are formally democratic cannot be expected to operate in a fashion that is substantively democratic' (1997, p. 24). Piotr Sztompka uses the metaphor that '*building a house* is not the same as *establishing a home*':

> The former is only the shell, the empty framework … it is a concern for architects. The latter is the living arena of social actions and interactions … it is the concern for sociology. The more or less explicit recognition of that distinction between the institutional and the cultural-civilisational spheres is also indicated by other terms, i.e. public sphere versus civil society. (Sztompka, 1996, p. 117)

Larry Diamond similarly stresses the importance of civil society above the conflict-ridden and self-interested sphere of politics.

Groups which are part of civil society are concerned with public interest and do not aim to capture formal political power for the narrow ends of any group, nor do they seek to impose their views on others, therefore they are held to play a central role:

> Civil society can also be a crucial arena for the development of other democratic attributes, such as tolerance, moderation, a willingness to compromise, and a respect for opposing viewpoints. These values become most stable when they emerge through experience, and organisational participation in civil society provides important practice in political advocacy and contestation. (Diamond, 1994, p. 8)

The growing consensus on the importance of the cultural values of civil society to the democratic process has meant that, for increasing numbers of commentators, institutional and legal safeguards are no longer enough. If states do not have the culture and values necessary to safeguard democracy then democratisation necessitates change which reaches down to the heart of society. Parrott notes:

> A civic political culture embodies high levels of interpersonal trust, a readiness to deal with political conflict through compromise rather than coercion or violence, and acceptance of the legitimacy of democratic institutions. It stands to reason that political culture affects whether citizens choose to support moderate or extreme political movements and parties, and whether they choose to engage in democratic or anti-democratic forms of political participation. (Parrott, 1997, pp. 21–2)

David Held writes that institutions alone are not adequate: 'a "will to democracy" and a democratic culture are indispensable supporting conditions' (1995, p. 158). Keitha Fine highlights 'the patent inability of conventional instruments of western politics and legal systems to function effectively' in the East as 'without a history and practice in participatory politics, warring groups have little incentive to negotiate' (1996, p. 560). For Fine, 'ingrained patterns of thought, response, and behaviours' of the former communist society are 'dysfunctional' and counterproductive for modern civil society, constituting deep cultural barriers (1996, p. 566):

> ... people in the so-called new democracies have remarkably few legal, political, and civic skills; they hold deep-seated prejudices and an enormous reservoir of anxiety about the future. They have as yet little willingness to re-conceptualise their prejudices or anxieties in language familiar to Westerners. (Fine, 1996, p. 559)

US Deputy Secretary of State Strobe Talbott agrees that institutional change is not enough and 'must be matched by a corresponding change in public attitudes, or what is sometimes called political culture' (1996, p. 62). Richard Gunther and others similarly argue that consolidation has more to do with attitudes than institutions: 'Consolidation involves a second dimension, relating to the stabilisation, routinisation, institutionalisation, and legitimation of patterns of politically relevant behaviour ... This definition thus includes an attitudinal dimension ... as well as a behavioural criterion' (Gunther et al., 1996, p. 152). Sztompka uses the concept of 'civilisational competence' to describe the alleged lack of 'internalisation of certain cultural codes, rules and values' which are essential for 'meaningful action within institutions' (1996, p. 118). He argues that the problem in Eastern Europe is not with the idea of democracy itself, or even with the institutions of liberal democracy, it is one of cultural mismatch:

> The institutional and cultural levels may fit together and may mutually reinforce each other. In such situations we may speak of a true *consolidation* of institutions and *adequacy* of culture. But both levels may also manifest a lack of fit ... This seems to be the case in post-communist societies where the widespread cultural rules still dictate pervasive suspicion toward authorities, reluctance to get involved in public life, ignorance and neglect of public issues, political apathy, and electoral absenteeism. (Sztompka, 1996, p. 119, original emphasis)

This framework of a cultural democratic divide seems to be encapsulated in Francis Fukuyama's view of four levels of democratisation: first, that of normative beliefs, a belief in the legitimacy of democracy; second, the institutional level; third, the level of civil society, and fourth, the level of culture. It now seems that each higher level depends on the one beneath it:

> Just as democratic institutions rest on a healthy civil society, civil society in turn has precursors and preconditions at the level of culture ... Change on level 3, that of civil society, has been much slower in coming. And here the pace of change clearly depends to a great degree on the characteristics of level 4, that of culture. (Fukuyama, 1995, pp. 8–9)

As Richard Rose pinpoints, the privileging of culture makes no small difference:

> Some theorists argue that a democratic culture is a consequence that follows from the establishment of democratic institutions, while others consider it a prerequisite for achieving a stable democracy. If the latter is the case, it could take genera-

> tions before democracy is secure in a given country, insofar as persons socialised in an authoritarian or totalitarian regime would persist in these ways even after democratic institutions are introduced. (Rose, 1997, p. 97)

Even if East Europeans demonstrated the right institutional procedures and cultural attributes to the satisfaction of the West they would still be under suspicion. Adam Burgess usefully highlights how the discussion of democratic consolidation becomes a tautological one where by definition 'new democracies' cannot be 'consolidated democracies' (1997, p. 191). Commentators are divided over exactly how long the process of consolidating democracy will take. For Fred Halliday, 'no-one can be sure [until] a democratic system is established for at least a generation' (1995, p. 217; 1994, pp. 232–3). Fine also argues that at least a generation is necessary (1996, p. 566). Strobe Talbott considers the time-scale for democratic consolidation to be 'not just years but decades, the passing of a generation or more' (1996, p. 62). Ralph Dahrendorf, in his influential book, *Reflections on the Revolution in Europe*, writes that democracy in Eastern Europe cannot be considered secure until at least two generations, or sixty years, have elapsed (1990, p. 99).

Qualifying democracy

As considered above, new democracies are seen as so fragile that, 'even without any immediate or direct threat', they may be susceptible to collapse. This has allowed the discussion of the regulatory implications of the democratisation approach to expand despite evidence of the formal workings of the democratic system. This approach to the problems of democracy in the 1990s is very different to that of earlier democratisation processes, for example, the transition from authoritarian rule in Southern Europe in the 1970s. The conditionality requirements for Eastern European membership of the Council of Europe and other institutions are far more exacting than they were for the new democracies of Greece, Spain and Portugal (Storey, 1995, p. 142; see also Bates, 1998; M. Walker, 1998b).

In Eastern Europe the establishment of democratic institutions and the holding of free and fair elections has been generally unproblematic, notable only by its exception. In terms of formal democracy, survey after survey shows Central and Eastern European states as meeting international norms. This is illustrated well by the ten-country survey carried out jointly by the European Commission and the Council of Europe (Kaldor and Vejvoda, 1997, p. 65). In fact, the stability of the democratic process both in countries which are relatively ethnically homogeneous, such as the Czech Republic, Hungary, Poland and Slovenia, as well as in countries with large ethnic minorities, such as Romania, Bulgaria and Macedonia, has been the norm for the region. The successful establishment of liberal democratic institutions, along Western lines, has been achieved despite severe economic and social dislocation since 1989. The fact that no significant anti-system party or social movement has emerged, would in a different period probably have been greeted as demonstrating the strength of the democratic framework.

A key theme of democratisation commentators today is that the traditional methods of political categorisation are no longer adequate. Of particular concern is the need to downplay the traditional connection between elections and democracy and to develop an alternative broader framework that stresses the importance of the cohering values of civil society. Parrott notes that 'a competitively elected government is capable of behaving in a despotic fashion toward large numbers of its citizens or inhabitants' (1997, p. 4). Schmitter and Karl argue that the belief that free and fair electoral competition is a sufficient condition for democracy is a fallacy:

> However central to democracy, elections occur intermittently and only allow citizens to choose between the highly aggregated alternatives offered by political parties ... During the intervals between elections, citizens can seek to influence public policy through a wide variety of other intermediaries; interest associations, social movements, locality groupings, clientelistic arrangements, and so forth. Modern democracy, in other words, offers a variety of competitive processes and channels for the expression of interests and values – associational as well as partisan, functional as well as territorial, collective as well as individual. All are integral to its practice. (Schmitter and Karl, 1991, p. 78)

There is a new East/West divide, not between states with liberal democracy and those without, but between the leading 'mature' Western democracies and those states whose liberal democracies remain qualified. This divide is not predicated on the question of formal democracy, but on inevitably subjective judgements about democratic consolidation and political culture. Richard Rose, for example, notes that, according to Freedom House's ratings, states in Eastern Europe, such as the Czech Republic, Hungary, Poland, Estonia, Lithuania and Slovenia, are credited with being as democratic as France or Spain, yet he stresses that they 'are not stable democracies ... nor can they be considered as perfect democracies' (1997, pp. 94–5). As leading commentators have stated:

> While it is generally argued that the institutional, formal prerequisites for democracy have been broadly fulfilled in the ten Central and Eastern European countries under consideration, it is more difficult to assess in such a clear manner the level of consolidation of democratic behaviour, or of the fledgling democratic political culture, that has been obtained. (Kaldor and Vejvoda, 1997, p. 60)

While there is universal agreement on the basic elements of formal democracy – regular elections, equality under the rule of law, freedom of association, etc. – there is no real consensus on the best indicators of democratisation, or how to measure them. Kaldor and Vejvoda list factors such as the media, political parties and civil society as indicative of substantive democracy. But the more these themes are explored, the less certainty there seems to be. Either political shortcomings appear little different to those in the West, such as the general lack of popular participation in the political sphere, or interpreting specific actions within a universal framework appears problematic; for example, is a high poll turnout a good sign or proof of a prevailing Stalinist mentality?

In relation to the political sphere itself, especially with regard to political parties and campaigns, it is difficult to raise questions about the lack of grass-roots involvement of the electorate in political party organisation, the lack of programmatic substance, or even the hierarchical organisation of political parties, without noting the universal nature of these problems, East and West. In which case, the distinction between East Europe's 'pre-democratic crisis' and Western Europe's 'post-democratic crisis' appears somewhat artificial (Kaldor and Vejvoda, 1997, p. 81).

Similarly, studies of the media reveal mixed messages. State control or influence over dominant sections of the media is not unusual in Western Europe, and giant media corporations mean that media pluralism is often restricted. Mostly media experts cite a lack of free time for opposition parties as a major problem, but media specialists, from the Dusseldorf-based European Institute for the Media and the Open Media Research Institute in Prague, write with regard to the Trans-Caucasus region, that the state media provided too much free time to parties and candidates, which 'may have saturated the audience and induced fatigue, rather than contribute to viewers' enlightenment' (Lange and Fuller, 1996, p. 9). Instead, they call for less free time and more editorialising on issues, as the state-run media has a responsibility to be more informative.

The growth of civil society is also difficult to measure and difficult to categorise. The measurement of public attitudes has produced little agreement among scholars on interpretation of the data, as well as results which show that there are broad similarities in political culture in Eastern and Western Europe (Miller et al., 1998). Some research indicates that Russia is equal to the United States in democratic values, because the minority rejecting some democratic values is similar in both countries; other research shows the public in some Eastern states to have higher levels of acceptance for rights for ethnic minorities, normally seen as a key indicator (Rose, 1997, p. 98; Parrott, 1997, pp. 23–4). If political participation is used instead of attitudes, there is still little agreement. One measurement generally used is the number of NGOs active in the society, but the fact that Slovakia, normally portrayed as one of the least democratic countries in the region, has one of the largest NGO sectors has begun to raise questions about this approach (Kaldor and Vejvoda, 1997, p. 77).

The variety of measures for democratisation and democratic consolidation, and the flexible and selective use of the data, has meant that states under international assessment can always be seen as lacking 'democratic maturity'. As Kaldor and Vejvoda note, the increasing qualification of democracy by leading international institutions means an ever-extending framework of hoops for the new democracies to jump through to prove themselves:

> In substantive terms, a process of democratisation is … not a linear process, and it is not possible to measure progress or specify overall benchmarks of success … Thus Slovakia is often contrasted with the Czech Republic as being relatively backward in democratic terms; yet although it is undoubtedly true that Slovakia has one of the worst records among CEECs in terms of treatment of minorities … Slovakia has an extremely lively civil society and unusually active public participation in debates. The Czech Republic, on the other hand … [has a] human rights policy … [which is] rather weak. (Kaldor and Vejvoda, 1997, p. 80)

Once there are no 'overall benchmarks', any facet of life, from leadership style to street protests, can become an indicator of a lack of democratic consolidation (for example, Rose, 1997, p. 95; see also Schedler, 1998, p. 102). On the basis of selected policy areas, which are seen to fail the test of 'mature' democracy, the division between the democratising states of the West and those which need to be democratised in the East is accentuated and the areas of government policy making open to international regulation are extended.

As work on democratisation expands, it seems that liberal democracy is in need of ever more qualifiers. Research published in 1995, by David Collier and Steven Livitsky, indicated the use of more than one hundred different qualifiers that had been attached to the term 'democracy', mostly used to indicate the lack of one full attribute of democracy or another (cited in O'Donnell, 1996a, p. 47). Taking into account the new vogue for adding adjectives to adjectives such as 'consolidated', one could guarantee that number would be much higher today. Gunther and others, for example, argue that 'full consolidation' would be 'the unachievable end point of our ideal-type continuum, where all individuals in a society join in the democratic consensus'. This is in fact what is called for by Geoffrey Pridham's conception of 'positive consolidation' (Gunther et al., 1996, p. 153). As O'Donnell notes, the dynamic of the discourse is no longer to define democracies positively, but only negatively; through this process more and more characteristics and attributes can be held up to demonstrate a lack of democracy and the necessity for some form of regulation (1996b, p. 164).

Although liberal democracy is increasingly problematised, as Carole Pateman notes, no one talks about post-democracy (1996, p. 5). For the theorists of democratisation, the problem is never democracy itself. Democracy is upheld as a universal aspiration at the same time as being held to be increasingly difficult to obtain outside the developed and mature democracies of the West. This contradiction is played out in the international sphere, through the contrast between the states which can assist others to democratise and those which are held to be incapable of democratically governing themselves:

> ... there is a paradox; on the one hand, a global language of democracy is being created, and claims about human or universal rights are encouraged by international declarations of rights by non-governmental bodies ... On the other hand, the idea of universal rights is under theoretical attack by the proponents of the local, the particular, and social and cultural differences. (Pateman, 1996, p. 10)

In unravelling this paradox, the ideological assumptions which inform the approach of democratisation become clearer. This paradox is the subject of the following section.

DEMOCRATISATION AND SOVEREIGNTY

Writers analysing international relations since 1989 have increasingly seen the key problem of the global order as the disjuncture between the political level, dominated by nation states, and other levels, such as culture, communications, economics or the environment which are enmeshed in global interconnections. There is a call for intervention on the international level to deal with problems beyond the apparently narrowing scope of the nation state. Fred Halliday, for example, calls for a new 'firm insistence on universal standards and rights' (1995, p. 220). David Held argues that as the influences that affect people's lives are global there cannot be real democracy and accountability without new forms of global governance (1995). As the United Nations' *Report of the Commission on Global Governance* explains, global governance is about strengthening existing international institutions, not just in terms of a broader remit, to deal with the host of new problems unleashed by the process of globalisation, but also strengthening them morally, through putting to the fore a new global civic ethic and the promotion of democracy and social inclusion (Commission on Global Governance, 1995, p. xvi).

The nation state and narrow national interest should not be allowed to take precedence over the more pressing 'people-centred' concerns of the global community. This call for putting democracy and rights back on the international agenda has been warmly greeted, not only by many commentators, disillusioned with the way abuses of power were condoned during the Cold War, but also by the major international institutions, which have pledged to act under this international pressure. The end of the Cold War, in 1989, ushered in an era of transition in international relations. The international institutions, developed to contain conflict after the Second World War, such as the United Nations, NATO and CSCE, now needed to find new ways of legitimating their cohesive international roles (Park and Rees, 1998). The language of global ethics and democratisation has provided a new set of 'mission statements' that are particularly suited to the needs of the new era (Chandler, 1997).

It is clear that we have witnessed a major transformation in the language and themes of international relations. The international policy agenda today is dominated by issues such as the consolidation of democracy and the protection of rights, particularly those of women, children and minorities. These issues are ones that to a large extent would previously have been classed as the internal domestic concerns of states. The sovereignty of the nation state *vis-à-vis* the United Nations and other international institutions is under constant pressure. As the *Report of the Commission on Global Governance* urges: 'The principles of sovereignty and non-intervention must be adapted in ways that recognise the need to balance the rights of states with the rights of people, and the interests of nations with the interests of the global neighbourhood' (Commission on Global Governance, 1995, p. 337). This is given official support in international documents such as the 'Final Declaration' of the Third Strasbourg

Conference on Parliamentary Democracy, in 1992, which states: 'Human rights are no longer the exclusive province of states. The infringement of human rights entails an actual international duty of intervention' (Council of Europe, 1992). The UN World Conference on Human Rights in Vienna, in 1993, confirmed the competence of UN bodies to subject human rights violations in all countries to scrutiny and to critical study (Boyle, 1995, p. 85).

The global rights thesis, despite its universal thematic, in fact has presaged a new language of division, that of democratisation. The global democratic values now being espoused as the crucial organising principles of the new era are, of course, not held by all. Held gives his proposals thus:

> In the first instance, cosmopolitan democratic law could be promulgated and defended by those democratic states and civil societies that are able to muster the necessary political judgement and to learn how political practices and institutions must change ... an association of democratic nations which might draw in others over time ... (Held, 1995, p. 232)

If only democratic states are to be allowed into the institutions of the new world order, this poses the question of how this can be judged and what the 'democratic minimum' should be. For commentators such as Marcin Krol, this means that those who judge 'must be the West, however frightened or unprepared it may be to do so at this time' (1995, p. 42). Writers like Halliday and Shaw put the case for the division of the international order according to democratic status even more bluntly. Halliday, questioning Fukuyama's assumption of the victory of liberal democracy, writes that only about two dozen states can be trusted when it comes to democratic values (1994, p. 233). Shaw states that the global responsibilities that come with global society necessitate:

> ... a new unity of purpose among Western peoples and governments, since only the West has the economic, political and military resources and the democratic and multinational institutions and culture necessary to undertake it. The West has a historic responsibility to take on this global leadership ... (Shaw, 1994, pp. 180–1)

Since 1989, the international institutions which have a relation to Eastern Europe, for example, the UN, the EU, the OSCE, the Council of Europe and the European Bank for Reconstruction and Development, have all developed policy proposals to encourage democracy, 'good governance' and the protection of international democratic rights in the region. The major landmarks in this process have been the 1989 Vienna Concluding Document of the Human Dimension of the Conference on

Security and Co-operation in Europe (CSCE, now the OSCE); the OSCE Copenhagen Conference Document in 1992, which outlined the most comprehensive list of government structures and processes ever adopted by an international organisation; the 1992 United Nations resolution *Declaration on the Rights of Persons Belonging to National or Ethnic, Religious and Linguistic Minorities*; the Declaration of the Helsinki Conference of the CSCE, the same year, which made rights protection and the domestic political framework of member states 'matters of legitimate international concern [which] consequently do not constitute exclusively an internal affair of the respective state' (OSCE ODIHR, 1995, p. 15); and, in 1995, the Council of Europe's adoption of the *Framework Convention for the Protection of National Minorities*.

All these proposals have been undertaken within the framework of 'mature' Western democracies regulating the 'new' democracies of Eastern Europe. The division, central to this regulation, can be seen clearly in relation to policy development around ethnic minorities. The regulative powers of the international institutions, such as the OSCE, are interpreted so that 'national minority' specifically excludes American 'indigenous peoples' and the Turkish, Arab and Asian minorities in Germany, France and Britain. Even more controversial has been the exclusion of the Irish, Basque and Kurdish questions, affecting Britain, Spain and Turkey, from the remit of the OSCE High Commissioner on National Minorities (Heraclides, 1992, p. 16; 1993, pp. 102–4). This has meant that the new standard-setting regulations not only operated in a selective manner, but also minimised problems in the West while exaggerating them in the East (Chandler, 1997; 1998a).

The standard-setting dynamic of the OSCE around minority rights often meant that new regulative powers bore little relationship to the problems and needs of the region. This mismatch meant that OSCE policy development '[ran] the risk of appearing trivial or far-fetched, and as if locked in an absurd exercise ... of trying to constantly raise the standards so as to proclaim more and more states as wrongdoers' (Heraclides, 1993, p. 138).

Initially, policy moved forward fastest in relation to minority rights but, with the potential for European Union membership, broader requirements were flagged-up as democratisation became increasingly central to the discussion on the membership requirements and role of European institutions. The Council of Europe summit in Strasbourg, in October 1997, billed as 'a summit to consolidate democracy', demonstrated the new international dynamic as the institution set out to develop new social codes for member-state policy; the President of the Assembly, Leni Fischer, stated: 'The Council of Europe seems to me to be best placed to elaborate a European social model, in defence of social rights and social cohesion' (M. Walker, 1997).

The OSCE as an organisation symbolises the belief that democracy and the regulative protection of rights are intimately linked to broader security issues, and has used this to push forward new mechanisms of rights regulation in the region. The OSCE made a rapid transition from the Cold War to the new rights-based era due to the flexibility of its informal framework before 1990 and to the fact that it had already begun to prioritise rights issues in the 1980s (Chandler, 1998a). The process of externally regulated democratisation can, with hindsight, be seen to have originated with minority rights and then to have expanded over only a few years to cover broader concerns around the political process and the creation of civil society. This has been reflected in the rapid expansion and strengthening of the role of the OSCE Office for Democratic Institutions and Human Rights (ODIHR). When it was originally established in 1990, as the Office for Free Elections, this arm of the OSCE was restricted to election issues; since then its remit has constantly been extended. In 1992 the institution was renamed ODIHR and its remit expanded to cover the structural conditions necessary for the implementation of rights and national and international programmes of institution building and democratisation (Kritz, 1993, pp. 21–2). These powers were extended at the OSCE Rome Council Meeting, in December 1993, and at the 1994 Budapest Summit. This shift away from a focus on the elections themselves has necessitated much greater powers of intervention in the domestic political sphere of East European states. ODIHR's director, Audrey Glover, explained this increasing role:

> With the advent of second-generation democratic elections, newly emerging democracies have more sophisticated needs in elections assistance and observation ... election day observation alone has a limited impact. It was a feature of the first wave of fresh democratic elections, but now the international community's desire to assist newly-emerging democracies is best served in assuring fair and adequate conditions for political parties/candidates to compete in elections. This includes the important issues of access to media, free speech in an electoral context, and how parties/campaigns are financed. Finally the ODIHR will provide CSCE States with advisory services on how to improve election laws and practices. (Guerra, 1996, p. 14)

Democratisation has followed the pattern of expanded forms of international regulation seen with minority rights issues and so too has the amount of institutional resources devoted to it. Most

Western states have democratisation aid programmes: the Canadian government sponsors the International Centre for Human Rights and Democratic Development; the United States funds the National Endowment for Democracy; Germany's political party foundations support *Stiftungen* for democratic development; the Dutch, Danish, Swedish, Norwegian and Finish official aid agencies all sponsor democracy programmes; Britain established the Westminster Foundation for Democracy in 1992; and the European Union funds the PHARE and TACIS democracy programmes for projects in Eastern Europe and the former Soviet Union (Carothers, 1997b, p. 110). The rise of non-governmental institutions in the field of international democracy assistance has been equally rapid over the last ten years, and in particular from the mid–1990s onwards. This shift in resource allocation is highlighted by the fact that democratisation was set to account for US $1.6 billion in 1998, 8 per cent of the US Foreign Affairs budget, up from 0 per cent in 1985 before the end of the Cold War (Talbott, 1997, p. 76).

Ethnic division and the continuum of risk

Emphasis on the instability created by states lacking the 'democratic culture' of the West and thereby prone to the problems of nationalism and ethnic rivalry has thrown into sharp relief the new positive aspect of the international community, the fact that traditional inter-state rivalry is apparently no longer a threat to peace. The focus of concern seems to have shifted from the highly militarised major world powers to the dangers of fragmentation in the states that are more peripheral. The UN Commission on Global Governance sees that '[although] war between states is not extinct, in the years ahead the world is likely to be troubled primarily by eruptions of violence within countries' (Commission on Global Governance, 1995, p. 81). Martin Shaw agrees that although there may be rivalry between Western powers no one seriously believes this could lead to war, whereas 'regional and, even more, civil conflicts now have greater potential for war' (1994, pp. 59–60). A central supposition of the post-Cold War era for Konrad Huber, an adviser to the OSCE High Commissioner on National Minorities, is that one of the greatest threats to security 'is posed not so much by disputes between countries as by conflicts involving – or appearing to involve – national minority issues within a country' (1993, p. 30). Fred Halliday's explanation is that today the major world powers are no longer 'in the grip of nationalism' and uninterested in military action against each other, whereas the 'torrent of nationalism' that does exist 'takes a communal, inter-ethnic, as distinct from strategic form' (1995, p. 211). Paul Hirst and

Grahame Thompson argue that conflict between the major powers is impossible because of the nuclear threat, which has meant that 'lesser states' are the remaining threat to world peace, particularly as they are more likely to engage in 'the politics of losers', inward-looking nationalism and cultural fundamentalism (1996, pp. 178–80).

It seems that while, in the advanced states of the West, there is no danger of petty national interests leading to conflicts, in other parts of the world, states are yet to reach this level of development. The internal political arrangements of states are now classed as a key concern for international stability. The Council of Europe, downplaying conflict caused by previous attempts of external powers to promote minority protection, particularly in the inter-war period, argues that 'upheavals of European history have shown that the protection of national minorities is essential to stability, democratic security and peace in this continent' (Council of Europe, 1995, p. 2). Similarly, Vernon Bogdanor writes that:

> ... the need to transcend nationalism is the fundamental challenge facing the emergent democracies of Central and Eastern Europe. Upon their success in achieving this, in overcoming the 20th century, the democratic stability of the region and perhaps also the peace of the Continent depend. (Bogdanor, 1995, p. 97)

In a remarkable, but fairly unquestioned, shift in approach to international security, it seems that the test of a state's commitment to a peaceful world is no longer how large its nuclear or conventional arsenal is, nor its record of military intervention or subvention, but its policy on minorities and whether its civil society satisfies the standards set by international bodies. Halliday, for example, asserts that 'the precondition for world peace is the consolidation of democracy on a world scale' (1995, p. 211).

In the international relations field, US and British policy advisers have been keen to talk up the new potential threats from democratic transition in the former Soviet bloc. Samuel Huntington and William Pfaff provide two differing approaches in the influential *Foreign Affairs* journal. Huntington reproduces the East/West divide as a cultural one, leading to inevitable conflict: 'The Velvet Curtain of culture has replaced the Iron Curtain of ideology as the most significant dividing line in Europe ... it is not only a line of difference; it is also at times a line of bloody conflict' (1993, p. 31). For Pfaff, the East European 'ethnic definition of citizenship' is the problem. NATO must be permanently on guard because 'the idea of the ethnic nation is a permanent provocation to war.' His assumptions lead him to conclude that, for example, 'Hungarians cannot be allowed to rest until they are reunited with the Hungarians of Hungary proper.' NATO has to act because 'it is the true Great Power in Europe today', and he urges 'a more activist and interventionist Western policy in defence of national minority rights in Eastern Europe and the Balkans' (1993, pp. 97–109).

In Britain, James Mayall, a leading international relations academic and policy adviser, shares American concerns about the fragility of democracy in the region:

> Wherever powerful and unassimilated national communities must coexist within a single polity, they are likely to use the institutions of democracy to gain preferential access to state power ... at the expense of their ethnic rivals. The competition to establish their respective national rights is likely to prove sufficiently ferocious to ensure that any commitment to uphold the merely human rights of all citizens will remain theoretical. (Mayall, 1991, pp. 423–4)

Since 1989 the future of Eastern Europe has often been posed in stark terms with the question of ethnicity as central. For example, the late Ernest Gellner, a leading authority on nationalism, saw the challenge facing Eastern Europe as that of two competing ideologies. Either 'civil society' would win out or the region would fall victim to 'the powerful ethnic passions' (1994, p. 126). His prognosis for the region was a negative one; while civil society could not easily be created, ethnic nationalism could be easily ignited: 'The sleeping beauty of ethnicity can, alas, often be awakened with the gentlest and most tender of kisses. She now sleeps ever so lightly' (1994, pp. 126–7).

The problematising of the nature of ethnic identity has been a key factor in facilitating a new international regime of regulation in the region. Highlighting the issue of identity has led to the questioning of the legitimacy of liberal democracy in the region. Rights theorists argue that in an ethnically divided regime, democracy must mean 'so much more than one man – one vote' (Mullerson, 1993, p. 811). Once division in society is seen to present special problems in Eastern Europe because of a lack of consensus, the focus of debate easily shifts to the broader theme of civil society itself and the alleged 'democratic deficit' of regimes which have recently escaped the grip of one-party rule.

The key factor legitimising the security fears is the idea that Eastern European states can not be trusted because they are 'susceptible' to democracy being undermined by 'ethnic politics'. Tom Gallagher writes that Western civil society is necessary, otherwise Eastern states are merely 'adapting the outward forms of north Atlantic democracies' (1995, p. 340). The fears about

Eastern Europe have far outweighed any rational analysis; for Keitha Fine, for example, overpopulation is the threat to democracy: 'East Central Europe as a whole, not just the Balkans, is a crowded region of the world overpopulated by people of many languages, religions, and cultures crammed into small, territorially artificial nation-states' (1996, p. 556).

The worst is always assumed. The level of risk is high, 'they' are susceptible to vote in madmen or to engage in genocide. It follows that conflict prevention and early warning are the solution. In today's risk-conscious world there is potentially no end to the possible problems. This means that even without obvious problems the risk is always there. For example, Mark Beissinger writes:

> The belief that post-communist states should represent the aspirations of the ethnic groups which gave them their names – even if their elites claim that these states are seeking to incorporate other groups living on their territories, and even if elites openly define these states as 'civic' rather than 'ethnic' polities – is fundamental to ethnic majorities throughout the region. (Beissinger, 1996, p. 134)

The OSCE Commissioner on National Minorities, Max van der Stoel, illustrates the way concerns about the region are generalised and therefore more threatening, despite the lack of proven relationship between perceived risk and reality. Asked in 1994, what, for him, the hottest issues were, he replied: 'it's hard to say what the real powder-keg issues are. I also think that their gravity can change from month to month' (Stoel, 1994, p. 36). This consensus that there can be a crisis anywhere is demonstrated in many treatments of the region – Laurence Rees, producer of the influential BBC series *The Nazis: a Warning from History*, writes:

> ... the underlying philosophy of Nazism – one of hate-filled nationalism – is not dead. It could arise again anywhere in Eastern Europe in an instant ... One cannot be sanguine about the countries of the former communist bloc. For if democracy does not bring the economic benefits that they expect, then it is possible that one day they will decide to vote democracy away and put their faith in violent nationalism. (Rees, 1997)

J. F. Brown's *Hopes And Shadows: Eastern Europe After Communism* provides another typical example, after listing potential minority problems in every country, he justifies such an extensive catalogue, on the following grounds:

> The list is not intended to be a Doomsday roster or a jeremiad, but rather a guide to conflict situations and tension spots, a list

> of bills that history is now presenting for settlement, if not full payment. No attempt is made to calibrate the seriousness of the different issues or their potential for conflict because, as events since 1991 have shown, conflict can flare up in the less likely of cases and places, while the apparently more likely ones remain smouldering. Better, therefore, to be on the *qui vive* for all of them and ready for the distinct possibility of new ones appearing. (Brown, 1994, p. 178)

This assumption, that no apparent problems can equally mean a smouldering conflict, puts inter-ethnic co-operation and conflict on the same continuum. Through this extension of the potential for conflict, and thereby the necessity of international regulation, nearly every domestic political relationship is opened up to international institutions. A typical example is Joan Kroc's work on ethnic conflict in Macedonia. She notes that Macedonians and Albanians have co-existed in separate communities without violent conflict, in fact, that relations are shaped by 'deeply steeped social patterns of conflict avoidance'; however: 'The behavioural pattern is to suppress, rather than openly confront conflict, which also presents its own risks ... The danger of conflict avoidance behaviour arises when the parties fail to use the opportunities that stalemates provide to engage third parties' (1996, p. 286).

For democratisers such as Kroc, the fact that Macedonians and Albanians have developed societal mechanisms to minimise conflict and avoid the escalation of tensions is not good enough. The belief in the inability of East European, and particularly Balkan, actors to manage their own 'conflict resolution' autonomously does not depend on the current situation on the ground, but the assumption that cultural incapacity means that there is always 'the risk that social tensions will end up at a higher level of conflict intensity' (1996, p. 286).

These assumptions legitimate a policing role for the international community in Eastern Europe and reinforce the 'democratic divide' between the East and the West. Mayall, writing for the Royal Institute of International Affairs, argues for a 'new transnational regime in which national minorities would have some measure of confidence that their interests and rights would be protected' (1994, p. 12). The proposed transnational regime he suggests would be led by the OSCE and the Council of Europe, through which, he urges a 'strengthened international capacity for rapid and politically robust intervention to prevent the massive abuse of human rights' (Mayall, 1994, pp. 12–13). Bogdan Denitch similarly argues:

> ... new and greatly strengthened international institutions, including a much stronger UN, are now desperately needed.

> The institutions have to be international because it is entirely possible, as free elections in many post-Communist states ... have shown, for a majority to democratically elect a xenophobic nationalist or fundamentalist majority. The result of such elections can be ... a massive attack on the rights of women ... internal and external conflicts and wars. This is not only an obscure regional problem; it can easily overflow its regional boundaries with terrorism, kidnapping, international arms trade, and other allied phenomena. (Denitch, 1996, p. 129)

CONCLUSION: DEMOCRATISATION AND THE BOSNIAN WAR

The new linkage between international security and democratisation has helped make the domestic political framework of East European regimes a central preoccupation for Western institutions. Once the global values of civil society, democracy and rights have been established as not just the best way of organising society but also an essential prerequisite for peace and stability it has then fallen to Western institutions to ensure other states comply. The major international bodies set up in the aftermath of the Second World War pride themselves on having learnt the lessons of the past when nationalism and state rivalries brought the world to the brink of destruction. The underlying assumption is that, while states in the West have spent the last 50 years distancing themselves from the experience of fascism, communism and war, states in the East have yet to come to terms with the past and reject extremist and 'fundamentalist' ideologies. In which case, the task of ensuring democratisation can only be entrusted to external bodies:

> The establishment of a cosmopolitan model of democracy is a way of seeking to strengthen democracy 'within' communities and civil associations by elaborating and reinforcing democracy from 'outside' through a network of regional and international agencies and assemblies that cut across spatially delimited locales. (Held, 1995, p. 237)

Democratisation has become a central theme of international relations today, with President Clinton proclaiming the promotion of democracy as 'the successor to a doctrine of containment' (Carothers, 1997a, p. 86). As US Deputy Secretary of State Strobe Talbott has stated: 'In an increasingly interdependent world, Americans have a growing interest in how other countries govern, or misgovern, themselves' (1996, p. 48). American leadership in the international promotion of democracy is, for Talbott, 'rooted in idealpolitik as well as realpolitik' as democracy promotion abroad is vital for US national interests of security as well as upholding the values 'the United States is uniquely and self-consciously founded on' (1996, p. 49).

The paradox of the prioritisation of universal democratic values but also the increased importance of cultural and regional differences, raised at the end of the first section of this chapter, can now be seen to be at the heart of the democratisation approach itself. The universal values of democracy and rights have today been asserted as the new priorities of international relations, important to defend both for self-interested reasons of global security and as good and noble causes in themselves. The approach of 'new ethical foreign policy', espoused in London, Washington and Bonn, is, according to Rein Mullerson, 'politics which is cross-fertilised with morality' (1997, p. 180).

However, the precondition of this projection of power on the international stage is the acceptance of the democratic divide between those states with the culture and social development necessary to make the 'morally right' choices and those, still caught up in the problems of economic and social development or lacking the culture of civil society, who cannot be trusted to manage their own political framework in the correct manner. As traditional democratic freedoms are supplanted by ethical and moral codes of behaviour, the universal content of liberal democracy, the presumption of individual and collective autonomy, has been replaced by regulation taking a universal form of judgements by international authorities which claim the mantle of mature democracy and civil society. Democracy has become a moral as opposed to a political category and democratisation now concerns societal values and attitudes rather than political processes.

The democratisation approach held up a vision of the conflict in Bosnia as above all a conflict of two value systems, the values of civil society and the values of ethnic division. Bosnia was the warning that civil war and social collapse were the inevitable result of unfettered liberal democratic freedoms in Eastern Europe without either Western cultural values or constraining international regulation. Nearly all analysts stressed the problem of democracy and lack of limits to autonomy as the crucial factor and the need for international action of one kind or another (see for example, Thompson, 1992; Malcolm, 1994; Cohen, 1995; Rieff, 1995; Sammary, 1995; Woodward, 1995; Barratt Brown, 1996; Denitch, 1996; Glenny, 1996; ICoB, 1996; Silber and Little, 1996).

The political fragmentation of Bosnia and the slide into war was often seen by commentators as the result of the failure of regulative and cultural frameworks that could have kept the democratic process on track. Susan Woodward titles a central chapter, in her authoritative *Balkan Tragedy*, 'Interrupted Democratization: The Path To War' (1995). The four-volume Cambridge University series *Authoritarianism and Democratization in Postcommunist Societies*, similarly titles its chapter on Bosnia 'Bosnia Herzegovina: a case of failed democratization' (Burg, 1997). David Potter et al.'s *Democratization* sees the lack of civic nationalism as the key to the failed transition to democracy in Yugoslavia (Ferdinand, 1997).

The republic elections held in Bosnia, in November 1990 – the only free elections in Bosnia before the imposition of the Dayton Peace Agreement – have been seen, nearly universally, as demonstrating the failure of democracy. The reason for this was the success of the nationalist parties at the expense of the cross-Yugoslav liberal-reform and reform-communist parties. Two hundred and two out of 240 seats in the republic's two-chamber legislature, or 84 per cent, were won by the three leading ethnic party organisations. Eighty-seven seats (33.8 per cent) went to the (Muslim) Party of Democratic Action (SDA), 71 seats (29.6 per cent) to the Serbian Democratic Party (SDS), and 44 seats (18.3 per cent) to the Croatian Democratic Union (HDZ). The liberal reform alliance, led by Federation Prime Minister Markovic, won 13 seats (5.4 per cent) and the reformed communists 18 seats (less than 8 per cent) (Cohen, 1995, p. 146).

Prior to the elections, Bosnia had been recognised internationally as a model of multicultural co-existence and symbolic of federal Yugoslavia's progressive minority policies. Public opinion polls in May and June 1990 and in November 1991 had shown overwhelming majorities (in the range of 70–90 per cent) against separation from Yugoslavia and an ethnically divided republic (Woodward, 1995, p. 228), and only six months before the elections, 74 per cent of the population had been in favour of a ban on nationally- or confessionally-based parties, later overturned by the Bosnian constitutional court (Bougarel, 1996, p. 99).

The democratisation approach holds that the Bosnian people were manipulated by the nationalist elites into voting for them, through the use of nationalist demagoguery. Mark Thompson illustrates the view that rational, modern values were alien to the voters of Bosnia: 'Bosnia [is] full of uneducated people who don't know what politics is, what they can do, what's right and what's wrong. Only the nationalist parties and the communists exist for these people' (Thompson, 1992, p. 102). The power of nationalism as an irrational force is central to this argument as the politicisation of ethnicity in Bosnia could not be purely a matter of elite manipulation; if this was the case, the question would have to be posed as to why the other elites with considerable social influence, such as the reform-communist and liberal politicians, failed to achieve the success they expected at the elections (Cohen, 1995, p. 146; Woodward, 1995, p. 125).

The 1990 elections took place as the Yugoslav state was fragmenting and the key political question was that of constitutional reform and a looser confederal arrangement. Without the security provided by the counterbalancing mechanisms of the federal state, questions of security became closely tied up with those of ethnic or nationalist orientation. In Bosnia, the reform of the constitutional framework put to question the guarantees of security and equal treatment for the three ethnic groups. Bosnian Croats were most in favour of a looser confederation: the smallest of the three ethnic groups, they felt their interests would be more secure through closer links with Croatia and Slovenia. The Bosnian Muslims were more divided over the question of constitutional change, while the Bosnian Serbs feared that any separation of Bosnia from the federal system would place them in a worse position (Cohen, 1995, p. 143). Bougarel's analysis captures the 'prisoner's dilemma' facing the Bosnian people and the ease with which ethnicity became a central political issue (1996, p. 99).

From the perspective of the democratisation approach, the vote for nationalist parties counted merely as evidence of the inability of the Bosnian electorate to accept democracy and the necessary values of civil society. Bougarel stands out, as an exception, in explaining the vote for nationalist parties as a rational response to the uncertainties of Bosnia's constitutional situation (see also Offe, 1996, Chapter 4). However, once the democratisation dichotomy, between the values of modern, rational, civil society and those of backward, irrational, ethnic division, had been established in relation to Bosnia the democratisation approach followed an inevitable logic.

If the population were not capable of voting rationally, then the elected representatives lacked a legitimate mandate. Because the nationalist elites had exploited the cultural incapacities of the electorate, they were seen to be unrepresentative of the electorate's real interests. Once convinced of the unrepresentative nature of the elected political leaders, the popular support they were able to wield during the protracted period of the dissolution of the Yugoslav state and the war and negotiations over Bosnia could only be put down to manipulation. For Woodward, fragmentation and war were essentially a continuation of electoral competition, as political leaders used their access to state resources to secure their hold on power and marginalise the opposition:

> In Bosnia-Herzegovina ... These leaders, to retain their position as representatives of their nation, not just in electoral terms but in terms of territorial rights to self-determination, had to go beyond holding a monopoly over an ethnic constituency within Bosnia-Herzegovina to destroying the constitutional alternative for an independent Bosnia – the idea of a civic state where ethnic difference was not politically defining and citizens were loyal to ethnic tolerance and multicultural civilisation. (Woodward, 1995, p. 233)

The Bosnian war was therefore seen as the direct result of the mismatch between Bosnian ethnic culture and liberal democracy, the electorate electing the wrong leaders who then used their control of the state institutions to create 'collective paranoia' (Woodward, 1995, p. 228). These elites, unrepresentative of Bosnian opinion, are then held to have fought amongst themselves for narrow political and self-interested reasons.

It was because the Bosnian war was portrayed as a struggle between civil society and ethnic division that it acquired an international importance well beyond the consequences on the ground. This was the test of the newly proclaimed international order based upon moral and ethical foreign policy. As David Rieff explains, he and other journalists were not driven by suffering alone – there were other wars being fought in different corners of the globe – but none had the urgency of Bosnia:

> ... I and many other foreign writers, photographers, and television journalists kept choosing ... to spend time on the Bosnian side. We did not just think that what was going on was a tragedy – all wars are tragic – but that the values that the Republic of Bosnia-Herzegovina exemplified were worth preserving. Those ideals, of a society committed to multiculturalism (in the real and earned rather than the American and prescriptive sense of that much overused term) and tolerance, and of an understanding of national identity as deriving from shared citizenship rather than ethnic identity, were the ones which we in the West so assiduously proclaim ... we in the rich world had not only a moral obligation to defend Bosnian independence but a compelling interest in doing so as well. (Rieff, 1995, p. 11)

Portrayed as an irrational ethnic struggle, the political motivation of actors in the region and the interrelationship between external factors, such as the fragmentation of the Yugoslav state and international intervention, and the Bosnian factions was often ignored (Chandler, 2000). Moral condemnation replaced rational explanation as leading experts wrote that all sides, although mainly the Serbs, committed 'unspeakable cruelty' and that 'ethnic cleansing' was the 'organising principle of state and society' in a direct challenge to 'the fundamental values of the pluralist democracies on both sides of the Atlantic' (ICoB, 1996, p. 2). The war was seen to have its roots purely in Bosnian society, in which 'claims and counter-claims are transmitted down the generations like a congenital deformity' (Thompson, 1992, p. 11).

Not only were the causes of the conflict located at the level of Bosnian culture, this culture was also held to prevent the parties from being able to resolve the conflict through rational negotiation and compromise. The elected leaders, described as products of the ethnic Balkan culture, were held to be incapable of bringing about a peaceful solution, as David Owen notes:

> ... leaders who had had no experience of democracy also displayed a callousness of mind in which the people's view never seemed to come anywhere near the conference table ... History points to a tradition in the Balkans of a readiness to solve disputes by the taking up of arms ... It points to a culture of violence ... [and] dark and virulent nationalism. (Owen, 1996, p. 3)

The irrational nature of Bosnian elected representatives and their incapacity to resolve political differences was highlighted by many authors as necessitating international intervention. Paul Szasz, for example, stated: 'the warring parties are unable to construct ... agreements amongst themselves' (1995a, p. 258). In similar language, Ivan Vejvoda writes:

> The warring parties were unable to sort it out themselves. In the end, they had to seek intermediaries to lead them out of the chaos they had, with varying degrees of responsibility, plunged themselves into. This plea for intervention was, in fact, very much in line with the nineteenth and twentieth century history of these territories. (Vejvoda, 1996, p. 258)

The war was held to have demonstrated the problems of unrestrained democratic autonomy in a society where often both the electorate and its leaders were alleged to be without civilised values or morality. Nearly all commentators agreed that the people of Bosnia would be unable to make democracy work without the international community regulating society. Denitch argued: 'The sad but important point is this: the meddling Western "outsiders" ... are *far better* representatives of the genuine interests of the Croatian, Serbian, and Bosnian peoples and states than their patriotic leaders' (1996, p. 210). Elsewhere he stressed:

> Out of that stalemate a new approach to international peacekeeping will have to be developed ... less rigidly restricted by

> respect for local sovereignty, especially when it comes to local political leaders, elected or not, who subject their peoples to endless war and misery. That may be a significant step forward for a world organisation previously paralysed by great power rivalries and an excessive respect for formal sovereignty. The peoples of the new post-Yugoslav states now have the dubious privilege of being pioneers of one more noble experiment. (Denitch, 1996, p. 60)

This is the 'noble experiment' that forms the subject of the following chapters.

2 Dayton and Sovereignty

The Dayton Peace Agreement reflected the new post-Cold War interventionist approach of international institutions, encapsulated in the United Nations' Agendas on Peace, Development and Democratisation, which since 1992 have stressed the importance of post-conflict peace-building and the necessity for the long-term involvement of international organisations in political institution-building and governance (UN, 1992; 1994; 1995a; 1996; see also Chandler, 1999a). In the case of Bosnia, however, this international involvement was to be built into the Dayton Agreement and non-negotiable.

This unique relationship between a nominally independent sovereign state and the international community initially raised few concerns amongst Western commentators. Paul Szasz, closely involved in the constitutional proposals as the former legal adviser to the International Conference on the Former Yugoslavia, puts the 'unique, or at least unusual' constitutional arrangements down to several factors specific to the Bosnian crisis: the nature of the conflict in terms of the centrality of human rights violations; the inability of the parties to construct agreements among themselves, and the 'artificial circumstances' of the Dayton negotiations, involving neighbouring states, different ethnic factions within Bosnia and the major international powers with a 'deep interest in and commitment to the peace process' (1996, pp. 314–15). Julie Mertus, visiting fellow in the Harvard Law School Human Rights Programme, stressed the most positive aspect of Dayton was that: 'neutrals play a key role in the new government, particularly with respect to decision making bodies considering questions of human rights and related issues' (forthcoming, p. 20).

For some legal commentators, Dayton represented a more global trend towards the diminution of traditionally accepted forms of state sovereignty:

> These arrangements ... may have a more general significance. Nation states, which once asserted an exclusivity of their internal administrative apparatus and a virtually unconditional requirement that their governors also be their citizens, may be undergoing radical transformation ... We may be entering a

> time in which the geographic nation state no longer has the exclusivity of governing power that it once claimed. With that change, constitutions may become increasingly complex. (Morrison, 1996, p. 157)

While some commentators may have read the situation in Bosnia as an example of globalised relations in the post-nation state world, this diminution of autonomy was not a new development for Bosnia itself. Xavier Bougarel's study of communitarianism in Bosnia notes that 'if there is one word that is not appropriate to Bosnia and its history, it is "democracy"' (1996, p. 87). Bosnia has never experienced stable liberal democracy. The land that makes up today's Bosnia was under the domination of the Ottoman Empire (1463–1878), the Austro-Hungarian Empire (1878–1918), then monarchical rule under the First Yugoslavia (1918–1941) followed by integration into the quisling Croatian state during the Second World War, then Yugoslav communism until free elections in 1990 and the fragmentation of Yugoslavia, followed by internationally recognised independence in 1992, war, and the imposition of an external international administration.

Of course, as Susan Woodward notes: 'having a history of overlords is not the same as needing one' (1998). Nevertheless, the international community, leading the democratisation process, would appear to be in little doubt that a transitional international trusteeship is essential to establish democracy in this small state. After three years of Dayton implementation, the transfer of decision making from international to Bosnian institutions had shifted from being a short-term prospect to a long-term objective dependent on the international administration meeting a wide range of vaguely defined policy goals. As Robert Gelbard, US Special Representative for Dayton implementation, noted in May 1998, in the medium term, policy-making is to follow an agenda effectively set by the Peace Implementation Council and NATO (USDoS, 1998d).

Relatively few commentators have questioned the diminution of sovereignty involved in the Dayton settlement or raised questions about the difficulties involved in imposing democracy from outside. Kimberley Stanton makes the point that international intervention beyond humanitarian assistance is unlikely to aid democratic development because of the difficulty of externally imposing institutions which are capable of being sustainable at the local level:

> International intervention that sets aside the principle of sovereignty is unlikely to foster democratic political arrangements … the very nature of democratic governance casts doubt on the likelihood that international actors can construct sustainable

> democratic institutions ... what is critical for purposes of building democracy is the process by which people learn to be 'democrats'. (Stanton, 1993, p. 15)

The UN Secretary-General's *Agenda for Democratisation* itself suggests that it would be a mistake to impose a model of democratisation:

> Indeed to do so could be counter-productive to the process of democratisation which, in order to take root and to flourish, must derive from society itself. Each society must be able to choose the form, pace and character of its democratisation process. Imposition of foreign models not only contravenes the [UN] Charter principle of non-intervention in internal affairs, it may also generate resentment among both the Government and the public, which may in turn feed internal forces inimical to democratisation and democracy. (UN, 1996, par. 10)

The Dayton process is an experiment in supporting democratisation through externally imposed strategies. This is a unique experiment which the UN, currently bound by its Charter to respect state sovereignty, has no mandate to pursue itself. Dayton has relied on the *ad hoc* and informal grouping of states which formed the International Conference on Former Yugoslavia (ICFY) now renamed the Peace Implementation Council (PIC). As US Secretary of State Madeleine Albright stated in March 1998: 'to a great extent the Dayton Accords and the peace process they built were made in America' (USDoS, 1998c). It has been US President Clinton, the Department of Defense and the Joint Chiefs of Staff who have in practice established the framework of international engagement in the Bosnian state, and the benchmarks or goals which would need to be met for the international administration to end (ICG, 1998a; USDoS, 1998a; USDoS, 1998c).

Despite the unique aspects of the Bosnian situation, in particular the fact that democratisation assistance is being imposed under international law by external powers, there is no suggestion that democracy in Bosnia should be measured or assisted any differently. Under Dayton, and broader international policy-making, there is no conception of Bosnian exceptionalism or special treatment. The objectives set by the international community are couched in universal terms. In fact, the international community, acting through the Peace Implementation Council, upholds Dayton as safeguarding the highest international level of democratic and human rights.

Although the Dayton settlement contained requirements which went beyond democratisation, such as the military balance of the region, there has been no suggestion that the broader requirements of regional stability conflict with the aims of democratisation. Democratisation is upheld as necessary, although not sufficient, for the successful implementation of Dayton, and as central to the civilian implementation of the Agreement. Under the Dayton Agreement, Bosnian citizens were to be granted the highest levels of political rights and the organisation of the political and administrative sphere was to take place according to the requirements for membership of the Council of Europe and the European Union. The objectives of democratisation in Bosnia were those of democratisation processes more generally, to establish a consolidated liberal democracy.

Because the democratisation process in Bosnia is being imposed under an external administration, it has facilitated the most extensive development of external democratisation strategies and therefore provides a testing ground for external intervention from which lessons can be learned. This study, focusing on democratisation strategy and the democratic process, does not encompass the totality of international institutional involvement in the Bosnian state. Two important mechanisms for stabilising the new state are not dealt with separately: these are the traditional peacekeeping elements of the military provisions of Dayton and the external economic assistance to free-market transition through the World Bank, IMF and EBRD. Although both these military and economic strategies have been important in shaping the Bosnian environment, they are not as pertinent to the democratisation discussion as policies specifically targeted at the political sphere. The policies being experimented with in Bosnia, which are considered in the following chapters – the institutionalisation of minority representation, the protection of human rights, the promotion of political pluralism, and civil society construction – are all either extensions of established mechanisms of democratisation assistance or under consideration for broader application internationally.

The aim of this internationally-led democratisation experiment has not diminished with the increasing powers awarded to the international institutions over the three years since Dayton. In fact, increased regulation has been expressly justified through its capacity to speed the process of democratisation and enable a measure of international disengagement. The stated objective of the democratisation process remains Bosnian self-government, the consolidation of democracy whereby the institutions of the Bosnian state have democratic legitimacy, and policy-making is accountable to the Bosnian people through the mechanism of electoral competition. The aim, described by the Office of the High Representative, in December 1997, was:

> … gradual disengagement as improving circumstances allow. The faster the progress, the sooner we will be able to leave matters in the hands of the people of Bosnia and those they elect, in free and fair elections, to lead and represent them. (OHRS, 1997a, par. 17)

As an overview, this chapter seeks to highlight the extensive network of powers established by the international community and establish the overall context within which the democratisation strategies, to be considered in the following four chapters, have been applied. The material is arranged in two sections: first, the contextualisation of the Dayton Agreement within the process of growing international institutional involvement in the new state, considering briefly the precursors to the Dayton Agreement, the agreement itself, and the gradual extension of international mandates after its signing; and, second, a consideration of the policy-making and implementing powers of the international community and the diminution of sovereignty at the level of Bosnian state institutions.

DAYTON IN CONTEXT

The Dayton Agreement was initially celebrated as marking a major step forward in the development of Bosnian sovereignty, creating the opportunity for Bosnians to establish a democratically accountable state after years of war and division. US Secretary of State Warren Christopher noted in September 1996: 'For four years, their fate was debated by outsiders and overshadowed by the war. Now the Bosnian people will have their own democratic say. This is a worthy goal in and of itself, because the only peace that can last in Bosnia is the peace that the people of the country freely choose' (USDoS, 1996b).

However, as Susan Woodward notes, Dayton and its implementation has done little to alter Bosnia's historic lack of autonomy (1998). The promise of democratic accountability is no nearer today than at the beginning of the externally imposed democratisation process in 1991. In fact, Dayton can be seen as one stage in a developing process of international institutional involvement in the Bosnian state. The following sections briefly trace this process to consider Dayton in the broader historical context of the erosion of Bosnian sovereignty.

The background to Dayton

In this section pre-Dayton developments will be briefly sketched. There is neither the space nor the necessity to give an in-depth historical analysis of the war, successive attempts at international mediation or policy shifts within and between the UN and NATO peace-keepers; many other works provide a thorough historical background to the Dayton Peace Agreement from a military and diplomatic perspective (for example, Cohen, 1995; Dyker and Vejvoda, 1996; Glenny, 1996; Owen, 1996; Silber and Little, 1996; Woodward, 1995). The developments highlighted below as the precursors to Dayton do not consider the role of international institutions as peace-keepers or aid providers but focus narrowly on the relatively new sphere of international democratisation and peace-building mandates (see further, UN, 1996, pars 5 & 13; and Chandler, 1998b; 1999a).

The call for 'neutrals' to play a key role in decision-making has been central to international policy in the region during the protracted process of the dissolution of former-Yugoslavia (Chandler, 2000). In this respect, Dayton merely formalised a process that had its roots in earlier initiatives which attempted to mediate between the Bosnian parties since independence first appeared to be a possibility in 1991.

In September 1991, the Committee of Ministers of the European Community convened a Peace Conference on Yugoslavia. The original task of this conference was to keep Yugoslavia together as a loose federation composing one state. Following extensive shuttle diplomacy, the chair, Lord Carrington, presented a text titled *Treaty Provisions for the Convention*. Even at this relatively early stage in international intervention into Yugoslav affairs, the Carrington proposals entailed a major role for international institutions in regulating areas of 'special status'. Areas within republics, where people not belonging to the dominant national or ethnic group formed a majority, were to be granted the special status of autonomy, having their own educational, legislative and administrative bodies. These areas were to be demilitarised and subject to international monitoring by a permanent international body which was to be established in the process of the negotiations (Szasz, 1995a, pp. 261–2).

The first international attempt to devise a constitutional settlement for an independent Bosnia was the European Community Lisbon Conference talks which culminated, on 18 March 1992, in a *Statement of Principles for New Constitutional Arrangements for Bosnia and Herzegovina*. This was motivated by the concern that 'there was great danger that once that goal [independence] was reached the ethnic differences in the new country would promptly tear it apart' (Szasz, 1995a, p. 240). In order to enforce the constitutional measures, a Mixed Commission for Human Rights was to be established under the control of the European

Community which was to appoint four representatives including the chair (Szasz, 1995a, p. 267).

The failure of the Lisbon conference led to the establishment of a joint European Community and United Nations London International Conference on the Former Yugoslavia (ICFY). In October 1992, the co-chairmen, David Owen and Cyrus Vance, presented a relatively detailed *Proposed Constitutional Structure for Bosnia and Herzegovina* ('Precursor to VOPP'). This gave the international community decisive influence over the Bosnian settlement. Section I, headed 'overall structure' stated that: 'The Constitution is to provide that on a transitional basis certain of the constitutional bodies be manned by persons appointed by the International Conference on the Former Yugoslavia and certain functions be internationally supervised' (Szasz, 1995a, p. 269).

These internationally supervised functions were to include management of the ethnic balance and integration of the military forces, the composition of the police, an International Commission of Human Rights, ombudsmen and a Human Rights Court (Szasz, 1995a, pp. 265–76). The Constitution was to be difficult to amend with special protections for the human and group rights provisions and the provisions for transitional international supervision (Section IIIA). The human and group rights provisions were laid out in both substantive and procedural detail. Substantively, they were to be 'the highest level of internationally recognised rights' as set out in the United Nations, Council of Europe and Conference on Security and Co-operation in Europe (CSCE) instruments which were to be incorporated into the Constitution and be immediately enforceable by the courts (Section VA). The international procedural arrangements to enforce these rights included:

(1) An International Commission on Human Rights with wide powers to investigate and hear complaints, obliged to report to UN, Council of Europe and CSCE bodies, including, if appropriate, the UN Security Council. This was to be established by the ICFY for a suggested limited period of five years but subject to prolongation by the ICFY or other appropriate international body.
(2) Four ombudsmen, appointed initially by the ICFY, to investigate human rights abuses and to intervene in courts to protect rights.
(3) A Human Rights Court with one national judge from each group, appointed by the Presidency, and at least five foreign judges appointed by the Presidents of the European Court of Human Rights and the European Commission of Human Rights.

(4) The incorporation of international human rights treaties into the Bosnian constitution with their provisions immediately applicable and enforceable by the courts. (Szasz, 1995a, pp. 272–6)

The Vance-Owen Peace Plan (VOPP), proposed in January 1993, extended the international mandates further with the creation of an Interim Human Rights Commissioner to head an International Human Rights Monitoring Mission. The Commissioner was to be allowed to intercede with the interim Presidency and the Central and Provincial governments (Szasz, 1995a, p. 278). The Owen-Stoltenburg (*Invincible*) Plan, which followed in September 1993, again expanded the regulatory powers of the international community, specifying that the Council of Europe would appoint the majority of members of the Human Rights Court which had competency over any constitutional or legal provisions (Szasz, 1995a, p. 284).

The unique powers given to neutral international arbiters have often been explained as responses to the intractable nature of the Bosnian conflict (Szasz, 1995a, p. 258; 1996, p. 301). However, restrictions on sovereignty were already being proposed before Bosnian independence was recognised in April 1992 and before hostilities had broken out. For example, the March 1992 Lisbon Agreement contained human rights clauses, such as the establishment of a Mixed Commission for Human Rights, which gave foreign appointees powers of adjudication at the highest level (Szasz, 1995a, p. 267). As Szasz notes elsewhere:

> ... all the diverse proposals that the international community has made, starting even before the conflict was ignited, have heavily emphasised the need to include in any new governmental arrangements unusually powerful substantive and procedural provisions for the protection of human rights in general, and those of minorities in particular. (Szasz, 1995b, p. 397)

This continuity between Dayton and the initial international mediation and eventual international recognition of an independent Bosnian republic, in 1992, was reflected in the fact that the Dayton Agreement did not formally establish a new state, as the first article of the Constitution states:

> The Republic of Bosnia and Herzegovina, the official name of which shall henceforth be 'Bosnia and Herzegovina', shall continue its legal existence under international law as a state, with its internal structure modified as provided herein and with its present internationally recognised borders. It shall remain a Member State of the United Nations ... (GFA, 1995, Annex 4)

The trend for every international conference on Bosnia to expand the remit of international institutions is one which clearly predated Dayton itself. The extension of international mandates over the Bosnian state was accepted by the three leading Bosnian parties without opposition, Szasz noting the provisions were 'not considered controversial by any of the parties and at most minor adjustments have been demanded' (1995b, pp. 397–8; see also Szasz, 1995a, p. 237). The ease with which international institutions assumed regulative administrative powers over the state under Dayton was not surprising considering the weakness of all three Bosnian parties and their dependency, either directly or indirectly, on international support.

The Bosnian Muslims were highly dependent on the United States, as they had been since US encouragement to go for independence in 1992. The Muslim-led government had little legal standing as Alija Izetbegovic's term as state President had expired, in December 1991, before the war and recognition (Woodward, 1996a, p. 7). Izetbegovic's leadership was openly challenged by other Muslims such as those in Bihac, represented by Fikret Abdic, who wanted a negotiated settlement. As David Owen recalled, the Muslim government was a small clique: 'Izetbegovic was in control of only about 11 per cent of the country ... The collective Presidency ... by 1992 was exercising less and less collective power ... by the end of 1992 ... power had gone to a small group of Muslim Ministers appointed by President Izetbegovic' (1996, p. 52). The Muslim SDA-led government had achieved its aim of independence but only through replacing the communal ties with the Bosnian Croats and Serbs with dependency on US sponsorship and international aid. Even the Muslim-Croat Federation, brokered by the United States in February 1994, was only sustainable through US pressure and Croatia's co-operation.

The Bosnian Serbs were both directly and, through their links with Serbia, indirectly dependent on the international community policy-makers. Isolated by the international community sanctions, which Serbia was forced to join, they were reliant on the US to halt the Croatian and Muslim offensives in north-western Bosnia when, with the Bosnian Serb army in disarray, it seemed likely that Banja Luka could fall without Washington's intervention (Silber and Little, 1996, p. 368). The Serbian President Slobodan Milosevic was empowered to negotiate on behalf of the Bosnian Serbs as international indictments for war crimes had been issued against Bosnian Serb leaders Radovan Karadzic and Ratko Mladic, preventing them from travelling abroad without facing arrest. Milosevic had little to bargain with at the negotiating table and, in order to get some relief from international sanctions, signed what was put in front of him. He was forced to cut the Bosnian Serbs out of the negotiations and then to accede to US demands to give up a claim to the Serb suburbs of Sarajevo and to accept arbitration of Brcko.

The Bosnian Croats were dependent on their links with Zagreb and on Croatia's negotiations with the United States. Franjo Tudjman was willing to impose a settlement on the Bosnian Croats which promised co-operation with the Muslim Bosnian government and support for the Muslim-Croat Federation in exchange for the freedom to mount offensives against the Croatian Serbs in western Slavonia and in the Krajina (which took place in May and August 1995) and for US support for the eventual reintegration of eastern Slavonia. The Bosnian Croats were a useful bargaining chip for Tudjman and were to be kept under tight control, otherwise Croatia's admittance to European institutions and the offer of reconstruction loans would be jeopardised.

Under these conditions there was little resistance to Dayton but equally there was little popular support within Bosnia for the Dayton settlement. The Bosnian people had had no opportunity to assent to the new divisions drawn on the Bosnian map, nor the constitutional framework. It was a settlement imposed on the Bosnian Croats, Muslims and Serbs by the international community and guaranteed by the neighbouring republics of Croatia and Serbia (Silber and Little, 1996, p. 336; Cohen, 1996, p. 109).

Dayton

The peace agreement signed at Dayton was unlike any other peace treaty of modern times, not merely because it was imposed by powers external to the conflict, but because of the far-reaching powers given to the international community which extended well beyond military matters to cover the most basic aspects of government and state. The majority of annexes to the Dayton Agreement, were not related to the ending of hostilities, traditionally the role of a peace agreement, but the political project of democratising Bosnia, of 'reconstructing a society' (Bildt, 1996a).

Reconstructing Bosnian society was undertaken in the same interventionist spirit as Dayton itself. Carl Bildt, the first UN administrator for the new state, described the Dayton Agreement as 'by far the most ambitious peace agreement in modern history' (1996d). It was 'ambitious' because, under the guise of a negotiated peace settlement, it sought to create a new political entity which was not a product of popular consensus or popular involvement and was seen by many Bosnians as an external imposition. For this reason the state-level elections, to be held within nine months of the signing ceremony, were held to be crucial for restoring ownership over the new state to its citizens. Under the Dayton General Framework Agreement, there was to be a year of internationally supervised transition during which there would be elections and the establishment of two types of joint institutions: the political institutions of the new state, which were to be elected and directly accountable to the people, and the economic, judicial and human rights institutions which were to be supervised through the appointment of representatives from international institutions for five or six years.

The Dayton Agreement itself was a short two-page text, the annexes to it were where the details lay. The eleven annexes gave effective power over the Bosnian state to institutions of the international community; these powers covered the entire range of government functions usually associated with an independent state, including the highest levels of military, political, judicial and economic regulation. An overview of international institutional power is provided in Table 2.1.

The Military Annexes

Annex 1-A, *Agreement on the Military Aspects of the Peace Settlement*, gave NATO complete control of military activity within the state. All foreign forces were to be withdrawn and the forces of local origin which were to remain on Bosnian territory 'must act consistently with the territorial integrity, sovereignty, and political independence of Bosnia and Herzegovina' (Article III 'Withdrawal of Foreign Forces'). This paragraph excluded the NATO forces UNPROFOR and IFOR, the International Police Task Force and any other forces operating under NATO agreement. While Bosnian forces had to respect the sovereignty of their own country under NATO edict, the NATO forces were necessarily excluded from any similar commitment.

Article VI gave IFOR 'complete and unimpeded movement' throughout Bosnia, no liability for damage to property and made any roadblocks, checkpoints or impediments to IFOR subject to legitimate military action. Annex B made NATO personnel exempt from passport and visa regulations, and operations, training or movement could not be impeded by requests for identification (par. 4). This annex also gave NATO personnel legal immunity for their actions 'under all circumstances and at all times' and made them subject to the 'exclusive jurisdiction of their respective national elements' in respect of any criminal or disciplinary offences in Bosnia (par. 7).

The NATO mandate extended well beyond that of military duties. Article VI, Paragraph 3 stated that the duties of IFOR

Table 2.1 The Dayton Annexes

Annex	Area of Authority	International Body
1-A	Military Aspects	NATO (IFOR/SFOR)
1-B	Regional Stabilisation	OSCE
2	Inter-Entity Boundary	NATO (IFOR/SFOR)
3	Elections	OSCE
4	Constitution	UN High Representative
Article IV	Constitutional Court	European Court of Human Rights
Article VII	Central Bank	IMF
5	Arbitration	
6 Part B	Human Rights Ombudsman	OSCE
Part C	Human Rights Chamber	Council of Europe
7	Refugees & Displaced Persons	European Court of Human Rights
8	Commission to Preserve National Monuments	UNESCO
9	Commission on Public Corporations	European Bank for Reconstruction and Development
10	Civilian Implementation	UN High Representative
11	International Police Task Force	UN

Source: GFA, 1995.

included, for example, 'to help secure conditions for the conduct by others of their tasks associated with the peace settlement, including free and fair elections' (par. 3a), and 'to assist the movement of organisations in the accomplishment of humanitarian missions' (par. 3b). Article VI stated:

> ... the IFOR Commander shall have the authority, without interference or permission of any Party, to do all that the Commander judges necessary and proper, including the use of military force to carry out the responsibilities listed ... and [the Bosnian representatives] shall comply in all respects with the IFOR requirements. (par. 5)

Annex 2, *Agreement on Inter-Entity Boundary Line and Related Issues*, gave the IFOR Commander the final say even on boundary-line changes agreed between the Muslim-Croat Federation and the Serb entity Republika Srpska (Article IV) and ruled that arbitration of the disputed Brcko area should be made 'no later than one year' after the entry into force of the peace agreement (Article V).

The Civilian Annexes

The civilian annexes, comprising five-sixths of the Dayton Accords, involved a wide range of activities in which international organisations were mandated to play key co-ordinating roles (Gow, 1998, p. 169). These included economic reconstruction, the establishment of political institutions, human rights enforcement and the holding of elections. In order for these regulatory powers to have legality under international law, these mechanisms were incorporated into the Dayton Agreement.

Annex 3 – Elections

This annex gave the OSCE far-reaching powers of regulation and control over the electoral process. Article II gave the OSCE the authority 'to adopt and put in place an election programme' for Bosnia and 'to supervise, in a manner to be determined by the OSCE and in co-operation with other international organisations the OSCE deems necessary, the preparation and conduct of elections'. The term 'supervision' was broadly defined in the case of Bosnia, as Article III went on to give the OSCE powers far beyond the supervisory role it had played in other Eastern European states.

A Provisional Election Commission was established, chaired by the Head of the OSCE Mission, who was invested with the power of final decision (Article II). Also involved in the Commission were the UN High Representative, Bosnian representatives and any other invitees of the OSCE Head of Mission. The Commission – in case of division, the Head of the OSCE – then had the power to adopt electoral rules and regulations regarding the registration of political parties, the eligibility of candidates and voters, the role of election observers and the nature of electoral campaigning. The Commission was responsible for 'supervising all aspects of the electoral process', 'ensuring compliance with the electoral rules' and 'ensuring that action is taken to remedy any violation of any provision'.

Annex 4 – The Constitution

'The highest level of internationally recognised human rights and fundamental freedoms' were ensured for Bosnia and Herzegovina and both entities in Article II. The second paragraph stated that the *European Convention for the Protection of Human Rights and Fundamental Freedoms* and its Protocols should apply directly in Bosnia and have priority over all other law. The Constitution also committed the Bosnian government to remain or become a party to another 15 international agreements listed in Annex 1 to the Constitution (par. 7) (see further Chapter 3). The fact that these international agreements were imbedded in the Constitution gave mandates of responsibility in Bosnia to the international supervisory bodies involved. Article II stated that:

> All competent authorities ... shall co-operate with and provide unrestricted access to: any international human rights monitoring mechanisms established for Bosnia and Herzegovina; the supervisory bodies established by any of the international agreements listed in Annex 1 ... the International Tribunal for the Former Yugoslavia ... and any other organisation authorised by the United Nations Security Council with a mandate concerning human rights or humanitarian law. (GFA, 1995, Annex 4, II, par. 8)

An even more far-reaching international precedent was set by Article X of the Constitution, which stated that 'no amendment to this Constitution may eliminate or diminish any of the rights and freedoms referred to in Article II'. One study protested that the limitations on the Constitution being changed by the people posed a fundamental question over whether it was a constitution at all under international law (Chossudovsky, 1997, p. 9). However, it has also been noted that similar restrictions on amendments applied in the Constitutions of Germany and Namibia, also formulated under international auspices (Szasz, 1995a, p. 256).

Article VI established a nine-member Constitutional Court with exclusive jurisdiction over constitutional questions arising between the entities or between different institutions, the authority to establish whether special parallel relationships with neighbouring states were consistent with the Constitution, and jurisdiction over issues referred by any court concerning the validity of domestic and international laws. The Court's decisions were final and binding (par. 4). Four members of the Court were to be selected by the House of Representatives of the Federation and two by the Assembly of Republika Srpska. The other three members of the Constitutional Court were to be selected by the President of the European Court of Human Rights, initially for five years, and 'shall not be citizens of Bosnia and Herzegovina or of any neighbouring state' (par. 1b).

The provisions covering the running of the Central Bank were contained in Article VII. Paragraph 1 stated that the Bank must operate as a currency board for the first six years, preventing it from extending credit by creating money. During this six-year period, the Governing Board of the Bank was to be managed by an International Monetary Fund-appointed Governor, who was not to be a citizen of Bosnia or any neighbouring state. The other members of the Board being one Croat and one Bosniak (sharing one vote between them) and one Serb, with the IMF Governor casting tie-breaking votes.

Annex 6 – Human Rights
This Annex established a Commission on Human Rights which consisted of two parts: the Office of the Ombudsman and the Human Rights Chamber. The Commission had the mandate to consider the violation of human rights and 'alleged or apparent discrimination on any ground' (Article II, par. 2b).

The Human Rights Ombudsman was tasked with investigating allegations of human rights violations, issuing findings and reports to the High Representative, and referring cases to the Human Rights Chamber (Article V). The post-holder was to be appointed for a five-year term by the Chairman-in-Office of the OSCE, could not be a citizen of Bosnia or of any neighbouring state, and was to be independently responsible for choosing their own staff (Article IV, par. 2). The Ombudsman had wide-ranging powers including access to all official documents including classified ones, as well as judicial and administrative files (Article VI, par. 1).

The Human Rights Chamber was mandated to decide on cases of violations of human rights, to facilitate an effective remedy, and forward reports of its decisions to the High Representative, OSCE and Council of Europe (Article VIII). The Chamber was composed of 14 members, four appointed from the Federation, two from Republika Srpska, and the remaining eight, appointed by the Committee of Ministers of the Council of Europe, could not be citizens of Bosnia or any neighbouring state (Article VII, par. 2). The Chamber was to normally sit in panels of seven, composed of two members from the Federation, one from Republika Srpska and four external appointees (Article X, par. 2).

Chapter Three of the Annex, *General Provisions*, gave unimpeded access to international human rights organisations. In fact, beyond this, Bosnian officials were instructed 'to promote and encourage the activities of non-governmental and international organisations for the protection and promotion of human rights (Article XIII, par. 1). The United Nations Commission on Human Rights, the OSCE, the United Nations High Commissioner for Human Rights, 'and other intergovernmental or regional human rights missions or organisations' were invited to:

> ... monitor closely the human rights situation ... including through the establishment of local offices and the assignment of observers, rapporteurs, or other relevant persons on a permanent or mission-by-mission basis and to provide them with full and effective facilitation, assistance and access ... and shall refrain from hindering or impeding them in the exercise of these functions. (GFA, 1995, Annex 6, XIII, pars 2 & 3)

Article XIII again repeated the wording of Annex 4, giving unrestricted access to the human rights monitoring and enforcing agencies, and the appendix listed the 16 human rights agreements.

Annex 7 – Refugees and Displaced Persons

Chapter Two established an independent Commission for Displaced Persons and Refugees. The Commission was to be composed of nine members, four appointed by the Federation, two by Republika Srpska, for terms of three and four years. The Chair and two others were to be appointed by the President of the European Court of Human Rights, for a term of five years (Article IX, par. 1). The Commission was mandated to decide on property claims and, where ownership had not been voluntarily transferred, to organise for its return or just compensation (Article XI).

Annex 8 – Commission to Preserve National Monuments

The Commission was to have five members, two appointed from the Federation, one from Republika Srpska, for terms of three years. The Chair of the Commission and the other two members were to be appointed, for a term of five years, by the Director-General of the United Nations Educational, Scientific and Cultural Organisation (UNESCO) (Article II). The mandate of the Commission gave it the authority to decide on petitions for property to be designated as a National Monument on the basis of cultural, historic, religious or ethnic importance.

Annex 9 – Bosnia and Herzegovina Public Corporations

This annex established a Commission on Public Corporations to examine establishing joint public corporations for the benefit of both entities, including their appropriate internal structure, the conditions necessary to ensure their permanent operation, and the best means of securing long-term investment capital. These were to include utility, energy, postal and communications facilities (Article I, par. 1). The Commission comprised five members, two appointed by the Federation, one by Republika Srpska. The President of the European Bank for Reconstruction and Development was charged with appointing the remaining two members and designating the Chair (Article I, par. 2).

One of the first tasks of the Commission was to establish a Transportation Corporation to organise and operate transport facilities such as roads, railways and ports. The Board of Directors, chosen by the Commission and the Board, was to appoint in turn its own officers and staff (Article II). The Transportation Corporation, if the Commission decided, was to serve as the model for other joint public corporations, in the fields of utility, energy, postal and communication facilities (Article III).

Annex 10 – Civilian Implementation

In recognition of the unique and expansive regulatory powers of the international community in the non-military sphere, the General Framework Agreement established the post of United Nations High Representative to co-ordinate the actions of international institutions and 'to facilitate the Parties' own efforts' (Article I, par. 2). The forms that this 'facilitation' was to take were outlined in Article II, which gave the High Representative a powerful and extensive mandate as the 'final authority in theatre regarding interpretation of this Agreement on the civilian implementation of the peace settlement' (Article V):

- Monitoring the implementation of the peace settlement
- Promoting the compliance of Bosnian representatives with 'all civilian aspects of the peace settlement' and 'a high level of co-operation' with international organisations and agencies
- Co-ordinating the activities of the civilian organisations and agencies
- Facilitating 'as the High Representative judges necessary' the resolution of any difficulties in connection with civilian implementation
- Participating in donors' meetings
- Reporting periodically to the UN, EU, US, Russian Federation and other interested governments, parties and organisations
- Providing guidance to the Commissioner of the International Police Task Force.

The method of co-ordination for these tasks was laid out in the second section of Article II which instructed the High Representative to convene and chair the Joint Civilian Commission. This Commission was to consist of senior Bosnian representatives, IFOR and other international agencies as the High Representative deemed necessary, including the IPTF Commander or representative. Subordinate Joint Civilian Commissions were also to be established at local levels, and the High Representative had the authority to establish other civilian commissions inside or outside Bosnia (Article II, pars 3 & 8).

This annex made clear that although the High Representative was to be in close contact with the IFOR Commander, through the Joint Consultative Committee, the UN High Representative had no authority over NATO forces and 'shall not in any way interfere in the conduct of military operations or the IFOR chain of command' (Article II, par. 9).

Annex 11 – International Police Force

In order to provide civilian law enforcement in accordance with 'internationally recognised human rights and fundamental freedoms', the DPA provided for the establishment of a UN International Police Task Force (IPTF). This put civilian law enforcement outside the control of elected Bosnian representatives. The IPTF 'shall be autonomous with regard to the execution of its functions' and its activities co-ordinated by the High Representative (Article II, par. 1). The members of the IPTF, and their families, were specifically guaranteed 'inviolability': they could not be subject to any form of arrest or detention, and would have absolute immunity from criminal jurisdiction (Article II, par. 6). Any obstruction, interference or failure to comply with IPTF requests on behalf of Bosnian representatives was to result in action by the High Representative (Article V).

In effect, the role of the IPTF was to police the police. They had the power to monitor and inspect law enforcement activities and to provide advice, training and assistance to law enforcement (Article III). Bosnian representatives were to provide the IPTF with full information about their law enforcement structures, including, on request, employment and service records. They were also to make personnel available for IPTF training (Article IV).

The only annex in which external power was not explicit was Annex 5, *Arbitration*, in which it was clearly implicit as the two entities resolved 'to engage in binding arbitration to resolve disputes between them'.

Post-Dayton extensions to the international mandates

This year of internationally supervised transition to, at least partial, self-governing democracy was due to end with the election of state and entity bodies in September 1996, symbolising 'the democratic birth of the country' (PIC, 1996a, par. 27). Although these bodies were elected under internationally supervised and ratified elections, the transitional international administration was prolonged for a further two-year 'consolidation period' and then, in December 1997, extended indefinitely. The extension of the time limits for international withdrawal and the creation of new mandates for international institutions since Dayton has been justified according to the DPA itself and also by growing reference to the 'spirit of Dayton'.

The Dayton Agreement provides little guidance for understanding the extension of international mandates nor the mechanisms of international administration over the new state. This is because the DPA was ostensibly a treaty between the Bosnian parties themselves and not a treaty between the international community and the Bosnian government. The Dayton Agreement was rigid where it concerned the limits to Bosnian self-rule but extremely flexible in relation to the powers which the international community could exercise over this nominally independent state. This ambiguity resulted from the fact that while the governments of Croatia, Serbia and Bosnia, as signatories, were bound by the DPA, the international institutions overseeing and implementing Dayton were not. As Paul Szasz notes, the Dayton Agreement was 'merely a part of total arrangements to bring peace to Bosnia' (1996, p. 304). It is worth quoting at length the international constitutional lawyer closely involved in the development of Dayton:

> Explicitly mentioned or merely implied by those texts are a host of other agreements or arrangements, which are to be concluded ... by or within the numerous international organisations assigned various roles by these texts, and which may take the form of bilateral or multilateral executive agreements, resolutions of the [United Nations] Security Council or decisions of NATO, the OSCE ... and other organisations ... evidently the parties to the GFA and the ancillary agreements could not bind these external actors ... nor, of course, are these external actors precluded from taking steps not foreseen in these texts. (Szasz, 1996, p. 304)

This flexibility has been exemplified by the extension of the powers of the UN Office of the High Representative, who has explained this process as one which has no fixed limits: 'if you read Dayton very carefully ... Annex 10 even gives me the possibility to interpret my own authorities and powers' (Westendorp, 1997a). Other international bodies such as the OSCE and NATO have similarly chosen to increase their authority in Bosnia since December 1995. It was in order to speed up the democratisation process that increased mandates were called for from the first months of the international administration. During 1996, concern was expressed that holding elections could not be equated with self-government and that an extended period of consolidation would be necessary. It was feared that withdrawal after one year would leave the new institutions without guarantees and encourage fragmentation. As the High Representative noted in describing post-election arrangements at state level:

> ... true signs of ethnic reconciliation are still sorely missing. Bosnia and Herzegovina is still a country divided into three to a very large extent separate ethnic communities ... The power-sharing arrangements must be fair to each and every one at the same time as they must ensure the effective governance of the

> country ... The common institutions of the country require a high degree of consensus in order to be able to work efficiently. (OHRR, 1996c, pars 83 & 84)

The powers of the international community have been amended at successive Peace Implementation Council meetings. The most important of these have been the strategic six-monthly review conferences: at Florence, in June 1996; Paris, in November 1996; Sintra, in May 1997; Bonn, in December 1997; and Luxembourg, in June 1998.

The PIC Florence Review conference, in June 1996, extended the European Union administration over Mostar and gave a mandate to the PIC Steering Board to discuss the extension of international involvement for a two-year stabilisation period (PIC, 1996a, pars 24 & 27). In July 1996, the High Representative suggested that 'our involvement must not only be longer in time than 1996 but also wider in geographic scope' (OHRR, 1996b, par. 86). In the run-up to the September 1996 elections, the international community increasingly clarified that the elections were not the end of the process of democratisation but the beginning. At the end of August, the OSCE Chairman-in-Office, Flavio Cotti, stressed that the elections were merely a step in the right direction: 'We have opted to hold the elections above all because they should be viewed as a small, but still the first, step towards the path of reconciliation' (OHRB, 1996o).

The Ministerial Meeting of the PIC Steering Board meeting a month after the elections, in November 1996, decided to extend the year of transition, due to end the following month, from one year to three years. Rather than policy-making being the prerogative of the state and entity authorities, with the joint institutions there to ensure the international community's influence over areas of potential controversy, policy-making was to be retained by the international administration. A two-year 'consolidation period' was announced, with the High Representative mandated to draw up two successive twelve-month 'action plans'. These Office of the High Representative 'action plans' were to be approved by the PIC, in consultation with the principal international institutions involved in implementing the peace agreement, and their implementation would then be reviewed at mid-term (PIC, 1996c, par. 4). The new extended role of the High Representative was accompanied by reinforced powers to make recommendations to the state and entity authorities, and in the case of dispute, to give his interpretation and make his recommendations public (PIC, 1996c, par. 6).

The NATO mandate, which was due to end officially on 20 December 1996, was also extended unilaterally. On 18 November, NATO Ambassadors from the North Atlantic

Council met to discuss plans for the Implementation Force (IFOR) to be replaced by a Stabilisation Force (SFOR). It was proposed that the force should be smaller, but would have a broader mandate to include a more enhanced role in civilian implementation (OHRB, 1996u). A further meeting, on 27 November, agreed a detailed timetable for stationing a further 30,000 troops from over thirty countries for no more than 18 months, with reviews of troop levels every six months. The United Nations Security Council voted unanimously, on 12 December, to give ultimate authorisation for the new 18-month SFOR mandate and the same resolution also authorised the continuation of UN civilian operations in Bosnia for a further twelve months, including the international police (IPTF) (OHRB, 1996x).

In October and November 1996, Presidents Izetbegovic, Zubak and Plavsic, on behalf of the state and entity governments, signed an agreement with the OSCE to supervise the municipal elections in 1997 (OHRB, 1996v). This new agreement also extended the operational mandate of the OSCE to cover post-election implementation (see further Chapter 5). This period of preparation for consolidation was rounded off at the 4–5 December PIC conference in London, entitled *Bosnia and Herzegovina 1997 – Making Peace Work*, attended by over fifty national delegations, international agencies and representatives from the Bosnian state and entity governments. The PIC approved an Action Plan for the coming year containing detailed recommendations (OHRB, 1996w).

The first action plan mid-term review took place at the Sintra Ministerial meeting of the PIC Steering Board, in May 1997. Here a new package of measures to ensure co-operation with the High Representative was announced, including the capacity to pursue deadlines announced by the PIC and enact measures in the case of non-compliance (PIC, 1997a, par. 92; PIC, 1997c, par. 8). These measures included visa restrictions on travel abroad for obstructive Bosnian representatives as well as economic sanctions targeted at a local level and the capacity to curtail or suspend any media network or programmes which contravened 'either the spirit or letter' of the Dayton agreement (PIC, 1997a, pars 35, 36 & 70).

The Bonn meeting of the PIC, in December 1997, extended the High Representative's powers further, allowing him to decide the time, location and chairmanship of meetings of the central institutions, to enact interim measures where the Bosnian representatives could not agree to OHR policy, and to take action against non-compliant officials at both state and entity level (PIC, 1997b, XI, par. 2). This meeting also called on the OSCE, IPTF and NATO to extend their mandates further (PIC, 1997b, IV, par. 5; VI, par. 3; PIC, 1997c, par. 13). There was a qualitative difference between the extended mandates, formalised at the Luxembourg meeting in June 1998, and the extended mandates granted earlier. The new mandates granted to the international bodies overseeing Bosnia were now indefinite: international withdrawal and the ceding of sovereignty and policy-making powers to Bosnian institutions was now to be dependent on a broad range of 'benchmarks' to be determined by the international institutions themselves (PIC, 1998, par. 109). The extension of mandates has been accompanied by the acquisition of further regulative powers which will be considered in more detail in the following chapters; for example, the High Representative's powers directly to enact policy, the OSCE's power to install multi-ethnic administrations and stipulate the allocation of governing responsibilities, and the extension of NATO's authority to include policing functions beyond SFOR's existing mandate (Rogers, 1998).

THE DAYTON PROCESS AND BOSNIAN SOVEREIGNTY

Although Bosnia remains formally a sovereign state, the extension of international mandates over the state has left little space for Bosnian state institutions to make or to implement policy. The extension of the administrative powers of the UN High Representative, in particular, has meant that policy is made at international forums and implemented within Bosnia through a parallel system of internationally-run committees and task forces.

International policy-making bodies

There is a growing network of international institutions and *ad hoc* bodies involved in the policy-making process, this complex inter-linking of different agencies does not make it straightforward to delineate responsibility for policy development and implementation. The following section seeks to chart the main bodies involved, however because of the *ad hoc* status of these forums and the informal government and institutional contacts between leading actors, the picture provided remains a fairly formal one.

The Peace Implementation Council

The Peace Implementation Council (PIC) was established at the London Peace Implementation Conference, in December 1995. The Conference Conclusions note that this body is composed of all the states, international organisations and agencies attending the Conference and that the PIC would subsume the role and authority of the International Conference on Former Yugoslavia (ICFY) (PIC, 1995, par. 21). The PIC, as an informal body, acts only through the mandates of its members. Once decisions have been reached the organisation must then request the UN Security Council, the North Atlantic Council, the OSCE, World Bank, International Monetary Fund and other international institutions to agree to proposals for involvement.

The Steering Board of the Peace Implementation Council

The Steering Board, through its monthly meetings, is the key international managing body, discussing policy developments in detail and providing political guidance to the High Representative (OHRR, 1996a, par. 12). The PIC Steering Board includes the US, Russia, France, Germany, Japan, Canada, Italy, the European Union Presidency, the European Commission and Turkey, on behalf of the Organisation of Islamic Countries, and usually meets at the level of Political Directors of the respective Foreign Ministries under the chairmanship of the High Representative. The OSCE and the UN are invited to attend Steering Board meetings and the views of major donors, at meetings co-ordinated through the European Commission and the World Bank, are of importance in informing the Board Meetings.

The PIC also has working groups, which prepare policy papers for consultative meetings, such as the Humanitarian Issues Working Group, chaired by the UN High Commissioner for Refugees (OHRB, 1997m).

Meetings of the Dayton signatories

Ad hoc meetings of the signatories have been called to discuss policy and apply pressure to the Parties, both directly and through pressure on Croatia and Serbia (OHRR, 1996a, par. 13). A typical meeting would be called by the US Secretary of State, and involve the Bosnian, Croatian and Serbian Presidents, the UN High Representative, NATO's Supreme Allied Commander, the Chairman-in-Office of the OSCE and the Head of the OSCE Mission (OHRB, 1996n).

The Contact Group

The Contact Group of the six states most involved in Bosnia (France, Germany, Italy, Russian Federation, United Kingdom and the United States) meets at the level of Foreign Ministers on a monthly basis. Meetings are also attended by the High Representative and the Head of the OSCE Bosnia Mission. The Contact Group regularly carries out preparatory work for PIC Steering Board discussion and decision (see, for example, OHRB, 1997p).

The Brussels Secretariat of the Office of the High Representative

The Office of the High Representative (OHR) Secretariat in Brussels is responsible for co-ordinating the international planning and policy decision-making process and is headed by a senior adviser (OHRR, 1996a, par. 14). The Brussels office maintains contacts at a strategic level with the different governments and implementation agencies and international organisations involved. The Brussels-based units for Political Affairs and Policy Planning develop policy for discussion at Contact Group and Peace Implementation Council level which then, after consultation, is implemented by the High Representative on the ground (OHRR, 1996a, par. 6). In order to develop closer co-ordination of policy, the Human Rights Co-ordination Centre and the Economic Task Force are based both in Sarajevo and Brussels (OHRR, 1996a, par. 15).

Meetings of the Main Implementation Agencies

The OHR organises regular meetings of the Main Implementation Agencies (MIA) at the Brussels offices, every other month, to assess policy proposals of the international agencies and organisations and to review developments in the implementation of the DPA (OHRR, 1996a, par. 15). These agencies include the Council of Europe, ECMM, ICRC, ICTY, IOM, NATO, OSCE, UNHCR and the UN, and enable co-ordination between the PIC Steering Board and the international agencies (OHRB, 1996j).

Informal and formal contacts

The UN High Representative is in regular contact with the Secretary General of NATO and regularly addresses meetings of the North Atlantic Council, also the OHR Brussels office and OHR military advisers are in frequent contact with NATO authorities including the Supreme Headquarters Allied Powers Europe (SHAPE). The High Representative is similarly in regular contact with the OSCE Chairman-in-Office and UN Secretary General, and reports regularly to individual governments, the Council of Ministers of the European Union, the UN Security Council and other bodies.

Bosnia-based international policy forums

The Office of the High Representative (OHR) Headquarters in Sarajevo is responsible for carrying out the immediate implementation of agreed policies (OHRR, 1996a, par. 14). The Headquarters (nicknamed 'The Presidency') is staffed by over two hundred international officers, headed by the Principal Deputy High Representative, and is responsible for operational level co-ordination of civilian implementation (Hedges, 1998). Under a Chief of Staff, there are units responsible for Political Affairs, including elections, Economic Policy and Reconstruction, Relations with the UN, Relations with NATO, Human Rights, Humanitarian Issues, Legal Affairs and Media Relations (OHRR, 1996a, par. 5).

At the London Peace Implementation Conference, in December 1995, Carl Bildt, the EU Mediator for Former Yugoslavia was designated High Representative, with Michael Steiner as his Principal Deputy. This team was succeeded, in June 1997, by a new High Representative, Carlos Westendorp, assisted by two Principal Deputy High Representatives, the US-nominated Ambassador Jacques Klein, former head of the United Nations Transitional Administration in Eastern Slavonia (UNTAES) and German nominee Gerd Wagner, replaced after his death in a helicopter accident, in September 1997, by Hanns Shumacher.

Forums organised by the Office of the High Representative on the ground in Bosnia mirror the international forums in bringing together the international agencies to discuss the implementation of the previously agreed policies.

Contact Group representatives meetings

Regular meetings of Contact Group representatives are held in Sarajevo, chaired by the High Representative (OHRB, 1996q).

Principals meetings

On the ground in Bosnia the civilian side of the Dayton process is co-ordinated through 'regular and frequent' Principals meetings convened by the Office of the High Representative at the Sarajevo office, with the participation of the Special Representative of the Secretary-General, the IPTF Commissioner, the Special Envoy of the Office of the UNHCR, the Commander of SFOR and the Head of the Mission of the OSCE (OHRR, 1996a, par. 24).

Liaison with military authorities

The High Representative has frequent contact with the IFOR Commander and the Allied Rapid Reaction Corps (ARRC)

Commander. Representatives of IFOR and ARCC take an active part in Office of the High Representative commissions and working groups. The High Representative is represented on the Joint Military Commission and IFOR on the Joint Civilian Commission.

Under the Office of the High Representative there are a series of special Task Forces, which operate in addition to the international commissions called for by the DPA:

The Economic Task Force

The Economic Task Force is the main co-ordinating body for economic reconstruction, and therefore seen as a key instrument for influencing developments. The High Representative stated, in early 1996, that control of this sphere was 'one of the most potent instruments at our disposal to influence the reintegration of the country ... it thus has great political significance' (OHRR, 1996a, par. 36). Control of this 'most potent instrument' is organised through OHR co-ordination of the Economic Development Agencies – the World Bank, the European Commission, the European Bank for Reconstruction and Development, the International Monetary Fund and the International Management Group – through meetings in Brussels and weekly meetings in Sarajevo (OHRR, 1996a, pars 37 & 38). The World Bank and the European Commission also organise 13 sector task forces which meet regularly to ensure effective co-ordination between international donors and to report to the OHR (OHRR, 1996c, par. 63).

After the London PIC conference, in December 1996, the OHR Economic Unit which co-ordinates the Task Force was strengthened by the establishment of a Deputy High Representative for Economic Issues, Claude Ganz, Special Representative of the US President and Secretary of State, seconded to the OHR. Representatives of the European Commission and the World Bank were also seconded to the Economic Unit (OHRB, 1997g).

The Human Rights Task Force

Chaired by the High Representative, this task force consists of the key international organisations involved in human rights issues – the OSCE, European Community Monitoring Mission, UNHCR, Council of Europe, IPTF, International Committee of the Red Cross, IFOR, the Helsinki Citizens' Assembly and the UN Mission in Bosnia. At regular progress meetings, members discuss 'priorities and strategies to force the Parties to comply with their obligations' (OHRB, 1996f). This forum was of particular importance in developing and implementing policy because the remit of human rights was broadly defined to include vital issues of government, such as institution building and the rule of law (OHRB, 1996s). The task force established a number of work groups, which met to devise policy strategies which were then put to the Bosnian representatives through OHR forums such as the Joint Civilian Commission or through the direct pressure of meeting with individual ministers (see, for example, OHRB, 1996d; OHRB, 1996i).

The Freedom of Movement Task Force

Established at the London PIC Conference, in December 1996, the role of this task force was the development of implementation mechanisms to promote freedom of movement for people, goods and mail. The Task Force included representatives of the OHR, UN IPTF, SFOR and interested countries (OHRR, 1997a, par. 17).

The Reconstruction and Return Task Force

This task force was established, at an informal meeting of international agencies in Geneva, on 20 January 1997, in order to develop an integrated approach to refugee return and economic reconstruction. Key roles were allocated to the UNHCR, the World Bank, the European Commission, the International Management Group, the Commission for Real Property Claims and the OHR (OHRB, 1997c).

The Media Support and Advisory Group

Founded by the Office of the High Representative in late summer 1997, its members meet weekly in the OHR office in Sarajevo. Membership includes representatives from SFOR, OSCE, European Commission and UN Mission in Bosnia, and the body is responsible for developing a strategic approach to the media including establishing operational standards and licensing regulations (SAFAX, 1998c).

Bosnian state policy forums

Since Dayton the central institutions of the Bosnian state have had little independent policy-making capacities; the extension of the international administration after the September 1996 elections meant that there would be little difference in the power or the workings of these bodies.

The Joint Interim Commission and the Joint Civilian Commissions

Under the DPA transitional arrangements, prior to the creation of new state institutions with the September 1996 elections, a consultative Joint Interim Commission (JIC) was established with a mandate to discuss the implementation of the Constitution and other Dayton annexes (GFA, 1995, Annex 4, II). This Commission, which included the Prime Ministers of Bosnia and Herzegovina, the Federation and Republika Srpska, was the highest civilian authority outside the High Representative. The regular meetings were chaired by the High Representative (OHRB, 1996a). It was decided that, following the Peace Implementation Review Conference in Florence, in June 1996, the High Representative would convene the JIC on a weekly basis to ensure compliance with the international community's desire for the implementation of constitutional amendments and the development of common policies (OHRB, 1996f).

The JIC was little more than a high-level consultative body, but was the central mechanism for making Bosnian representatives accountable to the international community. When the Republika Srpska Prime Minister, Gojko Klickovic, failed to attend a meeting at the end of June 1996, High Representative Carl Bildt issued a statement declaring 'this refusal to attend agreed meetings is against the undertakings of the Peace Agreement to work together within the framework of the JIC and the JCC, and calls into question the sincerity of the RS statements that they intend to co-operate fully with the implementation of the Peace Agreement' (OHRB, 1996g). In order to prepare policy in the post-election period, a JIC sub-committee was established (JIC-PE) involving all three governments at ministerial level and candidates for the Bosnian Presidency (OHRB, 1996o).

Below the Joint Interim Commission, the Joint Civilian Commission (JCC) operated on similar lines. Established under Annex 10 on Civilian Implementation, the Commission was convened and chaired by the Deputy High Representative and comprised ministerial representatives, from the Bosnian government, the Federation and Republika Srpska, the IFOR Commander and representatives of international agencies invited by the High Representative, including the Head of the OSCE Mission (Article II, par. 2). Parallel subordinate structures existed at a regional level, run by the Principal Deputy High Representative, Ambassador Michael Steiner. The agendas of the regional JCCs were all similar, informing the Bosnian representatives of the results of international meetings of the Contact Group and the Peace Implementation Council and applying pressure on elected representatives over media issues, economic reintegration and refugee return (see, for example, OHRB, 1996f). As well as the Deputy High Representative, other international organisations were represented at these forums including the OSCE, UNHCR, IFOR, IPTF, UN Civilian Affairs, ECMM and the World Bank. Working groups chaired by the Office of the High Representative or other international agencies were also established to develop joint policy, for example, the JCC Working Group on Free Media and the OHR Department of Legal Affairs-chaired JCC Working Group on Travel Documents to ensure freedom of movement (OHRB, 1996g).

After the September 1996 elections, the Joint Interim Commission and its subsidiary bodies were replaced as policy implementation forums by the joint-Presidency and the Council of Ministers. The regional Joint Civilian Commissions and their working groups were maintained until, with the extension of the OHR's mandate, their tasks were transferred to the OHR regional offices in Banja Luka, Tuzla and Mostar (OHRR, 1997a, par. 6; OHRR, 1997c, par. 5).

The Joint-Presidency and the Council of Ministers

After the first state-level elections, in September 1996, the new three-member Presidency was chaired by the SDA leader, Alija Izetbegovic, with the Croat HDZ representative, Kresimir Zubak, and the Serb SDS representative, Momcilo Krajisnik, as vice-chairs. The Chair of the Council of Ministers (CoM) was nominated by the Bosnian Presidency, but only with the approval of the UN High Representative, and the Ministers and Deputy Ministers all required the approval of the High Representative before assuming their posts. Presidency and Council of Ministers sessions always took place under the auspices of the Office of the High Representative with policy agendas shaped by the OHR's requests. These were attended by the High Representative or his Principal Deputy, who instructed members as problems arose (see, for example, OHRB, 1997f).

Well before polling day, the Steering Board of the Peace Implementation Council had discussed the 'Quick Start Package' (QSP) of regulations for the new Bosnian state institutions, prepared by the OHR in consultation with the International Monetary Fund and the European Commission. The High Representative, Carl Bildt, drew up a timetable for meetings of the Presidency in order to establish the membership of the CoM and delegations for international institutions (OHRB, 1996p; OHRB 1996q).

The Presidency also established a series of working groups to consider issues of constitutional structures, staffing and procedural rules, as well as implementation of OHR recommendations regarding the budget and other QSP measures. All the working groups were set up and overseen by the OHR (OHRR, 1996d, par. 27). The European Commission assisted the OHR by drafting policy for the Presidential working groups, including the Trade Law, the Foreign Trade Law, Customs Tariff Law, Customs Policy Law and Investment Law, while the European Institute for Media drafted the Media Law (OHRB, 1997h).

Giving assent to the economic packages prepared by the OHR, IMF and World Bank was the central task facing the Council of Ministers. The newly appointed Ministers attended an OHR-organised Economic Policy Forum at which representatives from the IMF, World Bank, European Commission and US Treasury explained the actions they were required to take (OHRR, 1997a, par. 22). Following this, there were briefing sessions at the OHR office, 'working retreats' and pre-meetings with the Deputy High Representative, in order for the elected representatives to receive instruction on the implementation of policy and the order of implementation procedure. The OHR *Bulletins* describe the process through which the Council was 'presented with' European Commission and OHR-prepared policy such as the Quick Start Package of laws and how OHR guidance hastened their adoption and 'steered debate in the right direction' (for example, OHRB, 1997b; OHRB, 1997o; OHRB, 1997s).

Bosnian representatives who opposed aspects of international community policy proposals had little opportunity to challenge or appeal against them and the joint state institutions generally complied, passing most policies unchanged or with only minor amendments. Nevertheless, some legislation was delayed, for example, the laws on foreign trade and customs policy which weakened the capacity of entities to negotiate 'special parallel relationships', formally allowed under Dayton (OHRB, 1997i). This resulted in Christine Wallich, the World Bank Country Director for Bosnia, attending the CoM in March 1997, to outline the World Bank's proposals and state that co-operation was a necessary precondition for the planned donors' conference (OHRB, 1997j). Carl Bildt sent a letter to the CoM stating that the postponement of the donor's conference 'could have severe financial repercussions for the country' and suggested they meet as often as necessary to pass the legislation necessary to reach agreement with the IMF requirements. This was duly done by the end of the month (OHRB, 1997j). The effectiveness with which international economic pressure was applied, to enforce the adoption of contested OHR policy, demonstrated the balance of power between the international community and the elected Bosnian representatives and the limited opportunities for Bosnian institutions to put any real input into policy-making (OHRB, 1997j; OHRB, 1997k).

This process continued in the late spring and early summer of 1997, as IMF and World Bank representatives attended CoM meetings to reinforce pressure from the Office of the High Representative on the Bosnian representatives (OHRB, 1997s). By the end of 1997 this external pressure was no longer necessary as the UN High Representative could unilaterally impose disputed legislation on the design of the new currency, uniform vehicle licence plates, citizenship laws, and even decide on the new Bosnian flag (*Economist*, 1998a).

The Council of Ministers had very little supporting structures outside the services of the Office of the High Representative, and their offices in their respective entities were staffed by no more than a few personal assistants (OHRR, 1997a, par. 26). Even the OHR admitted, in mid-1997: 'In the absence of administrative structures, the Council remains, effectively, little more than an extended working group' (OHRR, 1997b, par. 24). The State Parliament had even less of a role in policy implementation and with the Deputy High Representative 'assisting', was responsible for formally assenting to policy passed down from the Ministers (OHRB, 1997a).

CONCLUSION

The extension of the international institutional mechanisms of regulation during the process of democratisation, the transition to democracy and self-rule, has meant that the Bosnian state bodies have had little influence over either policy development or its implementation. In effect, Bosnia, under Dayton, has been governed by a network of international community institutions representing the major world powers, with NATO, the UN Mission in Bosnia and Herzegovina (UNMiBH) and the OSCE Mission in Bosnia and Herzegovina as leading implementing organs. At state level, Bosnian representatives have had the opportunity to discuss policy proposals, under the guidance of the Office of the High Representative and other international bodies such as the World Bank and IMF, but at the most the Bosnian institutions could only make minor alterations to OHR pre-prepared packages or delay their implementation.

Having been relegated to the status of 'an extended working group', capable only of discussing policies drawn up and implemented by international community institutions, it was little wonder that the Bosnian state bodies were increasingly sidelined by the OHR. Discussion and debate in Bosnian government assemblies was viewed by the UN High Representative as unnecessary and evidence that 'Democratisation has a long way to go before one can safely say it has truly taken root in a country with no political experience of its benefits' (OHRB, 1997B). The cut and thrust of democratic consensus-building, at the level of the tripartite Presidency, Council of Ministers and Parliamentary Assembly, was often seen as an unnecessary delay to vital policy implementation. These discussions created further work for the High Representative as affirmation of international policy in these bodies nearly always required 'prompting by, or support from, my Office' (OHRR, 1997b, par. 18). Compared to the swift signature of the chief administrator's pen, the joint institutions were 'painfully cumbersome and ineffective' (OHRB, 1997B).

The 'cumbersome' need to acquire the assent of elected Bosnian representatives was removed when the Bonn PIC summit gave the High Representative the power to impose legislation directly, giving the international community both executive and legislative control over the formally independent state. Since December 1997, the High Representative, Carlos Westendorp, has grasped the opportunities this has provided, explaining, 'You do not [have] power handed to you on a platter. You just seize it, if you use this power well, no-one will contest it. I have already achieved this' (Rodriguez, 1998).

This experiment in externally imposed democratisation raises questions about the relevance of sovereignty and political autonomy to the long-term success of the democratisation process. This relationship will be further investigated within the following four chapters. International community policy assumes that the 'benchmarks' for international withdrawal and Bosnian self-government are ones that can only be achieved at the cost of a transitional lack of sovereignty and the denial of self-government. Consideration of international strategy in relation to four of the key 'benchmarks' of democratisation – multi-ethnic administration, human rights protections, political pluralism and civil society construction – provides a solid basis from which to analyse whether international democratisation strategy has been able to facilitate the development of Bosnian self-government or whether the level of involvement has made it more difficult for the international community to exit from Bosnia.

3 Power-sharing and multi-ethnic administrations

The aim of reconstructing a multi-ethnic Bosnia has been a central facet of international democratisation strategy since Dayton and seen as key to preserving peace in the region. US Deputy Secretary of State Strobe Talbott, speaking during the Dayton negotiations, made clear that American assistance in constructing multi-ethnic administrations in Bosnia would be essential for democracy. Multi-ethnic government was seen as a bulwark against aggressive nationalism and therefore vital for both regional and international stability:

> If there is to be a post-Cold War peace in Europe – and not a cold peace, but a real one – it must be based on the principle of multi-ethnic democracy ... The United States is one of the first and one of the greatest examples of that principle. What's more, the civic behaviour and constitutional structures associated with pluralism are conducive to regional peace and international trade. Hence, it is in our interest that multi-ethnic democracy ultimately prevails. (USDoS, 1995)

At the heart of this multi-ethnic policy was the decentralisation of political power and the provision of security to all ethnic groups in order that their vital interests would be protected. This was particularly important for Bosnia as each of the three dominant groups was a potential minority: the Muslims, the largest group, could still be outvoted by the Serbs and Croats. To safeguard a unified Bosnia it was therefore essential to ensure that minority interests were protected in the constitution. It was accepted that only with guarantees of security could the barriers of the war be overcome. Warren Christopher, then US Secretary of State, explained:

> These divisions will not be overcome overnight. But the central structures created by Dayton were designed to insure that each ethnic group would see that its interests can and will be protected within a unified Bosnia. It is in this way, and only in this way, that it is possible to build a consensus for unity within Bosnia. (USDoS, 1996b)

The promise of Dayton was that the power of majorities at higher levels of government would be closely regulated, and where possible, power was to be shared through being devolved downwards, thereby allowing greater self-government at local level. This was intended to secure a level of self-government for each ethnic constituency, preventing the passage of legislation which could be seen as favouring one ethnic constituency over another. This devolution of power was to provide security to all three minorities and therefore provide a crucial mechanism for institutionalising support for a multi-ethnic society. As High Representative Carl Bildt stated: 'The two entities will probably be the most decentralised state in the world' (1996d); 'It will be a very loose and highly decentralised state with weak central powers for its common institutions – and thus unlike any other state in existence' (1996c); 'What is necessary in order to make peace work is to have effective and true power sharing between the two entities and the three communities ... Power sharing is the essence of the Constitution that is at the core of the Peace Agreement' (OHRB, 1996b).

The central constitutional plank of this new multi-ethnic state was the division of Bosnia into two separate entities: the Croat-Muslim (Bosniak) Federation, established by the Washington Agreement in 1994, occupying 51 per cent of the territory and the Serb entity, Republika Srpska, occupying the remaining 49 per cent. The responsibilities of the state and entity institutions were outlined in Article III of the Bosnian constitution. Institutions of the Bosnian state were to be responsible for foreign policy, foreign trade, customs, monetary policy, inter-entity communication, international and inter-entity law enforcement, and transportation. The entities were to be responsible for 'all governmental functions and powers not expressly assigned in this Constitution', for example, law enforcement, education and social policy. The entities also had the right 'to establish special parallel relationships with neighbouring states consistent with the sovereignty and territorial integrity of Bosnia and Herzegovina' (par. 2a).

In order to safeguard the interests of the three groups, the central state institutions were organised on the basis of an ethnic key which guaranteed representation to all three sides and the protection of 'vital interests'. The Dayton Agreement outlined the constitutional procedures and powers in relation to the Presidency, Council of Ministers and the Parliamentary Assembly in Annex 4.

The Presidency

There was to be a three-member Presidency, directly elected, one Croat and one Bosniak elected from the territory of the Federation, with each voter only allowed to vote for one seat, ensuring that only Croats voted for the Croatian Presidential candidates and only Bosniaks for the Bosniak candidates, and one Serb elected from the territory of Republika Srpska (Article V, par. 1). Alija Izetbegovic, representing the Muslim SDA, became the first Chair of the Presidency as he attained the highest number of votes.

The Presidency was bound to endeavour to adopt all Presidential decisions by consensus (Article V, par. 2). When consensus could not be reached, a dissenting member of the Presidency could declare a Presidency decision to be destructive of a vital interest of the Entity from which they were elected. If so, the decision would be referred immediately to either the National Assembly of Republika Srpska or the Croat or Bosniak delegates in the Federation House of the Peoples. If the declaration was confirmed by a two-thirds vote of those persons, the Presidency decision could not take effect.

The Council of Ministers

The Presidency nominated a Chair of the Council of Ministers and the Chair nominated Ministers and Deputy Ministers; both the Chair and the Ministers could only take office on approval by the House of Representatives. Under the DPA, no more than two-thirds of all Ministers could be appointed from the territory of the Federation and the Deputy Ministers could not be from the same constituent people as their Ministers (Article V, par. 4). Following the guidance of the High Representative, the Presidency decided that the Council would be led by two co-chairmen, one Bosniak and one Serb, rotating weekly, with a Croat vice-chair, and that each Minister would have two Deputies from the other two peoples (OHRB, 1996v). Consensual decision-making was to operate within each Ministry, with differences of opinion forwarded to the full Council (OHRR, 1997a, par. 24).

The State Parliament

Under Article IV, the ethnic composition and procedures of the Parliamentary Assembly were laid down by international law. The Parliamentary Assembly consisted of two chambers: the House of Peoples and the House of Representatives. The House of Peoples comprised of 15 delegates, five Croats and five Bosniaks, selected by the Croat and Bosniak delegates, respectively, of the House of Peoples of the Federation, and five Serbs, selected by the Republika Srpska National Assembly. The House of Representatives consisted of 42 elected members, two-thirds elected from the territory of the Federation, and one-third from the territory of Republika Srpska.

The procedures laid down by the Agreement to protect minority interests were complex (Article IV, par. 3). Each chamber was to select from its members one Serb, one Croat and one Bosniak to serve as the Chair and Deputy Chairs, with the Chair rotating among the three. All legislation required the approval of both chambers. This approval was to be by simple majority vote of those present and voting, unless a majority did not include one-third of the members of each entity. If this was the case, the Chairs had three days to try and gain approval of over one-third of both entities. If this failed, the majority decision would go through unless there was a dissenting vote which included two-thirds or more of the members of either entity.

The defence of 'a vital interest' of an ethnic group was also provided for (par. 3e). If a majority of the Serb, Croat or Bosniak delegates to the House of the Peoples declared a Parliamentary decision to be destructive of a vital interest, then in order for it to be approved it had to have the support of the majority of all three of the delegations. However, if a majority of another delegation to the House of the Peoples objected to the invocation of this provision, a Joint Commission of three delegates, one from each group, was to be convened by the Chair of the House of the Peoples. If the issue was not resolved within five days it was to be referred to the Constitutional Court.

On paper, Dayton appeared to provide the security that was so essential after the war and to bridge the dilemma of unifying the state, as well as guaranteeing the protection of minorities through institutional safeguards. This chapter considers how the implementation matched the promise of multi-ethnic guarantees through decentralised decision-making and power-sharing. The sections below consider the autonomy of decision-making and the capacity for protecting vital interests, provided to the three ethnic constituent minorities, at state, entity, city and municipal levels.

STATE LEVEL

The first state-level elections were held in September 1996. Despite the large number of parties and large turn-out, the election results gave a substantial popular mandate to the three main pre-war nationalist parties: the Muslim Party of Democratic Action (SDA), the Serbian Democratic Party (SDS) and the Croatian Democratic Union (HDZ). The party composition of the Bosnian state Parliamentary Assembly demonstrated the segmented nature of Bosnian politics (see Table 3.1). The three main nationalist parties won about 86 per cent of the seats and, including the Muslim Party for Bosnia and Herzegovina and Serbian Party for Peace and Progress, the ethnic political blocs accounted for about 95 per cent of the seats (Kasapovic, 1997, pp. 119–20).

Table 3.1 Party Composition of the Bosnian State Parliament (September 1996)

Party	Seats	%
Party of Democratic Action (SDA)	19	45.2
Serb Democratic Party (SDS)	9	21.4
Croatian Democratic Union (HDZ)	8	19.0
Party for Bosnia and Herzegovina	2	4.8
Joint List	2	4.8
Party for Peace and Progress	2	4.8

Source: Kasapovic, 1997, p. 119.

As considered briefly in the previous chapter, the central state institutions of the Presidency, Council of Ministers and Parliamentary Assembly had little opportunity to develop policy proposals independently of the Office of the High Representative. Because policy was being made outside Bosnia, the policy-making process was not regulated by the Constitution but the international community. The extension of the Dayton mandates meant that the scenario of self-government and the need for constitutional protections for one ethnic group against the other two did not arise. Unlike under self-government, where constitutional safeguards were deemed necessary, under the High Representative's administrative guidance, consensus was obligatory and opposition seen as illegitimate obstruction. The High Representative instructed the parties that: 'the Peace Agreement is not an a la carte menu where you can choose what you like. It was, is and remains a package deal where full implementation is what counts ... The time for political trench-warfare over prestige or details [is over]' (OHRB, 1996t).

This meant that disagreements were not held to be between the parties, but rather between the Office of the High Representative and the parties, and therefore not open to constitutional challenge. The High Representative as the 'final arbiter' of the civilian implementation of Dayton, could not be challenged on the grounds of 'vital interest' or any other clause of the Bosnian Constitution. The democratic mandates attained by the three main nationalist parties in the elections counted for little against the mandate of the High Representative as the 'final arbiter' of the democratisation process.

The three main nationalist parties have been seen by leading international representatives not as bearers of a substantial democratic mandate but as barriers to democratisation in Bosnia. The leading nationalist representatives have been described by High Representative Carlos Westendorp as 'like animals who cling to their turf' and accused publicly by his Deputy, Jacques Klein, in the Sarajevo daily *Oslobodenje*, of only serving their own interests (Hedges, 1998; AP, 1998a). Far from taking into account ethnic group interests, Alex Ivanko, the spokesperson for the UN Mission in Bosnia, explained: 'My experience in this country is that if all three sides criticise you, you're probably on the right track, and it's a healthy compromise' (Landcent, 1998).

At state level, the Serbian presidential representative, Momcilo Krajisnik, and the Serbian delegation in the Council of Ministers were generally under the most pressure as the political desire for greater autonomy for the RS came up against OHR-led policies for economic and political integration. Far from taking Bosnian Serb concerns on board, the UN High Representative publicly threatened to sack Krajisnik, the Serb member of the Presidency, and later stated: 'I do not co-operate with [Momcilo] Krajisnik any longer ... We don't need Krajisnik ever and I don't count him in the building of this state' (*RFE/RL Newsline*, 1997c; Numanovic, 1998).

Croatian, Bosniak and Serb leaders have all accused the High Representative and leading international institutions of breaking the Dayton Agreement guarantees of ethnic autonomy in policy-making. The Croatian Deputy Prime Minister of Bosnia, Neven Tomic, has argued that international community hostility to the three leading national parties contravenes Dayton's guarantee that Bosnia would be composed of three constituent nations (BBC, 1998). In May 1998, Bosnia's Muslim President, Alija Izetbegovic, wrote an open letter to the Deputy High Representative, Jacques Klein, accusing him of taking on authority beyond the Dayton mandates in his attacks on elected politicians, complaining that Dayton did not establish a protectorate 'and you are not the protector' (AP, 1998a). Republika Srpska President Biljana Plavsic, has similarly condemned international 'nation-builders', stating that she opposed the international community's use of 'the nebulous concept of the "spirit of Dayton" to blur the issue and legitimise ad-hoc reinterpretation of the agreement' (Plavsic, 1998). She has instead insisted on the implementation of the 'letter of the agreement' which granted specific rights to each ethnic group and to each of the two separate entities (*RFE/RL Newsline*, 1998e). In August 1998, Milorad Dodik, the Western-sponsored RS Prime Minister, reiterated these requests, calling for local authorities to have more decision-making powers (*RFE/RL Newsline*, 1998f)

ENTITY LEVEL

The Federation

The Federation followed the same model of ethnic balance as the Bosnian state, with guarantees of minority representation and the protection of vital interests. The Federation has a joint-Presidency with a Muslim and Croat as President and Vice-President. The Federation Parliament is constituted from two Houses: the House of the Peoples, composed of 30 Bosniaks, 30 Croats and up to 14 Others, selected by the Canton Assemblies; and the Federation House of Representatives composed of 140 directly elected members (see Table 3.2).

Table 3.2 Party Composition of the Federation Parliamentary Assembly (September 1996)

Party	Seats	%
Party of Democratic Action (SDA)	78	55.7
Croatian Democratic Union (HDZ)	35	25.0
Joint List	11	7.9
Party for Bosnia and Herzegovina	11	7.9
Democratic People's Union	3	2.1
Croatian Party of Rights	2	1.4

Source: Kasapovic, 1997, p. 120.

Even at the level of the Federation, Bosnian politicians were seldom allowed to autonomously introduce policy. Policy-making and implementation took a similar form to that at state level, except the American government played a more direct role in assisting the OHR. The Federation, although not a creation of the Dayton Peace Agreement, was considered by the international community to be 'an indispensable building block for its successful implementation', the central plank of international policy in Bosnia and the key to holding the state together (OHRR, 1996a, par. 86).

Federation policy implementation was developed by the US Embassy and the OHR Advisory Commission in Brussels. Ties between the Federation and the Republic of Croatia were encouraged in order to give more confidence to the Bosnian Croats and to use economic and diplomatic pressure on Croatian President Tudjman to ensure their compliance. While the proposed 'special relations' between RS and the FRY were seen as destructive, the US brokers of the Federation actively pressurised Izetbegovic into accepting these closer links with Croatia (OHRB, 1997x).

The Federation Forum

Since Dayton, there have been regular monthly high-level meetings held to enforce international policy within the Federation. These meetings are co-chaired by the Principal Deputy High Representative and the US Assistant Secretary of State. Participants vary but generally include the President and Vice-President of the Federation, the President of Bosnia, the OSCE Head of Mission, and other senior international officials (OHRB, 1996l). The United States, as architect of the Federation, has maintained a strong influence over policy in the entity and, through Forum meetings, applies diplomatic pressure on the parties. It is at this level that Federation policy is often decided, before being put to the governing institutions, examples being the common institutions at entity and canton level (OHRB, 1996x); the organisation of Mostar, Sarajevo and other divided municipalities, and most internationally-prepared draft legislation (OHRB, 1997d; OHRB, 1997h).

The Federation Implementation Council

The Federation Implementation Council (FIC), established in May 1996, was one of the most important committees established by the Federation Forum. The composition of the FIC demonstrated the desire of the international community to side-step the representative bodies (OHR FBH, 1996, p. 1; OHRB, 1996c). The Council was chaired by the Deputy Principal High Representative and included two other international community representatives as well as the President and Vice-President of the Federation. It convened in Sarajevo, whenever the Deputy Principal High Representative deemed necessary, to hear cases against persons holding elected or appointed offices at Federal, Canton, City or Municipal level. Cases could be brought by Council members, the Ombudsman of Bosnia, Ombudsman of the Federation, the Federation Arbitrator and the Federation Mediator.

The Council had the power to remove individuals from office under three headings of misdemeanour:

1. Violation of obligations under the Constitution of the Federation, the laws of the Federation, or the relevant Canton, City or Municipality, the Dayton Peace Agreement or any other international agreements on the Federation or decisions of the Federal Arbitrator
2. The substantial violation of human rights or the incitement, assistance or condoning of violations by others, including advocacy of ethnic, religious or racial hatred that may lead to discrimination, hostility or violence

3. As a member of the executive branch, systematically and seriously obstructing co-operation with the International Tribunal for the Former Yugoslavia.

The FIC, although ostensibly a temporary forum, was given permanent status by the Federation Forum in February 1997.

Special groups

Following the *Agreed Measures* signed in Geneva, in August 1996, a Special Group was established to finalise the schedule of implementation, involving representatives of the US government and the Office of the High Representative and the Bosnian and Federation governments (OHRB, 1996n). This forum was similarly extended beyond the elections and, in October 1996, chaired by Deputy High Representative Michael Steiner, it was mandated to decide on the implementation of the agreed measures for Sarajevo, the design of Federation emblems and unified customs and policing reforms to be put to the Federation Assembly (OHRB, 1996r).

At the Federation Forum, in February 1997, it was decided to establish a Special Group to deal with the broadcast media, co-chaired by the OHR and the US Embassy (OHRB, 1997d; OHRB, 1997h). An Advisory Commission was also established, headed by the Council of Europe, to address the question of municipality structures (OHRR, 1997a, par. 55).

Elected bodies

The Federation President and Vice-President, Vladimir Soljic and Ejup Ganic, had little power to influence policy-making and were under the pressure of the international community, the Office of the High Representative, and the Croatian and Bosnian Presidents who had their own interests in their party juniors following the instructions of the international community. The Federation Parliament was, like the state assembly, ill-equipped to debate fully or to oppose the international community policy recommendations passed down through the Federation Forum and its committees. Any attempts to hold up issues of contention, such as the Council of Europe-prepared legislation relating to the split and new municipalities, was met by pressure from the Office of the High Representative and the threat that the international community would decide if Parliament could not (see, for example, OHRB, 1997m). Following similar lines of operation, the lower-level canton assemblies met under the watchful eye of the Office of the High Representative and implemented pre-prepared policies (see, for example, OHRB, 1997a). In April

1998, when asked about the leading Federation parties' lack of support for the international community's Federation policy, Senior Deputy High Representative Hanns Schumacher stated:

> I don't care! I am simply not interested in who does not want the Federation: this is a concept that we will implement, despite the resistance on the field, which undoubtedly exists! ... We dictate what will be done! Therefore, this is a concept that will be implemented jointly and we simply do not pay attention to those who obstruct! (Suljagic, 1998)

Republika Srpska

The capacity for independent policy-making of the RS entity has been strictly regulated through the adoption of OHR-prepared legislation such as the Law on the Government of Republika Srpska and the Law on the Ministries. The Serb Democratic Party (SDS), previously led by Radovan Karadzic and seen as hard-line opponents of Dayton, won a comfortable majority in the September 1996 Assembly elections (see Table 3.3). The RS governmental functions were largely transferred from Pale to Banja Luka, as part of the process of weakening the influence of the hard-liners, and the number of ministries reduced. This move was facilitated by the expansion of the OHR regional office and completed after the November 1997 Assembly elections.

Table 3.3 Party Composition of the Republika Srpska Assembly (September 1996)

Party	Seats	%
Serb Democratic Party (SDS)	45	54.2
Party of Democratic Action (SDA)	14	16.9
Party of Peace and Progress	10	12.0
Serb Radical Party	6	7.2
Party for Bosnia and Herzegovina	2	2.4
Joint List	2	2.4
Others	4	4.8

Source: Kasapovic, 1997, p. 120.

The central area of dispute with the Office of the High Representative was over the powers and authority that elected representatives could wield over the entity. The desire for greater autonomy was considered as a 'pretence of statehood' by the High Representative and therefore contrary to the Dayton Agreement. Of particular concern was legislation on the economy and citizenship. Republika Srpska's desire to extend citizenship to residents of the former Yugoslavia, for example, Serb refugees from the Croatian Krajina, was resisted by the Legal Department of the OHR (OHRR, 1997a, par. 34). Similarly, economic legislation which sought to enable the National Bank of Republika Srpska to operate a foreign exchange market and control the domestic currency was ruled to be unacceptable, as have plans to generate closer economic ties with the FRY (OHRR, 1997a, par. 64).

Dayton commitments to a free market and international economic reconstruction assistance have enabled economic pressure to be put on Republika Srpska to break its economic ties with the FRY. High Representative Carl Bildt, in a joint press conference with Assistant to the US Treasury David Lipton, in January 1997, stressed the need to sever economic ties, stating that the people in Republika Srpska were in a fortunate situation because they were part of Bosnia-Herzegovina and only this could save them from 'economic catastrophe' (OHRB, 1997b). The February 1997 Agreement on Special and Parallel Relations between the RS and the FRY, which envisaged a Co-operation Council to work on planning and co-operation in areas of economic development, culture and communications, was strongly opposed by the High Representative Carl Bildt (OHRB, 1997h; OHRB, 1997j). Carl Bildt's concern was that the agreement could undermine international attempts to push through economic legislation to bind the two entities together (OHRB, 1997k).

The IMF Programme went beyond the Quick Start Package in restricting the economic regulatory controls of the RS entity. In June 1997, Scott Brown, the IMF Mission Chief for Bosnia, clarified the nature of this Programme, which had been developed with the OHR at the end of 1996. The four basic elements included: the currency board regulation of the Central Bank, maintaining the fixed exchange rate and preventing credit creation; budgets being financed only through domestic revenue and external assistance, not government domestic borrowing; large-scale external assistance for economic reconstruction, and structural and legal reforms to rapidly facilitate transition to a market economy (OHRB, 1997t). This package, in conjunction with the QSP, literally forced RS into dependence on politically conditioned economic reconstruction aid from the international community. With no ability to raise credits externally or domestically and the imposition of limits on state spending, Republika Srpska was forced to accede to international community wishes. This resulted in the RS accepting an internationally imposed entity budget and a common currency as preconditions for the following donors' conference (OHRB, 1997t).

The political domination of the international community over the internal affairs of the RS was demonstrated in July 1997, when international pressure on RS President Plavsic resulted in a rift between the President and the National Assembly. The political crisis led to further direct intervention in the domestic politics of the entity as the international community supported President Plavsic's control over internal affairs in order to combat the 'increasingly anti-democratic atmosphere' (OHRB, 1997v). NATO troops occupied the public buildings in Banja Luka, handed them over to President Plavsic and disarmed local police loyal to the Pale faction, while a British officer sat in Ms Plavsic's office answering her phone (Hedges, 1998). The Principals of the OHR, OSCE, SFOR, UNMIBH/IPTF and UNHCR supported President Plavsic's consequent dissolution of the Parliamentary Assembly and overruled the Constitutional Court which held her action to be unconstitutional (OHRB, 1997u). New National Assembly elections were held under OSCE regulation in November 1997 (see Table 3.4).

Table 3.4 Party Composition of the Republika Srpska Assembly (November 1997)

Party	Seats	%
Serb Democratic Party (SDS)	24	28.8
SDA-led Coalition	16	19.2
Serb Radical Party	15	18.0
Serb People's Alliance (SNS)	15	18.0
RS branch of Milosevic's Socialists	9	10.8
Independent Social Democrats	2	2.4
Bosnian Social Democratic Party	2	2.4

Source: OSCE MBH, 1998a.

The split in the ruling SDS, with President Plavsic's establishment of a new party (SNS), together with the substantial refugee vote for the SDA-led coalition (see Chapter 5) meant that the SDS lost their majority and that even with the support of the Serb Radical Party they were three seats short of forming a new government. Initially the international community urged the Assembly to support a government that stood apart from party politics, involving eleven non-elected experts and eleven representatives of the parties, headed by Mladen Ivanic, an economics professor at Banja Luka University who had not stood in the elections (*RFE/RL Newsline*, 1998a). The SDS and SRS were uncooperative and protested that this would devalue the parliamentary election results (OHR SRT, 1998a).

Plavsic then proposed Milorad Dodik as Prime Minister, the leader of the pro-Dayton Independent Social Democrats, which had won only two seats in the Assembly. Negotiations broke down and the SDS and the SRS, controlling 39 seats and the speakers' chair, adjourned the parliamentary session late at night on 17 January. Those remaining were one short of a majority as a member had already left to drive home to Zagreb. Deputy High Representative Jacques Klein asked NATO troops to intercept him on the road and return him to parliament. The session was reconvened and, without representatives of the SDS and SRS, a new government was elected (Kelly, 1998).

Klein's quick thinking was praised and the new multi-ethnic government, with the support of 18 Croat and Muslim deputies, was welcomed by the international community. Following this, the High Representative publicly insisted that the Parliament select a third Deputy Prime Minister from the Coalition for a United and Democratic Bosnia and Herzegovina, in order for the Federation MPs' strong presence to be adequately reflected (OHRB, 1998a). However, it remains to be seen whether Dodik's leadership will be seen as credible within the entity itself, with even the Deputy High Representative fearing that international actions to impose a government reliant on Federation parties and the promise of international funding could make the Assembly 'look like Western stooges' (O'Connor, 1998a).

There is very little autonomous policy-making at the entity level of the Federation or Republika Srpska. International involvement at this level has attracted most attention in the RS where internal power struggles among the Bosnian Serb leadership have been the subject of international intervention. International involvement in Federation policy-making had been much less overt or publicly contested prior to the Bonn Peace Implementation Council summit, in December 1997, which gave the OHR the power to dismiss representatives of both entities for non-co-operation. The willingness of the High Representative to use his powers of policy imposition at this level, as and when necessary, have been clearly demonstrated in the lists of demands and deadlines which have been presented by the Office of the High Representative to both entity assemblies.

THE KEY CITIES: MOSTAR, SARAJEVO AND BRCKO

The three key cities where the protection of minority ethnic interests were considered most important were Mostar, Sarajevo and Brcko. Mostar, at the heart of the Federation, was divided, the west bank under Croat control, the east bank under Muslim control. To bring unity to the Federation, it was necessary to create a new multi-ethnic administration that could win the trust of both sides. Sarajevo, the capital, was possibly even more important as a showcase for a united Bosnia, again special measures were felt necessary to ensure Serbs and Croats felt safe to return. Brcko was placed under international arbitration under Dayton, as a region claimed by both the Federation and RS and seen by the international community as a test case for rebuilding confidence.

Mostar

Under the regulation of the European Union Administration Mostar (EUAM), elections were organised in June 1996. This was the first test of international mechanisms for institutionalising multi-ethnic administrations. In February, the EUAM drew up an electoral statute that allotted 16 City Council seats to the Bosniaks, 16 to the Croats and 5 to 'Others'. On paper this looked like an ideal solution, guaranteeing an equal say for both sides and avoiding any one group having a majority, which could then be used to deny the other group equal rights, thereby creating insecurity and conflict.

Unfortunately, the international community experiment in multi-ethnic equality did not work out as planned. Out of 106,568 eligible voters, 58,301 voted, including 18,000 who travelled back to vote and 7,426 in refugee polling stations in Denmark, Norway, Sweden and Germany. The Croat HDZ list under the west Mostar mayor, Mijo Brajkovic, gained 26,680 votes, and the Muslim SDA coalition which included the Liberal Party, the Party for Bosnia-Herzegovina, the Liberal Bosniak and the Serb Citizen Forum, headed by the east Mostar mayor, Safet Orucevic, took 28,505, while the multi-ethnic United Democrats coalition, led by Jola Musa, captured just 1,937 votes, around 3 per cent. Due to the complicated electoral system, a narrow SDA coalition victory meant that all five of the new council's Others were Serbs from their list while none came from the HDZ list. This meant that despite the complicated election engineering of the European Union, the Muslim SDA had control over the City Council.

The complex electoral management involved can be demonstrated by a closer examination of the election regulations covering the City Council and the Mostar Municipal Councils. The City Council of 37 councillors (16 Bosniak, 16 Croat and 5 Others) was to be composed of 24 councillors elected from the six municipalities comprising the City of Mostar and 13 councillors elected from throughout the city regardless of municipality. The six Municipal Councils were to elect 25 councillors also on a preset ethnic criteria (see Table 3.5).

Table 3.5 Mostar Municipal Councils

Municipality	Croats	Bosniaks	Others
1. Mostar North	4	11	10
2. Mostar-Old Town	4	12	9
3. Mostar-South-East	3	19	3
4. Mostar-South	12	6	7
5. Mostar-South-West	12	6	7
6. Mostar-West	10	6	9

Source: ICG, 1996b.

In each municipality, three separate ballots took place, one for the 25 councillors for the Municipal Council, one for the 4 councillors to the City Council and another for the whole city to elect the 13 at-large councillors to the City Council. The candidates for the council seats were selected on a proportionate system based on quotients of the electoral lists. Once a share of a given ethnicity was achieved, then the first candidate of a different ethnic group on the same party list was elected. If there were no more candidates of a different ethnic group on the same party list, candidates from the party list with the next highest votes were selected. If the party lists did not hold enough candidates to fulfil the quota of an ethnic group, then the seats were to remain vacant. Because the Bosniak SDA list achieved more votes than the Croat HDZ list this enabled its Serb candidates to pick up the five City Council seats reserved for Others. This meant that the SDA-led List of Citizens for Mostar won 21 of the 37 seats and the HDZ won 16 seats.

From the standpoint of the international community, even the allocation of seats in advance failed to produce the desired result. Having lost the election, and after having opposed the reunification of the city to begin with, the Croats argued that the City Council was illegitimate. In order to preserve the ideal of ethnic equality, the European Union had to re-fix the elections to take account of the results not fitting their expectations. In August a new agreement was reached on forming a joint town administration for the city. It was decided that the City Council meet to elect a Mayor and Deputy Mayor, with the precondition that the Mayor was to be a Croat (OHRB, 1996l).

The international community has been accused of manipulating democracy to serve the interests of the Bosnian Croats by giving them the Mayor's position despite the fact that the Muslims won the majority of the votes (Heitmann, 1996, p. 24). While this is true, it misses the point that the democratic wishes of neither the Bosnian Croats nor the Muslims were furthered by this move. Policy to be implemented by the newly elected council was to be made in Brussels through the offices of the European Union and the Office of the High Representative. The August agreement imposed the control of the European Union Special Envoy over both sides:

> The Mayor and Deputy Mayor shall co-operate closely with the Special Envoy of the European Union in fulfilling his mandate. The Mayor in particular shall, as soon as possible, carry out the tasks in Article 39 of the Interim Statute of the City of Mostar on the basis of consensus with the Deputy Mayor, during the life of this Agreement. (OHRB, 1996l)

The beauty of the externally-administrated electoral process was that the people living in Mostar could have an election in which the parties supporting the international community plans for Mostar received only marginal support yet could have their policies imposed under the guise of ethnic equality and consensus politics. The elections were considered a success not because of the results but because they provided a mechanism for enforcing the will of the international community. The Office of the High Representative celebrated the elections, stating:

> [They] were without doubt a success for the Mostaris and the European Union Administration of the city. The astonishingly high turnout of almost 60 per cent of the 100,000 electorate provided substantial proof that people want elections, thus sending a strong positive signal for the general elections in September. The atmosphere was peaceful, sometimes even festive ... Voters travelled freely between East and West Mostar while the local and international police, supported by IFOR, worked well together and provided the necessary level of security. (OHRB, 1996h)

The elections gave the impression of being free and fair and enough people voted to give the new city institutions a democratic mandate. In terms of international opinion, the international community was clearly doing a good job in assisting democracy. Which parties or political programmes the people voted for was entirely secondary for the international community because the seats had been allocated in advance to ensure that there was an ethnic balance and the mandate of the EU Administration meant it could enforce policy on the parties. The pattern of voting itself symbolised little support for the EU Administration, as the OHR stated:

> ... the results of the elections, however, sent mixed signals. Most people chose to vote along ethnic lines with the SDA-led

> List of Citizens receiving over 48 and the HDZ almost 46 per cent of the vote. The opposition share was practically reduced to zero and [they] will not be represented in the new city and municipal institutions. (OHRB, 1996h)

Through international community policies for promoting multi-ethnic governance, the wishes of the people and their elected representatives on both sides of the divided city were undermined. This lack of autonomy meant that there was little possibility for a negotiated solution between the parties. Even more problematic, for a stable solution to the division of Mostar, was the fact that the international imposition of ethnic equality did little to increase the security of people on either side of the divide. International regulation of the police and the media merely asserted the control of the international community as opposed to giving responsibility to the Mostaris themselves. For example, when the Croatian city authorities formed a 'Union of Mostar city municipalities with a Croat majority', Deputy High Representative Gerd Wagner proclaimed this was illegal if it did not limit itself to services outside the Agreed Principles for an Interim Statute for the City of Mostar, and warned that 'any decision ... to melt the three municipalities on either side of the Neretva into one would be a severe violation not only of the letter but also of the spirit of the agreement reached in Dayton' (OHRB, 1997w).

The influential International Crisis Group reported after the elections that the rules governing Mostar in future municipal elections should not be altered, advising that: '[The OSCE] must apply the EUAM rules and not the OSCE rules. Although it would be anomalous to distinguish Mostar in this fashion, only the EUAM rules guarantee an equitable distribution of seats in joint institutions' (ICG, 1996a, p. 3). These rules meant that international regulation was institutionalised on the grounds that ethnic equality necessitated external regulation to prevent one side dominating the other. The drawback to this approach was that external regulation marginalised the Mostari voters and elected representatives and imposed co-operation from above as opposed to increasing local accountability for policy-making.

Sarajevo

Sarajevo was of central importance to the administrators of the international community, who were keen to demonstrate that multi-ethnic co-operation existed in the state's capital city. After Dayton the international management of Sarajevo was directly in the hands of the High Representative, operating through the Joint Civilian Commission Sarajevo (JCCS).

The international community was highly embarrassed by the actions of the Muslim-led government towards the Serbs that wanted to remain in Sarajevo and the success of the SDS encouragement for people to leave. Against the reality of an increasingly mono-ethnic city, the international community imposed the Rome Statement on Sarajevo in February 1996. This resulted in the integration of the Ilidza municipality at the end of May, through swearing-in 14 local Serbs who had remained while the suburb changed hands. Deputy High Representative Michael Steiner made an address declaring at the assembly meeting that this step heralded 'serious progress toward building a democratic, multi-ethnic future' (OHRB, 1996e).

In Sarajevo the international community avoided the embarrassment of elections entirely and decided to allocate seats by political party as well as ethnicity (see Tables 3.6 and 3.7).

Table 3.6 Sarajevo Municipal Council Seat Allocation by Political Party and Nationality

By political party:		By nationality:	
HDZ	3	Bosniaks	16
SBiH	1	Croats	6
SDA (including at least 2 'Others')	12	Others	6
SPD (including together at least	7		
UBSD 3 Croats and 4 'Others')	5		

Source: OHR FBH, 1997b.

Table 3.7 Seat Allocation by Political Party in the Four Sarajevo Municipal Councils

Centar:		Novo Sarajevo:	
HDZ	1	HDZ	1
SBiH	0	SBiH	0
SDA	3	SDA	3
SDP	1	SDP	2
UBSD	2	UBSD	1
Novi Grad:		**Stari Grad:**	
HDZ	1	HDZ	0
SBiH	0	SBiH	1
SDA	3	SDA	3
SDP	2	SDP	2
UBSD	1	UBSD	1

Source: OHR FBH, 1997b.

In March 1997, the Constitution of Sarajevo was amended to provide a framework that guaranteed multi-ethnicity, regardless of the amount of votes cast for candidates and parties. The City Constitution now stated, in Article 4b, that the City Council would consist of 28 councillors, with seven delegates being nominated from each of the four Municipal Councils in such a way that:

> A minimum of 20 per cent of seats in the City Council [that is, six seats] shall be guaranteed to Bosniaks, Croats and the group of Others, regardless of the election results ... If the minimum number of seats ... can not be filled by electing city councillors from among the municipal councillors, city councillors shall be elected from among the candidates from the list of political parties who participate in the municipal councils, on the basis of election results. (OHR FBH, 1997a)

As was the case in Mostar, this detailed regulation of the ethnic key gave minority groups a strong voice in policy-making on paper that was not matched by autonomous decision-making in practice. The Sarajevo Canton Assembly had the task of implementing policy drawn up by the Federation Forum and Special Group, in particular the Protocol on the Organisation of Sarajevo. At the first session in October, Deputy High Representative Steiner addressed the assembly and outlined the tasks ahead (OHRB, 1996r).

Brcko

Under the Dayton Agreement the international mandate over the town was expressly given for one year, ending in December 1996 (GFA, 1995, Annex 1-B, par. 2). A week before the mandate expired, the tribunal decided to extend the international mandate for a further two months, then for a further year, until March 1998 (OHRB, 1996x; OHRB, 1997f). Roberts Owen, the international arbiter, stated that the reason for continued supervision was that the tribunal 'had not been convinced that any of the three candidates [the Federation, Republika Srpska, or the joint Bosnian institutions] were sufficiently stabilised to take on the situation' (OHRB, 1997f). In February 1998, the international mandates were extended for a further 13 months as there was little pressure for self-government to be restored once the international mandates had been indefinitely extended (Graham, 1998).

In order to 'strengthen local democratic institutions' and to supervise the implementation of Dayton in the area, the Office of the High Representative established an office and staff under an OHR-appointed Supervisor, Robert Farrand, nominated by the

United States (OHRB, 1997f). The Arbitration Tribunal ruling outlined nine key factors to be included in the work of the Brcko Supervisor (presented in Table 3.8).

Table 3.8 Brcko Arbitration Rulings (14 February 1997)

No.	External agency	Role
1	OHR Supervisor	promulgation of binding regulations and orders
2	OHR, OSCE, UNHCR, SFOR, EBRD, IMF, and others	advisory Council
3	SFOR and IPTF	democratic policing
4	UNHCR, Commission for Displaced Persons and Refugees, and other agencies	organisation of return
5	Deputy High Representative and OSCE	organisation of elections and issue of regulations and orders following them
6	international development agencies	economic revitalisation
7	public and private investors	revive Sava River port
8	international customs monitors	customs controls
9	State of BH and Republic of Croatia	customs and border crossings

Source: OHRB, 1997f.

The Brcko ruling, referred to as a 'mini and accelerated Dayton' by the Supervisor, Robert Farrand (OHRB, 1997l), demonstrates in microcosm how international strategy for implementing multi-ethnic administrations has done little to further autonomy or self-government on a local or national level. The elections provided for representation of the three main ethnic groups, but their influence over policy-making was to be strictly limited. The OSCE was to organise elections and the Supervisor was empowered, 'following such elections, [to] issue such regulations and orders as may be appropriate to enhance democratic and a multi-ethnic administration' (OHRB, 1997f).

In May 1997, the OSCE decided municipal elections should be held in the pre-war Brcko municipality of Brcko Grad, under the control of the Serb side, but not on the Federation side in Rahic Brcko and Ravne Brcko, except to allow displaced persons from the RS side to vote. The aim of these elections was to establish a 'multi-ethnic governing body in Brcko Grad' and the Head of the OSCE mission, Robert Frowick, warned that taking part in the elections was compulsory: '... any attempt by either party to boycott the elections would undoubtedly be viewed by the Arbitrator as an extremely serious obstruction of efforts toward a democratic solution in Brcko, and could prejudice the case of whichever side took such action' (OHRB, 1997o).

Following the municipal elections of September 1997, which resulted in a Serb majority, Ambassador Farrand issued the *Supervisory Order on Multi-Ethnic Administration.* This Order, in effect, annulled the election results by ensuring that the international community, not the winning party, could determine the composition of the political officers and policy issues:

- The Municipal Assembly was to have three leading officers, a President, Vice-President and a Secretary, all of different nationalities.
- Assembly decisions on issues considered to be of vital national interest were to require the approval of at least half of the Assembly Members of each national group represented by a minimum of five percent of the seats.
- The President of the Executive Board (Mayor) was to have two deputies, all three individuals were to be of different nationalities. (OHRB, 1997B)

The High Representative welcomed the rulings' provisions, stating: 'Taken together, these measures should, during the coming year, make it possible to transform Brcko from an area of confrontation to an area of co-operation between the different constituent nations of Bosnia-Herzegovina' (OHRB, 1997f). However, co-operation between the parties was to be imposed by the international community. The OHR Supervisor was given the 'authority to promulgate binding regulations and orders to further implementation and local democratisation' (OHRB, 1997f). In the conclusion to his introductory speech, the new Supervisor Robert Farrand explained that key policies were 'not a point for debate' (OHRB, 1997l). The mandate of legislative and executive powers was placed in the hands of an external administrator, after the Dayton requirement to return the area to Bosnian authorities had been overruled, in order to promote democratisation. As the *Washington Post* described, his 'kingly powers' extended 'right down to determining who will live in which house, the list of required attendees at meetings of local police chiefs, the ethnic composition of the local municipal council and the pace at which privatisation will proceed' (Hockstader, 1998).

The international administrator used his powers to order that several City Council departments be headed by non-Serbs, and in fact, to give Brcko the most ethnically balanced staff of any city in Bosnia. However, there have been doubts over how much ethnic minorities have been empowered by this process and concerns over the proposed sacking of 52 of the 141 Serb council employees (OHR SRT, 1998b). There has been little reconciliation, Croat and Muslim returnees only feel safe in outlying districts where US soldiers are on constant patrol and Brcko Serbs, mainly refugees from Croat and Muslim-held areas, resent an internationally-appointed US diplomat ruling by decree and the imposition of a Muslim Mayor, Mirsad Djapo, as titular head of the City Council, whose office is 15 miles away in the Federation (O'Connor, 1998b).

MUNICIPAL AUTHORITIES

Before the end of 1997, the imposition of international community policy at the local level was largely limited to the threat of withdrawing reconstruction aid. In April 1996, Principal Deputy High Representative Steiner informed four authorities which had failed to agree on new interim municipal assemblies, Bosnian Croat-controlled Stolac and Capljina and Bosnian Muslim-controlled Bugojno and Vares, that they would no longer receive any 'financial resources from shared taxes and transfers' or reconstruction aid (ICG, 1997b, p. 16; see also OHRB, 1997d). As a spokesperson from the OSCE Democratisation Branch stated, this was a 'tough weapon' with little to show in the short term, although the international community hoped that in the 'black-listed' authorities, the lack of funds would encourage people to put pressure on politicians and 'eventually they will have to come begging'. He termed this approach 'sustainable multi-ethnic development' as it was hoped that support for more openness would come from the local communities themselves.[1]

At the end of 1997, the international community developed two new lines of approach, which were much more interventionist, to ensure that minority group rights were protected and multi-ethnic administrations created at the local level. The first approach was the dismissal of obstructive officials at local level following the extension of the powers awarded to the High Representative at Bonn in December 1997. In March and April 1998, the Office of the High Representative sacked the Croat HDZ Deputy-Mayor of Drvar, Drago Tokakcija, and the HDZ Mayor of Stolac, Pero Raguz, and, in September, the HDZ Mayor of Orasje, Mark Benkovic, as examples to other non-co-operative municipalities (Fazlic, 1998; *RFE/RL Newsline*, 1998c; 1998g). The second approach was the imposition of OSCE awards of multi-ethnic administrations following the municipal elections in September 1997. In towns such as Vares, Novi Travnik, Kresovo, Gornji Vakuf, Zepce, Foca, Brad, Prozor-Rama, Srebrenica and Stolac, the OSCE chose the mayors itself and disregarded local election results to create multi-ethnic administrations with greater parity.

The power-sharing mechanisms varied from city to city, for example, in Vares three of the city's departments were run by Croats and three by Muslims with the positions of Mayor and Deputy Mayor switching every five months between the Muslim and Croat representatives (O'Connor, 1998c). In the Sarajevo City Council in which the Muslim SDA won 17 seats, the Social Democratic Party won six, and the Croatian HDZ won three, the High Representative decided that the President should be a member of the SDP, but should be a Croat and should be selected by the other parties (OHRB, 1998a). In April 1998, the OSCE went further and suspended the assembly in Srebrenica altogether, imposing an interim executive board run by an international representative, appointed by the OSCE and the High Representative, who was to rule by decree (OSCE EASC, 1998; *Economist*, 1998b). In July, Deputy High Representative Schumacher announced the dismissal of the HDZ and SDA leaders of the Gornji Vakuf municipal assembly and threatened to suspend the whole assembly and replace it with an executive board (OHR BiH, 1998).

Despite their apparent short-term success, whether these internationally regulated power-sharing arrangements can become the basis of locally self-sustaining governing bodies is still an open question. These imposed solutions have rarely satisfied any of the parties, especially those with majority powers. In a dozen or so municipalities, where the votes of displaced persons meant that parties elected by absentee ballots gained a majority or a substantial minority, the conflict caused by the election regulations has been even more intense. It could be argued that the success on paper has yet to be matched by an increase in the confidence of minority populations in these towns and in some cases has led to increased tensions and fears that homes would be seized by absentee voters (see, for example, R. J. Smith, 1998a; Fleishman, 1998).

CONCLUSION

It can be argued that the minority protections promised to the three constituent peoples of Bosnia by the Dayton Agreement have not been delivered by the state's international administrators. Through the different case studies, at state, entity, city and municipality levels, a clear pattern has emerged of majorities being given little control over policy-making. However, this power has not been decentralised to give minority groups a stake in government but rather transferred to the international institutions responsible for democratisation and recentralised in the hands of the UN's High Representative.

The Bosnian state now seems to be much less unique than when imagined by the then High Representative, Carl Bildt, in July 1996, as 'a highly decentralised one with more extensive devolution of key responsibilities to the two entities than seen anywhere else in the world' (OHRR, 1996b, par. 84). The language of multi-ethnicity and power-sharing has been used to justify far-reaching international regulation of Bosnian political life but it remains to be seen whether this regulation can promote a genuine participatory pluralism based on the stable coexistence of different political interests.

In Bosnia, under Dayton, the institution of multi-ethnic administrations would appear to have achieved considerable success on paper, but as the case studies reveal, an imposed consensus on policy is not the same as one autonomously attained. Even at city and municipal level there is little accountability to constituents or autonomy for elected representatives. The international promotion of multi-ethnic administrations through sanctions and dismissals may well reassure neither majorities nor minorities that their needs will be taken into account in the long term.

4 The protection of human rights

Respect for human rights and their protection and promotion is generally seen to be an essential prerequisite for a democratic society. Nowhere is this considered more so than in Bosnia. One of the central preconditions, laid down by the international community, for the process of democratisation to be completed in Bosnia is the establishment of a culture in which human rights are universally respected:

> Human rights is the key to most other aspects of political and civilian implementation of the Peace Agreement. It is only when human rights are fully respected that the political life of the country can free itself of the factor of fear now so obvious. It is only when human rights are secure that the refugees and displaced people will start to return in greater number to their places of origin or choice. (OHRR, 1996d, par. 93)

For the drafters of the new Bosnian Constitution and the Dayton Agreement, the removal of 'the factor of fear' through the promotion of human rights was a foremost consideration. John Shattuck, the US Assistant Secretary of State, explained:

> We believe the success of the peace process is integrally related to the successful implementation of the human rights provisions of the Dayton accords. For this reason, implementing the human rights elements of Dayton is one of the Administration's highest priority goals for Bosnia ... a fundamental pillar of US foreign policy ... in Bosnia and Herzegovina, where Europe witnessed its most terrible crimes against humanity since the Holocaust. (USDoS, 1996a)

The High Representative, Carl Bildt, articulated this approach in even stronger terms at the first meeting of the Human Rights Task Force in Brussels in January 1996:

> The history of the conflict in Bosnia – as well as in all of former Yugoslavia – is the history of the most flagrant violations of human rights we have seen in recent European history. And the setting up of institutions and mechanisms to safeguard

> human rights in the future is one of the most crucial elements of the peace process that we are now embarking on. (cited in Amnesty, 1996, p. 2)

While the evidence was still being gathered and sifted through as to the extent of human rights abuses during the war, human rights took on a unique importance in the reconstruction of the Bosnian state. According to John Shattuck: 'From a human rights perspective, the Dayton accords are a remarkable document. Never before has a peace treaty placed such heavy emphasis on human rights concerns' (USDoS, 1996a). The unique emphasis on human rights protections has been welcomed by the international NGOs focusing on human rights concerns and by most commentators.

This chapter seeks to analyse the role of human rights protection in creating a new atmosphere of security that can assist the democratisation process. The following three sections consider the Dayton Agreement's inclusion of international human rights treaties in the Bosnian Constitution, the post-Dayton monitoring and assessment of the level of human rights abuses, and international intervention to promote a human rights culture in Bosnia through the war crimes tribunals and support for refugee return.

INTERNATIONAL TREATIES

Under the Dayton Agreement, the citizens of the Bosnian state were ensured 'the highest level of internationally recognised human rights and fundamental freedoms' (Annex 4, Article II, par. 1). Annex 4 (*The Constitution*) and Annex 6 (*Human Rights*) incorporated 16 human rights agreements into Bosnian law, listed in Annex 4, Article I, and in the appendix to Annex 6. The agreements were:

1. 1948 Convention on the Prevention and Punishment of the Crime of Genocide
2. 1949 Geneva Conventions I–IV on the Protection of the Victims of War, and 1977 Geneva Protocols I–II thereto
3. 1950 European Convention for the Protection of Human Rights and Fundamental Freedoms and the Protocols thereto
4. 1951 Convention relating to the Status of Refugees and the 1966 Protocol thereto
5. 1957 Convention on the Nationality of Married Women
6. 1961 Convention on the Reduction of Statelessness
7. 1965 International Convention on Elimination of All Forms of Racial Discrimination
8. 1966 International Covenant on Civil and Political Rights and 1966 and 1989 Optional Protocols thereto

9. 1966 Covenant on Economic, Social and Cultural Rights
10. 1979 Convention on the Elimination of All Forms of Discrimination against Women
11. 1984 Convention against Torture and Other Cruel, Inhuman or Degrading Treatment or Punishment
12. 1987 European Convention on Prevention of Torture and Inhuman or Degrading Treatment or Punishment
13. 1989 Convention on the Rights of the Child
14. 1990 Convention on Protection of the Rights of All Migrant Workers and Members of Their Families
15. 1992 European Charter for Regional or Minority Languages
16. 1994 Framework Convention for the Protection of National Minorities.

This provided the citizens of Bosnia with more human rights protections than those of any other state in the world. It is useful to compare the commitments of the Bosnian government with those of the US and the UK. Of the 16 agreements, the US had agreed to be bound fully by 3 and the UK by 10. This international comparison is illustrated in Table 4.1.

If there is a direct relation between constitutional protections for human rights and democracy, then clearly this institutional framework is a good starting point. However, the nature of the incorporation of these agreements raises some questions in relation to democratisation and the aim of facilitating popular sovereignty and democratic accountability in Bosnian society. To illustrate these questions it is useful to compare the incorporation of the European Convention on Human Rights into Bosnian law with the same process in Britain. The European Convention on Human Rights and Fundamental Freedoms and its protocols (Agreement no. 3), under the DPA, 'shall apply directly in Bosnia and Herzegovina' and 'shall have priority over all other law' (Annex 4, Article II, par. 2). This direct application is unique and highlights the relationship between the international community and Bosnian institutions which is at the core of this thesis.

In terms of democratic accountability, the UK government, in deciding to incorporate the Convention, made it clear that it would exercise its right to include derogations, such as the length of detention without trial for persons suspected of terrorism, and reservations, with respect to the right to education in accordance with cultural and religious beliefs. The British government would also continue to exclude the optional protocols 4 and 6 relating to conditions placed upon entry and the abolition of the death penalty (UKHO, 1997, Chapter 4). These derogations, reservations and exclusions are the product of a trade-off between universal human rights of individuals and the recognition of political needs of governments to act counter to these in specific circumstances, according to the demands of the general interest of the community.

Table 4.1 Human Rights Agreements: International Comparison

Agreement no.	United Kingdom	United States
1	accepted	accepted in 1989
2	accepted – both 1977 protocols signed but not ratified[1]	accepted – both 1977 protocols signed but not ratified
3	accepted – in process of incorporation, but derogations and reservations and without all optional protocols	not a party
4	accepted	not a party – 1966 protocol accepted
5	accepted	not a party
6	accepted	not a party
7	accepted	accepted in 1994
8	accepted – optional protocols on individual petition and abolition of death penalty excluded	accepted – not a party to optional protocols
9	accepted	signed 1977 but not ratified
10	accepted	signed 1980 but not ratified
11	accepted	accepted
12	accepted	not a party
13	accepted	signed 1995 but not ratified
14	not a party	not a party
15	not a party	not a party
16	signed 1995 but not ratified	not a party

[1] It should be noted that the signing of a treaty merely shows an interest in it, a state is not bound by it until ratification.

Source: Information provided from the UK Foreign Office Treaties Section and UK Home Office Human Rights Unit, November 1997.

In European states, such as Britain, incorporation into domestic law does not place the Convention 'above all other law' and states have a right to restrict the protected rights to the extent that this is 'necessary in a democratic society' (UKHO, 1997, par. 2.5). More importantly, the Convention itself does not require that priority be given, such that it takes precedence over domestic laws (UKHO, 1997, par. 2.12). The UK government has decided that the domestic courts should interpret legislation as far as possible as to be compatible with the Convention and where this is impossible for this to be formally declared. However, the courts' declaration of incompatibility will not result in the legislation being set aside, the reasons for this are as follows:

> This conclusion arises from the importance which the Government attaches to Parliamentary sovereignty. In this context, Parliamentary sovereignty means that Parliament is competent to make any law on any matter of its choosing and no court may question the validity of any Act that it passes. In enacting legislation, Parliament is making decisions about important matters of public policy. The authority to make those decisions derives from a democratic mandate. Members of Parliament in the House of Commons possess such a mandate because they are elected, accountable and representative. (UKHO, 1997, par. 2.13)

The people of Bosnia may have the highest level of human rights freedoms but it is possible to question the extent that this contributes to the process of developing democracy or enhancing security. If anything, the in-built human rights protections, which cannot be changed by Bosnian elected representatives, represent a permanent undermining of popular sovereignty in a manner which, as has been demonstrated, would never be accepted by the international powers which are enforcing the Dayton mandates. The Bosnian state is not expected to have the capacities for making judgements or considered trustworthy to rule on the basic fundamental rights of its citizens.

The fact that the human rights agreements were felt too important to be debated or discussed by Bosnian governing bodies or put to popular opinion, is also indicative of the lack of involvement of Bosnian people in their own constitutional and legal framework. This is in striking contrast to the procedure followed in other European states, in which the Convention has been wholly or partly incorporated into domestic law. For example, in the discussion on incorporation of the European Convention into UK law, in the Government White Paper, *Rights Brought Home: The Human Rights Bill*, the conception of ownership and 'broad agreement between the parties' is emphasised (UKHO, 1997, par. 1.2).

The fact that the Bosnian Constitution and the human rights framework of legislation had been externally prepared and imposed created problems for Bosnian lawyers and politicians who were unaware of the laws of their country. The OSCE, Office of the High Representative and the Council of Europe have worked to publicise these laws and explain them. For example, the OSCE Democratisation Branch and Council of Europe have established a Legislation Commentary Project where 'high profile academics and practitioners ... comment on these laws and explain their functioning', however, the problem lies less with the capacity to understand the laws than the fact that 'the texts of the laws of their own country are often inaccessible' (OSCE DB, 1997g, pp. 3–4; OSCE DB, 1997i, p. 2). This situation has created anxiety and mistrust, especially when the majority of existing legislation is found to be non-compliant with expected international standards. Dieter Wolkewitz, the OSCE Democratisation Branch Co-ordinator for the Rule of Law, explained that the whole of the former Bosnian system of para-legal bodies, of workplace tribunals and local courts was being reformed, not because it was not legally effective, but because the system differed from Council of Europe requirements.[1]

Under the framework of human rights protection, the court system is being reformed, judges vetted and reappointed, and Bosnian law rewritten, with little input from Bosnian politicians or lawyers. As the Bosnian courts and public prosecutors' offices suffer from a lack of professional staff, due to the weak financial situation, international institutions have stepped in to fill the gap (OSCE DB, 1997h, p. 2). Wolkewitz was highly supportive of the new law-making process, and stated that the Dayton regulations 'allow six or seven new independent bodies to overrule local unfairness and injustice'. On the basis of individuals seeking support from the OSCE, he was confident that democracy was being served as 'the population believes more in these [Dayton] institutions than their own institutions'.[2]

The reason for the unique powers given to the international institutions under the heading of human rights protection is the assumption that human rights are uniquely under threat in Bosnian society and that without international regulation 'massive human rights abuses' would occur. The next section looks further at the development of this perspective and its policy consequences.

THE CONTINUUM OF HUMAN RIGHTS ABUSE

The understanding of the Bosnian war as a succession of systematic human rights abuses, and the regular comparisons with the Holocaust made during the war, not only facilitated the creation of an international consensus for military intervention but has also been central to the development of international democratisation strategy to protect human rights. The allegations of war crime atrocities, ethnic cleansing, mass rapes, death camps and genocide, clearly cast many Bosnians (in particular the Serbs) as active or passive supporters of human rights abuses.

For many of the international institutions, this picture of a susceptibility to human rights abuses and their generalised nature is as correct three years on as it was during wartime. The Bonn Peace Implementation Council report, of December 1997, stated 'human rights violations threaten to remain endemic', while the US State Department Annual Report for 1997 found that 'human rights and civil liberties remain tenuous in Bosnia and Herzegovina' (PIC, 1997b, Section I; USDoS, 1998b, Introduction). These headline allegations make the press releases and have been used to argue for the extension of international mandates and to explain a multitude of political phenomena from the lack of return of displaced persons to the continued election successes of the three main nationalist parties.

This has been a misleading approach upon which to base democratisation strategy. The deeply held belief of many human rights NGOs, that Bosnian people were highly likely to abuse human rights, led to a one-sided focus that constantly portrayed Bosnian people and their elected authorities in a negative light. Many respected human rights monitoring agencies, such as Amnesty International, Human Rights Watch and the International Crisis Group, tended to use the existence of isolated cases of injustice to argue that serious human rights abuses were endemic. This 'tip of the iceberg' argument led to a misrepresentation of the situation on the ground in Bosnia. Leading human rights theorist Rein Mullerson, for example, writes that: 'some NGOs concentrate too much attention on certain issues or aspects of human rights situations which may distort the overall picture' (1997, p. 145). Questions over this approach and the real nature and extent of human rights abuses have been raised, for example, when the British government's Overseas Development Administration criticised Human Rights Watch for an overemphasis on what it described as 'unfounded allegations' (Vulliamy, 1997).

The use of isolated examples to allege widespread abuses was justified by international human rights NGOs on the basis that this assumption was the safest one considering the lack of evidence available. Diana Johnstone, writing in *The Nation*, described this circular approach in relation to wartime allegations of rape:

> The projected numbers and supposed pattern act in a reinforcing cycle. The initial impression that rapes were

> 'massive' suggests a deliberate policy and thus a pattern. When, later, the evidence does not support such large numbers, then the 'pattern' implies a 'policy' that in turn implies that the numbers must have been massive. (Johnstone, 1997)

Amnesty International, for example, argued that the monitoring situation was inadequate and required greater resources and organisation (Amnesty, 1996, section VII, A). The weak point with the 'tip of the iceberg' theory was that nowhere else in the world was there as extensive a system of human rights monitoring as in Bosnia. As the HRCC Florence Report revealed, the monitoring situation, with unimpeded access and expansive methods of information co-ordination, was 'surprisingly good ... [the] combined reporting provides a fairly thorough and accurate picture of the human rights situation throughout Bosnia' (PIC, 1996b, section II, D). The report stated that monitoring access was 'a crucial measure of the human rights situation' and that 'human rights monitors have been able to travel without restriction in all areas of the country' (PIC, 1996b, section III, 2).

Since Dayton, a growing network of human rights monitoring organisations have operated in Bosnia under a variety of international remits. The Office of the High Representative established a Human Rights Task Force to co-ordinate international monitoring and a Human Rights Co-ordination Centre (HRCC) for day-to-day co-ordination and support. International institutions were invited under the DPA to take part in extensive human rights monitoring, to date these have included: the UN Mission in Bosnia and Herzegovina, with overall responsibility for the monitoring role of the UN International Police Task Force and the UN Civil Affairs staff; the OSCE, which includes in its remit the monitoring and reporting of human rights abuses; the UN High Commissioner for Refugees, whose office in Bosnia is responsible for human rights assessments; the UN High Commissioner for Human Rights, again involved in monitoring; the European Community Monitoring Mission, with 20 teams deployed throughout Bosnia; and the Council of Europe's human rights support programme. There are also other organisations active in the human rights field, for example, the International Committee of the Red Cross; Human Rights Watch/Helsinki; Amnesty International; the International Helsinki Federation; the International Crisis Group and local NGOs supported by the International Council of Voluntary Agencies and the OSCE.

In fact, Bosnia's human rights record is fairly respectable by international or even European standards. There was little evidence to suggest the strategic or locally organised political use of state institutions such as the police to abuse the human rights of minorities. There were no reports of politically motivated disappearances in 1996 or 1997. There were two confirmed reports of police involvement in deaths of minority national groups in 'suspicious circumstances' in 1996. One incident occurred in the Federation, where two Croat special police officers were identified as perpetrators of the murder of a Bosnian Muslim driving between Zenica and Zepce; the other was the death of a Bosnian Muslim through physical abuse while in police custody in Banja Luka (USDoS, 1997, section 1). In 1997 there was just one report of a minority death at the hands of the police, which occurred when Croat police fired in a confrontation during a graveyard visit in West Mostar (USDoS, 1998b, section 1).

The main problem raised in human rights reports is not so much that of conflict but the lack of desire to reintegrate communities or to unquestioningly accept international policy requirements. Since Dayton, there has been little conflict between the three communities, which were now mostly separated by the Inter-Entity Boundary Line and administrative divisions within the Federation, the main exceptions being politically sensitive towns and villages along administrative divisions and the disputed city of Mostar. Where communities were intermixed, away from disputed lines of demarcation, most people were getting on with their lives and putting the war behind them (USDoS, 1998b, p. 15).

It seems that the more extensive the monitoring of human rights abuses has become, the more difficult it is to establish evidence of ongoing abuses. This has led to a variety of developments in the human rights reporting strategies of organisations and institutions. Typical was the way forward indicated in Amnesty International's statement that 'human rights abuses have not ceased *completely* nor have the conditions in which further serious abuses *could* be perpetrated' (Amnesty, 1996, section V, A, emphasis added). From the end of 1996, the emphasis of human rights reporting moved largely into the field of what might be happening now or in the future or through extending human rights 'abuses' into a catch-all category. Amnesty International, for example, criticised human rights reports that failed to indicate a sufficient level of 'abuses'; for example, some of the UNHCR Repatriation Reports. Amnesty argued that the UNHCR reports were problematic because they:

> ... include municipalities in Bosnia and Herzegovina which are relatively calm at present and do not necessarily reflect the conditions in Bosnia and Herzegovina generally. In addition, they do not include an assessment of whether rights violations

> would recur if refugees or internally displaced persons returned ... the apparent lack of reference to the human rights situation ... does not imply a human rights assessment in a given area. (Amnesty, 1996, section VII, A)

Of course, if human rights reports left out all the areas where there were no reports of human rights infringements and included a prediction of what could happen in the future, based on the unlikely scenario of full return in the context of housing shortage and unresolved political tensions, then there would be reports that 'reflected the general conditions' in Bosnia, or at least the conditions as Amnesty tended to portray them.

A popular strategy, used by the NGOs and the international institutions, has been to make up for the shortfall in serious incidents of human rights 'abuse' by expanding the definition of the problem. Many reports have taken to focusing on acts of 'more subtle discrimination', the types of harassment, with which people in workplaces and colleges in the US and Britain are becoming increasingly familiar, in which harassment is not overt but 'may be subtle and indirect' (PIC, 1996b, IV). In this vein, the UN High Representative's Office has concerned itself with such questions as loyalty oaths at workplaces, threatening phone calls and nationalist rhetoric (PIC, 1996b, III, 2). The level of harassment may be 'unacceptably high' in Bosnia today, but there is a need to put this in perspective, first against the injustices of wartime and, second, against the 'unacceptably high' level of harassment and discrimination that exists the world over.

RESTORING A CLIMATE OF CONFIDENCE?

Two areas in which human rights concerns were given priority were the pursuance of war criminals and the return of refugees and displaced persons. Compliance in these areas has become a central precondition for international support for reconstruction. Following the discussion above, these areas demonstrate the ease with which human rights abuse became a catch-all category and the consequences that this perception of Bosnian politics has had for Bosnian ownership of the democratisation process.

War crime indictments

One of the major barriers to democracy and human rights protections was alleged to be the influence of suspected 'war criminals'. In the narrow sense, 'war criminals' were those under Hague indictments, but in a broad sense those in positions of power through nationalist party structures could all be seen as suspect. In a broader usage, those who voted for the nationalist parties have been seen as failing to accept that nationalism led to the war and war crimes, and therefore to be condoning human rights abuses. It is this broader understanding of Bosnian politics that has led some commentators to talk about a 'universal' or 'endemic' problem and a culture of 'human rights abuse'.

The question of the legitimacy, under international law, of the UN Security Council's decision to establish a war crimes tribunal at The Hague is beyond the scope of this work (discussed, for example, in Rubin, 1996). The tribunal's supporters often claimed that the prosecution of Bosnians, on all sides, for alleged war crimes was essential for reconciliation and that, particularly in the Serb case, the conviction of individuals prevented people in general from being tarred with the crimes committed by a few. However, it could be argued that the Hague process, through its representation of a civil war over the boundaries of emergent states as human rights abuses on a massive scale, has played a major role in legitimising a broader questioning of the capacity of the people of the region to be trusted with democracy. The International Crisis Group, for example, state that: 'The respect shown Karadzic by the people and leaders of Republika Srpska ... is the tangible expression of their complete denial of responsibility for genocide, crimes against humanity and war crimes' (ICG, 1996c, p. 8). Leading US academic and activist, Bogdan Denitch, went further, to question the capacities of Bosnian people more generally, and saw popular support for nationalist leaders on all sides as evidence of a lack of democratic responsibility: 'Ideally, for real civic life to be possible again in a post-war Bosnia-Herzegovina, there will have to be both war-crime trials and something resembling the de-Nazification processes in Germany and Italy after the Second World War' (Denitch, 1996, p. 8).[3]

The issue of war criminals has inevitably sharpened the distinction between the international community, which could be trusted to wield power and responsibility, and the Bosnian parties, which were alleged to be incapable of acting against war criminals or of protecting human rights. In October 1997, Carlos Westendorp stated that the presence of old political leaderships and the continued influence of alleged war criminals still lent an 'unpleasant flavour to Bosnian politics' (OHRB, 1997B). The connection between war criminals and obstructionist politicians has been made explicit by the International Crisis Group:

> The nationalist cancer extends much deeper in Bosnian society than the leadership of the nationalist parties, and obstructionist officials are in positions of authority at all levels. A mechanism

> is therefore required to secure their removal. A properly funded ICTY would be as start. Given the resources, this body could build cases against, indict, and prosecute many more individuals. (ICG, 1997b, p. 43)

The extension of regulation over the Bosnian political process was given legitimacy by the campaigning of international NGOs and other human rights activists, many of whom called for elections to be postponed until all alleged war criminals had been removed to The Hague. The President of the Hague Tribunal, Judge Antonio Cassese, stated: 'These leaders will jeopardise free and fair elections ... they will mastermind the aftermath of the elections and the division of Bosnia-Herzegovina into three separate "ethnically pure" entities' (Silber and Clark, 1996).

These concerns have had a major impact on the scope of representative democracy, through legitimising new limits imposed by the international administration. The fact that Bosnians indicted by the tribunal were still at liberty was used to undermine the legitimacy of the elections that took place in September 1996, and those held subsequently. This process started with the restriction of the mandates given in the 1996 elections from four years down to two years, justified on the basis that the presence of alleged war criminals meant that democratic conditions were not yet in place (Silber and Clark, 1996).

Under the banner of human rights protection, the issue of war criminals has been used to challenge the elected representatives and to enhance the legitimacy of international administrative regulation over Bosnia as a whole. The threat of being charged with war crimes has been a powerful weapon for compliance in the hands of the international community. This threat was brought home to the Bosnian local elites in July 1997 when an SAS snatch squad seized Milan Kovacevic and shot and killed the former Prijedor Police Chief Simo Drljaca when he resisted arrest. Both were under sealed indictments from the ICTFY, issued some months previously, charged with being 'complicit in the commission of genocide' (OHRB, 1997u). This action was supported by the leading civilian implementation organisations, including the OHR, OSCE, UNMIBH/UN IPTF, UNHCR, human rights groups and other NGOs, on the grounds that this had enabled the political atmosphere to be changed (OHRB, 1997u).

Susan Woodward considered the war crimes tribunal policy to be closely aligned to the US strategy for elections in Bosnia, noting that the combined strategy was 'aimed at removing radical nationalists from the scene [in order to] ... enable more moderate leaders to emerge among Bosnian Serbs' (Woodward, 1996a, p.

8). Even commentators highly supportive of the tribunal have questioned why the focus has been placed on indicting Bosnian Serb leaders alone. For example, Cedric Thornberry writes: 'During its three years, has the court demonstrated an equality of prosecutorial zeal? How can indictments against only [the Serbs] Karadzic, Martic and Mladic – among all the leaders in the former Yugoslavia – be justified?' (Thornberry, 1996, p. 84).

The indictment of Karadzic was part of an ongoing US-led campaign to replace the Serb leadership, based in Pale, with more moderate Serbs based in Banja Luka. The OSCE, charged with organising the September 1996 elections, ruled in July, that Karadzic could not stand. Karadzic, the elected president of the Bosnian Serbs, was barred on the basis of a war crimes tribunal indictment, not on the basis of any proven conviction. The OSCE went as far as threatening to ban the ruling party, the SDS, from the elections, if Karadzic failed to stand down. Even after he accepted this, the OSCE election regulations made it illegal to mention his name in public rallies or to have his picture on election material (see Chapter 5).

The preparations for the elections were dominated by the linking of them with the International War Crimes Tribunal in The Hague. On 2 June 1996, at a meeting with the International Contact Group in Geneva, the High Representative, Carl Bildt, described Radovan Karadzic's attempt to hang on to public office as 'polluting the atmosphere in Bosnian Serb politics and as a provocation to the international community' (OHRB, 1996e). This use of war crime indictments to remove the Serb nationalist politician with the highest international and domestic profile not only served to remove an individual which the international community perceived to be a focus of opposition to the Dayton framework. The concern with removing SDS references to Karadzic was also intended to weaken the electoral support given to the main party, which had to rely on the promotion of other individuals less well known to the general population. As Adam Burgess points out, the importance attached to banning references and photos of Karadzic also contributed to the idea that the Bosnian Serbs had so little understanding of human rights that an image might set them on the path to violence (Burgess, 1997, p. 49).

The fact that the three main Bosnian nationalist parties opposed some aspects of Dayton led to accusations that they were stuck in the wartime mentality of 'ethnic cleansing' and therefore ill-suited to democratic politics. In February 1998, Bosnia's Deputy Prime Minister Neven Tomic, a Croat, challenged the High Representative's 'insistence that those who conducted the war cannot build peace – if the personalities cannot then, by implication, neither can their parties' (BBC, 1998). All three nationalist parties have been condemned by the international community for what is seen as continuing the ethnic politics of the war. However, the Bosnian Serb SDS has been put under the most pressure through the linking of its leaders directly with alleged war crimes.

The SDS leaders which have been perceived to be reluctant to accept the policies of the international administration have been accused of being influenced by Karadzic and providing support to war criminals. To take one, widely referred to, example, the Human Rights Watch/Helsinki report, *Bosnia-Herzegovina: the Continuing Influence of Bosnia's Warlords*, argued that underground paramilitary organisations under the direct control of the Serbian Democratic Party (SDS) were operating throughout Republika Srpska. It was claimed that Radovan Karadzic still exercised complete control through 'an underground Mafia-type network' which included 'liquidation units' and encouraged and would carry out systematic human rights abuses until Republika Srpska was ethnically 'clean' (HRW, 1996a, pp. 2–3).

The evidence for these claims were interviews with around a dozen unnamed international representatives from various human rights monitoring organisations and interviews with unnamed victims. The information that had allegedly come from human rights organisations had not been made public by them, quite possibly because it consisted of rumours and gossip against people in positions of influence or known to be hostile to Dayton. Words and phrases such as 'believed to be', 'rumoured', 'reported to be', 'may involve', 'allegedly', and 'unsubstantiated' run right through the document. Evidence against people included being 'vehemently opposed to the Dayton Peace Agreement and known to be openly defiant about it' or being 'uncompromising in his views'.[4] However, despite the lack of hard evidence the press-released summary stated that: '... the national and local political leadership of the Republika Srpska as well as the state organs and agencies under its control ... are responsible for directing, aiding and abetting continuing human rights abuses in post-Dayton Bosnia-Herzegovina on an RS-wide scale' (HRW, 1996b).

Commentary on Bosnian politics regularly referred to the SDS as 'Karadzic's party' and to Krajisnik and the SDS leadership as 'Karadzic's supporters'. In April 1997, the High Representative described Karadzic as remaining 'a force of evil and intrigue' who 'can only taint those personalities and institutions of the Republika Srpska which continue to tolerate his activities' (OHRR, 1997a, par. 146). He declared that in his judgement this applied to the Serb member of the RS Presidency, Krajisnik, and recommended that 'contacts with him are limited to essential business'. Although Karadzic's name could not be mentioned in the speeches of Bosnian SDS politicians, it has cropped up regularly as international community representatives seek to link opposition to Dayton with war crimes and human rights abuses.

The protracted process of hunting for war criminals, and of adding or threatening to add more suspects to the list, has done little to restore confidence and enable co-operation. The ICTY has little support within Bosnian society. An October 1998 ICTY press release concedes: 'the tribunal understands that there exist serious concerns about it among the population of former Yugoslavia' (ICTY, 1998). For the Bosnian Serbs, the process is seen to be one of political bias, with the international community treating Karadzic unfairly considering similar evidence against Tudjman and Izetbegovic. Poll findings that for Bosnian people of all three groups the question of war crimes is of little importance, with 6 per cent of people at the most giving it a high priority, would seem to indicate that the tribunal is acting more under international pressure than to meet Bosnian needs (Boyd, 1998, p. 51). Accusations of war crimes, so far, seem to have done little to develop community reconciliation and much to promote tensions between the communities and international administrators.

The right to return

The return of refugees and displaced persons has become a key priority aim for the international community and the numbers returning have been regularly used as an indicator of democracy and human rights (for example, OHRB, 1997p). International policy has worked on the assumption that the majority of displaced persons would want to return if human rights were respected and democratic values were in place. When people have expressed the wish not to return, this has not been seen as a genuine choice but as indicative of systematic intimidation and manipulation by nationalist politicians (ICG, 1998c, p. 11). For example, the unwillingness of Brcko Serbs to return to Sarajevo was seen by Deputy High Representative Jacques Klein in this way: 'One third would like to go home, one third does not know what it wants, and one third will never know. And they were all intimidated by Pale and held as some kind of political prisoners by Pale ... the Serbs from Brcko should return to Sarajevo' (Klein, 1998a).

The London PIC conference, which extended the international administration of Bosnia for a further two-year 'consolidation' period at the end of 1996, focused on the failure of return as the first area in which little progress had been made in implementing Dayton. The return of only 250,000 people to their pre-war homes, from 2.1 million refugees and internally displaced people, was considered to be damning evidence of the failure of the human rights situation to improve (PIC, 1996d, par. 3). However, the focus on these statistics as an example of the human rights situation may be misleading if the barriers to return are often social and economic, and not solely inter-ethnic ones.

Barriers to return

The real and substantial improvement in inter-community relations since the end of the war has received little attention in human rights reports. Since Dayton, freedom of movement had been increasingly enhanced and all fixed police checkpoints removed (USDoS, 1998b, p. 3). The image often given in the international press of widespread fear of crossing the Inter-Entity Boundary Line (IEBL) dividing the Federation and Republika Srpska has been shaped by a preoccupation with the small number of contested areas where there have been problems. The Bosnian people themselves have crossed the IEBL daily in their thousands (USDoS, 1997, section 2D). In an informal survey over a two-day period, in May 1996, IFOR counted approximately 28,000 Inter-Entity Boundary Line crossings and IPTF and ECMM reports support this conclusion (PIC, 1996b, section IV). Amnesty International reported in 1996 that 'many visits or attempts to return, mainly those in which small groups of Muslims [have gone] into Bosnian Serb-controlled areas, have taken place peacefully' (Amnesty, 1996, section V, A). The total number of passengers on the UNHCR-funded IEBL bus lines grew dramatically to nearly half a million by August 1997 (USDoS, 1998b, section 1D).

Many refugees, displaced by the war, do not wish to return in the short term. Despite the desires of the international community, Bosnia in 1996, and even more so by late 1998, was not the Bosnia of 1991. Many Serbs, Muslims and Croats expressed the desire to stay elsewhere than return to their homes after the war. For example, 300,000 Bosnian refugees abroad had already been granted permanent status or new citizenship by the Spring of 1997, and this had risen to 540,000 by the end of the year (RRTF, 1997a, par. 2.2; ICG, 1998c, p. 3). Some displaced persons have similarly chosen to stay in their place of displacement and, at the end of 1997, OHR reports, by the Reconstruction and Return Task Force, accepted that 'relocation is a fact' (RRTF, 1997a, par. 2.2; RRTF, 1997c, par. 5.6). There are many reasons for this, which reflect the nature of changes to the region since 1991, both political and economic. Economic factors have played a major role as people have sought to move to areas where there is more chance of finding work. UNHCR reports show that around 30 per cent of the Bosnian Croat population have moved to Croatia since the war in order to seek a higher standard of living (Boyd, 1998, p. 44). Relocation and demographic changes would have happened irrespective of the war, as the Bosnian economy made the transition to market competition (RRTF, 1997c, par. 5.6).

A major barrier to return to areas of previous residence or even to areas of choice, for many refugees, has been the shortages in housing and employment opportunities caused by the destruction and dislocation of the war. The OHR recognised, a year after Dayton, that return was limited by the lack of options available to people: 'Possibilities for people to return to their homes of origin are limited not only by concerns about the security environment, but also by the lack of available housing, employment and social services, as well as the level of infrastructure and communications' (OHRR, 1996d, par. 51).

In the course of the Bosnian conflict 50–65 per cent of housing stock was estimated to have been damaged and World Bank figures suggest 6 per cent and 5 per cent of housing stock was destroyed in the Federation and Republika Srpska respectively (Silber, 1996; ICG, 1997b, p. 8). The reconstruction process since the war has been subject to the political conditionality of the international community which has meant that money has not been allocated solely on the basis of reconstruction needs but also according to political priorities. Nearly two years after Dayton, 90 per cent of returnees were unemployed and, according to the IPTF, the economic conditions had made returns more of a problem than an asset, with fears that with 'time on their hands' returnees were likely to become involved in illicit activity and to create a policing problem (CFWG, 1997; RRTF, 1997b, par. 4.1).

The Federation's economy is estimated to have grown by about 50 per cent since the war: however, at the start of 1998 it was still at less than half the 1990 level, with growth rates progressively slowing (RRTF, 1997c, par. 4.1.1). The fact that Republika Srpska had received less than 5 per cent of international reconstruction aid, since the war, meant that the entity economy had stagnated and had declined to less than a quarter of the pre-war level. In 1997, the monthly average wage in RS was around one-quarter of that of the Federation, the Federation average being DM 280–290 and the RS around DM 64–67; unemployment was also approximately 20 per cent higher in the RS than in the Federation (ICG, 1997b, p. 20; RRTF, 1997a, par. 4.1). The absolute level of poverty in Bosnia and the growing economic divide between the two entities has not only discouraged return but also led to tensions, with even majority returns being seen as putting existing livelihoods under threat and returnees becoming frustrated with their poor living conditions (RRTF, 1997b, annex 1c).

Opposition to returns from local residents is not as straightforward as it has often been portrayed. In cases where the issue of return was problematic, this has often been because it was either seen as an attempt to redraw the Dayton borders or as a challenge to existing guarantees of work and housing. The Bosnian government initially made little secret of its desire to use the return of Muslims to areas of Croat and Serb domination to argue for a greater say in their running. For example, the US State Department noted 'indications that some resettlement efforts in "strategic" areas of RS, including by persons not originally residents of those areas, had tacit support from Bosniak authorities' (USDoS, 1997, section 5; see also ICG, 1997b, p. 12). The fear of regions within Republika Srpska being transferred to Bosnian Muslim control contributed to angry responses to return in Brcko, Doboj, Sanski Most and strategically sensitive Gajevi (Boyd, 1998, p. 48). This fear of return heralding a transition in the status of these areas was particularly strong for those residents who were refugees and displaced people from elsewhere. These people were likely to lose out from return and feared further displacement at the same time as being unable or unwilling to return to their original homes or areas of residence (RRTF, 1997b, annex 7a).

International intervention

The international focus on return as a human rights issue greatly politicised the question and has led to greater international regulation of Bosnian politics than would have otherwise been the case.[5] Return for the international community has become less a matter of choice, to be decided by individuals or negotiated between community representatives, and more a matter of international policy-making, and if necessary to be imposed. The Office of the High Representative has stated that compared to return: 'Relocation is clearly unacceptable when it takes place as a result of official manipulation. Even where it takes place as a result of individual, informed decision-making it remains problematic' (RRTF, 1997c, par. 5.6). Return could not be opposed by Bosnian political leaders, nor by the individual victims of the war themselves who disagreed with international policy. Regardless of Bosnian opinion the OHR position was that 'return to homes of origin has to be vigorously pursued' with no grant aid available for displaced persons who wished to relocate (RRTF, 1997c, par. 5.6).

The position taken by the international administration did not necessarily tie in with Bosnian needs. There was little evidence that the majority of people who had not returned to their former homes actually wished to and even less evidence that internationally supported or imposed return initiatives helped long-term resettlement. By far the majority of minority returns had, prior to 1998, been 'individual, voluntary and spontaneous' (OHRR, 1997a, par. 140; RRTF, 1997a, par. 2.1). High-profile organised repatriation by the international community 'made up for only a minor proportion of return movements' (OHRR, 1996d, par. 51). Far from concern at the lack of return without external pressure, internal minutes of international forums demonstrate the UNHCR's concern that as so many returns took place on a voluntary basis they found it difficult to keep track of the situation (CFWG, 1997). By 1998, the majority of those still displaced and in need of settlement were originally from areas in which they were part of the minority, and for a variety of reasons many did not wish to return to their original homes. Unlike the UN administrators, UNHCR officials therefore considered relocation 'an important component in the search for durable solutions for displaced persons and refugees' (ICG, 1998c, p. 10).

The international community has pursued a broad approach to encourage return instead of relocation, including applying pressure on local authorities over the running of municipal affairs, civil service structures, policing, employment practices and media coverage (RRTF, 1997c, par. 5.7). This pressure has either been applied indirectly through conditionality for reconstruction funds, as in the UNHCR's 'Open Cities' initiative (see RRTF, 1997b, annexes 7 & 7a) and the spring 1998 OHR-hosted international conferences on return in Sarajevo and Banja Luka (ICG, 1998c, pp. 14–17), or more directly through international administrative powers in the inter-entity Zone of Separation and Brcko and the use of powers to dismiss obstructive officials and shape the political composition of municipal authorities.

There is little evidence to suggest that international regulation of return is assisting the process even in areas where return has been contested. One reason for this is that the confidence to return has depended on establishing good relations with the existing community, something which is undermined when return is accompanied by international police pressure and the stick of sanctions. For example, arson attacks on abandoned Serb houses in the Croat-controlled town of Drvar, in early May 1997, coincided with fears generated by the holding of talks between the International Mediator for the Federation, Dr Schwartz-

Schilling, and the Drvar local authorities. In this case, the OHR and UNHCR met with the local authorities to discuss the need for prior confidence-building measures to address the fears of Croatian displaced persons living in Drvar (OHRB, 1997o). However, the extended international mandates and increased authority of the High Representative in late 1997 meant that less attention was focused on local concerns as returns were increasingly imposed.

The application of economic sanctions to municipalities and moves to make essential funding conditional on refugee return were seen by many international officers as achieving little in terms of reconciliation (ICG, 1997b, p. 16). UN Development Project staff have also revealed a high level of cynicism over this approach.[6] Where returns were accepted under the threat of sanctions, the tensions created through international pressure often led to distrust between the communities and the isolation of returnees. The Croat-run town of Stolac has been a showcase for this type of approach, but the returns imposed under economic pressure have resulted in segregation, not reconciliation. There may have been returns but the Muslim residential quarter had no phones or lighting and needed water to be trucked in by NATO forces. As one international official noted, 'we are creating a slum on two streets with little chance of success' (Fleishman, 1998). Muslim returnees mixed little with the Croat residents and shopped and sent their children to school in East Mostar (C. Smith, 1998).

The attempts to impose return through the creation of multiethnic administrations (see Chapter 3) has so far equally failed to achieve success. An International Crisis Group report on the return of Serb displaced persons to the HDZ-controlled towns of Drvar, Bosansko Grahov and Glamoc, three of the six towns in which nationalists lost control to displaced minorities, demonstrates the problems involved in the imposition of multi-ethnic administrations which are not accountable to the current residents (ICG, 1997e). To tackle this problem, the ICG urges that return should be promoted through an increased SFOR and IPTF presence, and pressure applied to the major employer to take on Serbian workers; however, this is likely to lead to greater resistance to return as the displaced Croatian population seek to defend their rights to homes and work.

CONCLUSION

Human rights abuse appears to have often been used as a catchall term to include anything that the international community conceives as a barrier to the return to the pre-war situation and the acceptance of the 'spirit of Dayton'. The concern is that, as long as insecurities remain, people choose to make new lives in areas where they have relocated, or choose to vote for the nationalist parties, the international community will view the human rights situation as deeply unsatisfactory. This chapter has suggested that implying human rights abuses from these choices, which reflect Bosnia's political and ethnic fragmentation, and then using human rights abuse to explain this fragmentation, can easily become a circular argument. An argument which, in turn, vastly exaggerates the extent of human rights abuses as well as narrowly interpreting political and social phenomena through the framework of human rights abuse.

Of course, it could be argued that even without a risk of human rights abuses, international human rights regulation over Bosnian society is still a positive international achievement. The viewpoint taken on this depends on the approach taken to democracy in Bosnia. This understanding of the potential of human rights abuses on the basis of implications and assumptions drawn from people's choices at the ballot box, or preferences to live somewhere other than they did in 1991, seems likely to ensure the maintenance of international regulation and set back the possibilities of Bosnian self-government.

Of greater concern, for long-term peace-building and self-government, is the fact that external regulation in the human rights sphere, through externally imposed reform of the legal system, the prosecution of war criminals and international pressure on people to return rather than to relocate, has done little to give Bosnian people more control over their lives. Far from creating a basis of greater security for cross-ethnic co-operation, the climate of implied human rights abuse has meant that the Bosnian parties are restricted in their capacity to negotiate a settlement on controversial questions, such as refugee return, themselves. This has resulted in solutions being imposed that have tended to feed insecurities and at times have provoked conflicts. These insecurities have then been used to provide further strength for arguments favouring greater international regulation.

5 Political pluralism

Democratisation strategy in Bosnia has relied heavily on the institutionalisation of ethnic division through the use of the 'ethnic key', the allocation of seats in advance on the basis of ethnicity (see Chapter 3). While the ethnicisation of politics has been welcomed, and multi-ethnic administrations formed at all levels, the politicisation of ethnicity, the success of political parties which appeal to one ethnic group, has been roundly condemned as a central barrier to democratisation and the Dayton process.

There is only marginal political support in Bosnia for parties which do not appeal to an ethnic constituency. In the September 1998 state and entity elections, the Muslim SDA and Croatian HDZ were comfortable winners within their constituencies while the more 'hard-line' Serb nationalist parties out-polled the moderate Serb nationalist coalition led by Biljana Plavsic, who lost out to Serb Radical Party representative Nikola Poplasen for the Republika Srpska presidency. In the municipal elections in September 1997, the non-national parties, which represented more than one national group, won 6 per cent of the seats across the country (ICG, 1997d). These figures were little changed from those a year previously when the non-nationalist parties won 5 per cent of the seats (see Chapter 3). Within the three ethnic constituencies, the Muslim SDA and the Croat HDZ have consistently secured substantial majorities, while the Serb SDS remains the largest Bosnian Serb party although politics in Republika Srpska have become increasingly fragmented.

From the viewpoint of the international community, the dominance of three political parties within three different ethnic constituencies has perpetuated ethnic divisions and been a barrier to the development of democratic competition. The Peace Implementation Council in December 1997 stated that the international community should help establish new multi-ethnic parties and strengthen the existing ones (PIC, 1997b, VI, par. 4). The High Representative has argued:

> ... there are many obstacles towards the democratisation process. It is essentially the lack of a really structured civilian society ... The presence of mono-ethnic parties, which do not really contribute to the pluralistic system. There is a democratic

> system in the sense that there are democratic elections, but the result of the elections is that they give the advantage to one ethnic group over another. This is only a continuation of the war with other means. So in order to develop democratisation, it is necessary to implant more pluralism in the political parties. It is necessary to encourage the development of multi-ethnic parties. (Westendorp, 1997a)

Democratisation has involved international regulation to ensure a level playing-field so that political parties which want to further non-nationalist programmes have a chance to compete against the accumulated resources of the parties which have held power since the war, and non-national multi-ethnic parties have been supported by the OSCE and the High Representative.

The High Representative has personally intervened to try to create an alliance of non-national parties that could make an effective cross-Bosnian challenge to nationally based politics (SAFAX, 1998a; Numanovic, 1998). The OSCE has also worked to identify and provide technical assistance and funding for non-national parties. The OSCE Democratisation Branch has been closely involved with encouraging the formation of new parties, indicated in this internal report on the Mostar region:

> In areas such as Siroki Brijeg where there are virtually no opposition parties, Democratisation Officers might help facilitate efforts to strengthen diversity by assisting political party training organisations such as [the] National Democratic Initiative [to] identify potential independent candidates or new opposition parties. (OSCE DB, 1997c, section I, B)

Alongside this, there has been a concerted strategy to prevent the Bosnian media from stirring up nationalist sentiments which the nationalist politicians can gain from. The starting point of the international community's media strategy has been that the media were largely responsible for the ethnic violence of the war and have since been a major barrier to the implementation of Dayton (ICG, 1997a, p. 1). As the Office of the High Representative explained in July 1997:

> The media climate in Bosnia and Herzegovina remains far from perfect, especially in the Republika Srpska and Western Herzegovina. It is widely accepted that there is a close relationship between control of the media and political activities, also indeed with the will to comply with the Peace Agreement. (OHRR, 1997b, par. 57)

If the media could be reformed to inform people that Dayton and the international community were working in their interests, then it was assumed the nationalist parties would lose support. The first goal of the 1997 OSCE Media Development strategy was: 'To strengthen and expand media pluralism, which gives voters access to information and opinions from a variety of perspectives and a multiplicity of sources' (OSCE MDO, 1997, p. 2). This strategy was based on an assumption that Bosnians were denied access to alternative sources of information that challenged the nationalist parties' hold on power. The High Representative has stated:

> ... my major concern is that the large political parties in this country control the public media, they send messages to one nation only, and the population has the right to hear other opinions too, and therefore we are trying to establish a principal of pluralism in public life through the opening of the media. (Kebo, 1997)

International intervention was considered necessary to break the link between the media and the nationalist parties and to establish alternative media enterprises. As the *Financial Times* argued in its leader column:

> [Making Dayton a success] involves facing down all the traditional parties, and actively encouraging those who are prepared to build bridges across ethnic lines. If Western governments do not have the will or the funds, then non-governmental institutions should back or, if necessary, found independent broadcasting stations – and help moderate parties reach out to Bosnia's widely scattered refugees. (*Financial Times*, 1996)

The need for funding to help struggling alternative parties and independent media sources has been a constant theme of democratisation reports. For example, the OSCE Media Branch states:

> Preservation of media pluralism requires not only OSCE support of media organisations against political pressure, but also awareness that one of the greatest threats to media pluralism in the next few years will come from economic pressures. The OSCE must join other international organisations in supporting media organisations identified by our regional and field officers and by other international organisations as enriching media pluralism in Bosnia, but who must be supported to survive. (OSCE MDO, 1997, p. 4)

This chapter considers the regulatory powers available to the OSCE and other international institutions and the context in which these powers have been applied. The following sections chart the extension of the powers available and trace how these powers have been used to challenge the hold of the leading nationalist parties and encourage the emergence of non-nationalist politics, in conclusion the demand for a non-nationalist political approach is considered and the strategy assessed.

THE REGULATORY FRAMEWORK

The task of challenging nationalism and promoting political pluralism has largely fallen to the OSCE, working in close co-operation with the Office of the High Representative. The OSCE powers of regulation over the political parties and the media stemmed originally from its powers under Dayton to supervise the elections. Annex 3 of the DPA, *The Agreement on Elections*, gave little indication of the extensive nature of these powers, stating only:

> The Parties shall ensure that conditions exist for the organisation of free and fair elections, in particular a politically neutral environment ... [and] shall ensure freedom of expression and of the press ... The parties request the OSCE to certify whether elections can be effective under current social conditions in both Entities and, if necessary, to provide assistance to the Parties in creating these conditions. (GFA, 1995, Article I, pars 1 & 2)

Over the last three years, the OSCE, in close co-operation with the OHR, has expanded the powers of regulation of the international community over both the election process and the media environment. In doing this the international community has pursued two strategies. First, the encouragement of independent non-national political alternatives, and second, the restriction of the capacities of the nationalist parties to take advantage of their control over Bosnian institutions to influence the political climate. By pursuing these two strategies together, the aim of international policy has been to create a political environment in which the politics of the leading national parties could be replaced by civic pluralism. The election regulations have been regularly modified to marginalise the space for nationalist ideologies and the 'spirit of Dayton' has been invoked to ensure that non-nationalist perspectives could be institutionalised (Woodger, 1997).

All political parties have to be vetted by the OSCE before being allowed to stand candidates. In order to be accepted, the party president must include a signed statement that the party will abide by the Dayton Agreement, the electoral code of conduct and the other Provisional Election Commission (PEC) rules and regulations (OSCE PEC, 1997, par. 46). The codes include the provision of access to all electoral activities for OSCE supervisors, staff and other representatives and specify that it is the duty of the parties to ensure that they behave with due deference to the international supervisors, down to 'ensuring their safety from exposure to insult' (OSCE PEC, 1997, par. 121).

The PEC established an Elections Appeals Sub-Commission (EASC) to rule on compliance with the election regulations, its four members were appointed directly by the OSCE Head of Mission, in his capacity of PEC Chair, and includes three Bosnian judges (OSCE PEC, 1997, par. 137). However, the three hand-picked Bosnian judges have little influence over the sub-commission decisions. Article 142 of the *PEC Rules and Regulations* gives the Chairman of the EASC, Judge Finn Lynghjem, powers of judge and jury over the interpretation of the election regulations and the penalties to be awarded. If there is no consensus, he is empowered to make the final decision, which is binding and cannot be appealed.

The *Rules and Regulations*, drawn up by the Provisional Election Commission, gave the OSCE far-ranging powers to penalise any infringements:

> The Election Appeals Sub-Commission will have the right to impose appropriate penalties and/or fines against any individual, candidate, political party, coalition or body that violates the *Rules and Regulations* ... in applying penalties the responsibility of political party leaders for their actions and those of their party or coalition members [will be taken into account] ... The Election Appeals Sub-Commission may prohibit a political party or coalition from running in the elections, decertify a political party or coalition already listed on the ballot, remove a candidate from a candidates list or an independent candidate from the ballot when it determines a violation of the principles established in the General Framework Agreement for Peace in Bosnia and Herzegovina or the *Rules and Regulations* ... has occurred. The Election Appeals Sub-Commission may set and apply pecuniary or other appropriate penalties for actions carried out with intent to disrupt the electoral process. (OSCE PEC, 1997, pars 140 & 141)

Alongside the PEC regulations, the OHR also intervened to establish guidelines for the parties to follow. Working in close co-operation with the OSCE, the Office of the High Representative often took the lead in flagging up issues for the PEC to act on. For example, in July 1996, the Human Rights Co-ordination Centre established an informal working group of the main human rights-implementing organisations and 'devised guidelines on issuance of rally permits, display of campaign posters, and security at party meetings ... [intended] to compliment existing regulations and procedures and specify acceptable campaigning procedures for all parties' (OHRB, 1996k). In early August the PEC issued rules for political party campaigning in accordance with the HRCC guidelines (OHRB, 1996m).

As long as the OSCE was supervising elections, it had a mandate to help ensure freedom of expression and the press. To this end the Provisional Election Commission drew up an Electoral Code of Conduct containing standards for the media and journalists and created a Media Experts Commission (MEC) to monitor compliance. The Media Experts Commission was a powerful body – it first met in May 1996, with the Head of the OSCE Mission, Robert Frowick, in the chair (OHRB, 1996a). Exactly what the international community would expect of journalists in Bosnia was indicated in a OHR-organised round table of broadcast editors and journalists organised in May 1996 in Banja Luka. This meeting focused on the use by state broadcasters in both entities of the 'rhetorical jargon of war' which was held to include the use of terms such as 'the Serb entity' and 'the Muslim-Croat Federation' (OHRB, 1996b). Terms in common use in the international media were held to be inflammatory in Bosnia itself and the framework was already established that the state media in Bosnia should be pressurised to play down the segmented reality of Bosnian politics and to challenge the nationalist outlook.

The postponement of the municipal elections, from September 1996 to September 1997, provided the PEC and the MEC with opportunities to expand their staff and their remit. The election regulations for the municipal elections gave the international community greater regulatory authority through the '500 Series' of new amendments which were added to the PEC *Rules and Regulations*. These amendments sought to undermine the hold of national parties further by increasing international regulation in three areas: encouraging displaced persons and refugees to register in their 1991 residences, strengthening the weight of absentee voters and the chances of minority parties gaining seats; the certification of new authorities depending on their actions following the elections – the authorities could no longer operate on a majority-rule basis, but only through a consensus with minority parties; and the regulation of the media.

In the 1996 elections, it had been possible for people to register to vote where they resided in 1991 before the war, where they lived currently, or where they wished to live in the future. The OSCE sought to encourage refugees and displaced persons, 36 per cent of those eligible to vote, to register to vote in their prewar municipalities, where it was likely that they would vote against the dominant nationalist party. This was done through restricting their right to register to vote where they wished to live in the future. People displaced within Bosnia, 18 per cent of the electorate, were not allowed to register to vote in a future municipality and refugees abroad, 19 per cent of the electorate, including 123,000 Bosnian Serb refugees living in the FRY, could only do so if they could establish genuine ties with the intended locality by providing 'clear and convincing documentation to demonstrate the Refugee Voter's pre-existing, legitimate and non-transitory nexus with the future municipality' (OHRB, 1997d). Out of 420,000 out-of-country voters, fewer than 1,000 were allowed to register in this way (ICG, 1997c, pp. 11–15).

The seats were to be allocated on the basis of the percentage of votes won, so that in most municipalities a party could win a seat with 3 or 4 per cent of the total vote. This guaranteed minorities representation but there was still the possibility that a majority may exclude them from positions of authority. To counter this, ratification was to be conditional on co-operation between majority and minority parties and could be withheld for the violation of 'basic democratic principles' including: preventing access to councillors through threats, harassment or violence; preventing councillors from establishing residence in the municipality; minority parties or coalitions not being proportionally represented among executive officers and committees; council sessions conducted with religious or ethnic oaths, hymns or icons or by other means inconsistent with the council's secular and multi-ethnic nature; or the denial of funds, materials or other assets to enable officers or councillors to perform their duties adequately (ICG, 1997c, pp. 26–7; OSCE PEC, 1997, par. 235.5).

In the sphere of the media the powers of the OSCE were greatly extended. The OSCE-headed Provisional Election Commission rules provided for authorities at all levels to adhere to the *Standards of Professional Conduct for the Media and Journalists* adopted in March 1997. These standards included:

- *Fair reporting*: 'Media and journalists shall ensure that the information they report is factually accurate, complete, fair, equitable and unbiased. Media and journalists shall not engage in distortion, suppression, falsification, misrepresentation and censorship, including systematic omission of information' (OSCE PEC, 1997, par. 130).
- *Avoiding inflammatory language*: 'Media and journalists shall avoid inflammatory language which encourages discrimination, prejudice, or hatred, or which encourages violence, or contributes to the creation of a climate in which violence could occur' (OSCE PEC, 1997, par. 133).
- *Accurate and Balanced Information*: 'Printing presses, press distribution agencies, and outlets such as news-stands have a

> responsibility to operate in a way that provides the public with accurate and balanced information concerning the views and activities of the political parties and candidates in the area, and to help transmit to the public a diversity of political and social viewpoints and orientations' (OSCE PEC, 1997, par. 136.1).

The updated MEC and PEC powers, included in the new PEC *Rules and Regulations*, gave the OSCE unprecedented control over media output: Article 149.1 gave the Media Experts Commission the power to:

> ... require any person or organisation connected to a case or complaint under investigation by the MEC to provide any information, including copies of documents, or any materials, including audio and video tapes, requested by the MEC ... [and] to meet with a designated MEC representative or come to a meeting of the MEC. (OSCE PEC, 1997, par. 149.1)

Articles 149.2 and 150 enabled the OSCE to consider a wide range of penalties for any infringements of the OSCE regulations including:

> ... to oblige any violators to publish or broadcast specific materials, at a time and in a manner determined by the MEC. Publications or broadcast stations can by required by the MEC to publish or broadcast such materials to redress Government or authorities violations ... These materials shall be broadcast free ... If the PEC decides that there has been a serious breach of the Media regulations ... the PEC will have the power to impose fines or any other appropriate penalties or to take other appropriate action. (OSCE PEC, 1997, pars 149.2 & 150)

On top of the compulsory publication of MEC-prepared material, in event of a breach of the regulations, the PEC also had the power to enforce the publication of election-related materials produced by the OSCE under Article 150.1:

> The PEC may require broadcast stations to air election-related materials produced by the OSCE, including materials on voting processes, political parties, candidates, campaign issues, and other matters relevant to the election. The PEC may specify the time and manner of such broadcasts. (OSCE PEC, 1997, par. 150.1)

While the 'other appropriate action' available to the OSCE was initially unspecified, the far-ranging possibilities were confirmed in May 1997 when the Peace Implementation Council's *Sintra Declaration* granted the Office of the High Representative the right to curtail or suspend any media network or programme whose output contravened either the spirit or the letter of the Peace Agreement (PIC, 1997a, par. 70).

CREATING A POLITICALLY NEUTRAL ENVIRONMENT?

The regulatory powers of the OSCE and the OHR were intended to help create a climate in which ideas could be openly contested and in which independent opposition groups were encouraged. The successive elections were seen as major tests of the powers of the international community and the implementation of these powers developed throughout the three major electoral competitions held in 1996 and 1997. Below the strategy is discussed in relation to each of these electoral competitions.

The 1996 state and entity elections

Karadzic and the SDS hard-liners

As Susan Woodward has commented, the September 1996 elections were seen as 'the last step in the defeat of the Bosnian Serbs', with international action removing radical Serb nationalists from above and the right to vote for refugees in their home locality in 1991, initiating a process from below that sought gradually to change the composition of voters to one more open to Bosnian government influence (1996a, pp. 8–9). The Dayton Agreement stated that no person under indictment by the International Tribunal for the Former Yugoslavia 'may stand as a candidate or hold any appointive, elective, or other public office' (Annex 4, Article 10). The indictment of Dr Radovan Karadzic, the President of Republika Srpska and President of the Serbian Democratic Party (SDS) led to a public stand-off between the OSCE and the SDS. When the OSCE threatened to ban the SDS from competing in the elections if Karadzic did not stand down from the leadership, OSCE Head Ambassador Robert Frowick, insisted that it was his 'unalterable position that any political parties who keep indicted war criminals in office shall be ineligible to participate [in the elections]' (OHRB, 1996i). The following day the powers enforced by the international community were given legal status when the PEC amended its *Rules and Regulations* to stipulate that as long as any political party maintains a person under ICTY indictment 'in a party position or function, that party shall be deemed ineligible to participate in the elections' (OHRB, 1996j).

Later in the month, under the pressure of the Office of the High Representative, OSCE, and US Special Envoy Richard Holbrooke, Karadzic signed a joint statement with leading representatives of the Republika Srpska and Serbian governments, relinquishing the office of President of the SDS, the office of President of Republika Srpska and all powers associated with office (OSCE PEC, 1996a, p. 25; OHRB, 1996j). Karadzic was also forced to agree to withdraw immediately and permanently from all political activity, not to appear in public, or on radio or television, or participate in any way in the elections (OHRB, 1996j).

This ongoing international attempt to weaken the influence of the hard-line opponents of Dayton in the SDS was continued through the focus, of the Office of the High Representative and OSCE, on removing any influence of the party's former President. At a meeting in Zvornik in August, High Representative Carl Bildt told the local SDS leader, Stevo Radic, that if posters of Radovan Karadzic were not removed within two days 'it would put into question the possibility of the SDS taking part in elections [there]' (OHRB, 1996n). Four days before the elections, the EASC ruled that even the display of Karadzic posters was a 'serious breach' of the election regulations and threatened to remove SDS candidates from the party list for the Republika Srpska National Assembly (OSCE PEC, 1996b, case number 96–29B; see also OHRB, 1997z).

Opposition to Dayton

In the run-up to the September 1996 elections, the OSCE expressed concern about statements from Republika Srpska candidates campaigning on the demand for greater sovereignty and control over their own affairs, part of the electoral platform for ruling and opposition parties within the entity (ECMM, 1996). Intervention in the contents of party manifestos seemed to lie outside the mandate of the OSCE, but the institution 'called for all sides to adhere to the spirit and the letter of the General Framework Agreement in order that the highest level governing bodies may achieve legitimacy and acceptance by the international community' (OHRB, 1996m). This invocation of 'the spirit' of Dayton meant that the powers of the international community could, in fact, be further extended, making it impossible to question the institutions of government.

On 6 September 1996, in Advisory Opinion number 5, the EASC ruled that:

> Statements that call for independence and territorial separation of part of the country, or that refer to part of the country as a sovereign territory ... represent a breach of the General Framework Agreement for Peace and the Rules and Regulations of the Provisional Election Commission. (OSCE PEC, 1996b, p. 103)

The ability of political parties to challenge the Dayton provisions was not excluded under the Dayton Agreement itself but by the OSCE Provisional Election Commission. Article 46 of the *Rules and Regulations* stated that the application for registration of a political party had to include a statement that the party will abide by the General Framework Agreement, the Code of Conduct for Political Parties and Candidates and the *Rules and Regulations*; the capacity of OSCE bodies to interpret these regulations, without appeal or redress, created restrictions that went beyond those of other European states.

Under the sub-heading 'Freedom of Expression and its Limits', the Advisory Opinion tried to defend freedom of expression as 'one of the essential foundations of a democratic society' and at the same time to justify its restriction in the Bosnian context, where it appeared that 'while the freedom of expression is fundamental, it is not absolute'. The argumentation provided an insight into how democratisation allowed external judges to decide who had the capacity for democratic debate and who had not:

> Not all statements which call for a re-examination of territorial borders fall outside the protection of freedom of expression. Each statement must be examined within the context in which it is made to evaluate whether it poses a genuine and imminent threat to national security, territorial integrity or public order. A statement made in an academic journal or to an audience in a stable democracy, however offensive, may pose little likelihood of motivating unlawful action, whereas the same statement made in the context of the first election campaign following a war characterised by ethnic cleansing may well pose a genuine and imminent threat to territorial integrity as well as to public order. (OSCE PEC, 1996b, p. 104)

This interpretation was guided by the European Convention for the Protection of Human Rights and Fundamental Freedoms, which was included in the General Framework Agreement and the Bosnian Constitution in Annex 4. Article 10(2) of the European Convention permitted a wide range of restrictions to freedom of expression in order to safeguard 'national security, territorial integrity or public safety, and the prevention of disorder or crime'. The weakness of the protections of democratic discourse under the European Convention were clearly highlighted in this example where the law was made and enforced by the international community and the people of Bosnia prevented from challenging it through the ballot box. As the Advisory Opinion went on to state: 'It is not possible to vote changes to the territorial integrity of Bosnia and Herzegovina. The international community is committed to preserving the country's territorial integrity' (OSCE PEC, 1996b, p. 104). However, there was a large difference between making an act, for example, changing the country's borders, illegal and making it an offence to even challenge or debate this. Because Bosnia was not classed as a stable democracy, Bosnian people were seemingly less entitled to democratic protections than the citizens of other states.

Four days later, on 10 September 1996, the EASC ruled (case number 96–24B) that the Serbian Democratic Party should forfeit US $50,000 for statements interpreted to threaten the territorial integrity of Bosnia (OSCE PEC, 1996b, pp. 119–20). The examples given in the judgement demonstrated how far the restriction on the freedom of expression was pushed by the OSCE in the run-up to the elections. The SDS were penalised not for directly challenging the Dayton Agreement but because 'SDS speakers have continually stressed the substantial autonomy granted to Republika Srpska in the General Framework Agreement, to the total exclusion of any reference to the unity of Bosnia and Herzegovina'. It now seemed that inadequate reference to territorial integrity in political campaigning was an infringement in itself. Even 'implied' references to moving closer to a union with Serbia, a possibility under the Dayton Accords, were seen to be problematic (OSCE PEC, 1996b, p. 119).

The 1997 Municipal elections

As Betty Dawson, the OSCE Press and Public Affairs Officer, stated: 'These will be the most supervised elections ever, anywhere.'[1] This extended supervision was specifically aimed at weakening the hold of national parties through altering the election regulations for both pre-election registration and post-election ratification.

Voter registration

OSCE control over who could vote and where they could vote provoked mistrust and anger amongst many people who were denied what they saw as their democratic rights. In response to this, in some areas, both residents and elected representatives tried to evade OSCE restrictions so that they could register to vote. This resulted in attempted election fraud in some of the municipalities which were seen as most at risk of having their postwar political status challenged through the OSCE use of the 1991 register as the basis for the proposed municipal elections.

The response to these ham-fisted attempts was a strict one. Under the rules, refugees could only vote in cities where they now resided if they could prove that they had lived there since 31 July 1996. Many displaced Serbs had moved to Brcko since then and had no wish to vote in their pre-war hometowns, cities that were now under Muslim-Croat control, from which they fled. The OSCE found that Bosnian Serb police were helping Serbs falsify addresses and backdate their identifications. In response the OSCE disqualified three leading SDS candidates and threw out the appeals of 3,270 Brcko residents, denying them the right to register. Even the right of a registered political party to stand candidates was under threat as the OSCE decertified the SDS entirely from the municipal elections in Srpski Drvar when they ruled that 19 people had been registered in breach of the regulations (OSCE EASC, 1997a, case number ME-049). Because regulation of the political process was not accountable to Bosnian voters, the network of election regulations and restrictions could easily be seen as external manipulation over the result. The insecurities created by this process did little to undermine the support for the nationalist parties (Wilkinson, 1997a).

Pressure on National Parties

Article 119 of the OSCE's election *Rules and Regulations* gave the international community the capacity to put pressure on the leaders of political parties in the run-up to elections because they could be held responsible for the actions of people alleged to be their supporters. The EASC ruled (case number ME-050) that the destruction of houses earmarked for returning Serbs in Drvar and the stoning of buses transporting returning Serbs was directly organised by the HDZ as: 'in the Drvar municipality the HDZ as the governing body, has complete control over local authorities and the police ... [and] the area where the destruction of houses occurred is under the absolute control of HDZ Drvar' (OSCE EASC, 1997b, pp. 1–2). The EASC removed the first name on the HDZ list for the municipal elections, without the need to establish any direct or indirect link between the leading candidate and the local unrest over refugee returns.

The broad powers of allocating blame for incidents or behaviour on leading national parties meant that the OSCE was able to apply pressure on the parties to co-operate and could freely choose which candidates to remove from the ballot, while the parties had no chance to appeal. With over a month to go before the September 1997 elections, the OSCE had already removed nearly fifty candidates, the vast majority of them from the SDS and the HDZ. In most instances, the penalty was the removal of the leading name on the candidates list, although in the case of SDA registration fraud in Zepce the second and third names were removed (OSCE EASC, 1997c). This method of regulation turned the elections in some areas into a farce, for example, in Zepce all the top nine candidates of the HDZ were removed (OSCE EASC, 1997d). The guilt-by-association approach was a draconian one, which placed the emphasis on the political party to 'prove that it has complied fully with its duties and responsibilities'. In the Drvar ruling, referred to above, the EASC threatened to punish the HDZ for any more anti-Serb incidents and was 'attracted to the remedy of striking two or more candidates for the destruction of one house etc.' (OSCE EASC, 1997b, p. 2).[2]

More controversial was the use of this regulation in conjunction with the media regulations to penalise the national parties. The MEC judged that, in June 1997, Croat-controlled HTV Mostar had broadcast an inflammatory speech by the former commander of the Herceg Bosnia police department in Mostar. The MEC wrote to the editor-in-chief of HTV informing him that the speech had violated the PEC regulations and instructed him to broadcast an editorial reply condemning it. In response, HTV rebroadcast the speech and followed it with an editorial response supporting the content of the speech in language which the MEC also found inflammatory. The EASC investigation found that HTV-Mostar received assistance from the mayor and the municipal council of Mostar and that a radio station, Croat Radio Mostar, had broadcast that the HDZ supported HTV both financially and ideologically. This meant that, under Article 119, the EASC found the HDZ in Mostar responsible for the failure of HTV to comply with MEC orders.

The consequences of this were far-reaching for the HDZ in Mostar. The first names on the party lists of the HDZ in the municipalities of Mostar South, Mostar Southwest and Mostar West were removed, their candidacies for office terminated and they were not allowed to be replaced. The EASC ordered HTV to broadcast an EASC-prepared statement on the evening news that night and on three consecutive nights, under the threat that if it was changed or they refused to comply, the EASC would strike a further three additional names from each of the HDZ lists, with three more removed for each day of non-compliance.

Ratification

The new rules for the registration process guaranteed a large vote for minority parties in areas where there were often few minorities. In six municipalities, the vote of displaced persons resulted in displaced-person governments: displaced Serbs won 52 per cent of the seats in SDA-controlled Bosanski Petrovac; and 63 per cent and 80 per cent respectively in HDZ-controlled Drvar and Bosansko Grahov; displaced Muslims won 93 per cent of the seats in HDZ-controlled Zepce and 52 per cent of the seats in SDS-controlled Srebrenica; and displaced Serbs and Muslims combined won 60 per cent in HDZ-controlled Glamoc (ICG, 1997d, p. 2).

The rules for ratification meant that the distribution of executive posts were contested in nearly all the municipalities. Instead of the party or coalition of parties which could form a majority deciding on the allocation of seats, there had to be a consensus or the OSCE and the Office of the High Representative stepped in with suggestions or imposed awards. Minority parties could easily disrupt the formation of municipal authorities and had little incentive to co-operate. In Prijedor, for example, attempts to convene the first session of the assembly broke down because the SDA-led Coalition refused to take the oath. They argued the oath should be changed even though the text had been suggested by the OSCE itself (OHR SRT, 1997b). This encouragement for minority parties to hold out for greater powers resulted in months of uncertainty and instability, with most councils not being ratified until February or March 1998 (OSCE MBH, 1998b). This eventually led to nearly all the municipal councils being formed through international assistance, often with complicated power-sharing solutions (see Chapter 4).

The municipal elections resulted in power-sharing solutions which have challenged the hold that the three leading national parties had over local government, but this was not a reflection of the wishes of the local communities or the voters in Bosnia as a whole, who gave overwhelming support to the leading national parties. The fact that power-sharing had to be imposed through threats of sanctions or directly through international awards did little to challenge the national politics of the parties. In fact, it could be argued that this policy intensified national or ethnic antagonisms at a local level with the fear of imposed returns galvanising a nationalist backlash and leading to an upsurge in conflict which put return plans at risk in spring 1998 (RFE/RL BR, 1998a).

The Bosnian Serb Assembly elections

The November 1997 ballot for new Republika Srpska Assembly elections was controversially called by the international community after RS President Biljana Plavsic dissolved the sitting Assembly, dominated by the Pale faction of the SDS, which was less open to international community involvement in Bosnian affairs. The new elections were openly viewed by the US as an opportunity to wrest legislative power from the Serb hard-liners, while Russia opposed this move and France and Germany expressed scepticism that the US could use the elections to change the political scene (Bonner, 1997). One central strategy was to ensure that the new party established by Plavsic, the Serbian Peoples' Alliance (SNS), had the opportunity of using the media to increase its support.

In September, the Pale-based Serb Radio and Television network (SRT) was pressurised to sign up to a series of agreements which undermined the influence of President Plavsic's opponents. The Udrivigo Agreement, of 2 September, reached by the Serb member of the Bosnian Presidency, Momcilo Krajisnik, in his capacity as Chairman of the Board of Directors of SRT, Deputy High Representative Jacques Klein, and SFOR General Shineski, agreed that SRT would: refrain from 'inflammatory reporting' against SFOR and international organisations supporting the Dayton Peace Agreement; provide an hour of prime-time programming every day in which other political views would be aired; provide the High Representative with a half-hour prime-time slot in the next few days, and agree to participate in the Office of the High Representative-conducted Media Support Advisory Group (MSAG) which regulated the media in accordance with the letter and spirit of the Dayton Agreement (OHRB, 1997y). On 24 September, the Belgrade Agreement, between President Plavsic, Momcilo Krajisnik, and Yugoslav President Milosevic, was signed. This lessened the Pale faction's editorial control over SRT through providing for news programmes to be broadcast on alternative days from SRT studios in Pale and Banja Luka (OHRB, 1997A).

The Pale faction's hold over SRT was removed entirely when, on 1 October, at the request of the High Representative, SFOR occupied four SRT transmitters preventing the transmission of SRT from the studios in Pale. The grounds for this action were stated to be the 'grotesque distortion' of the press conference by Hague war crimes prosecutor, Justice Louise Arbour, which SRT broadcast on 28 September. A video of the briefing had been presented to SRT for broadcast in its entirety, under the terms of the Udrigovo Agreement; however, the tape had been edited and editorial comments supportive of Karadzic and Mladic had been added as well as accusations that the Hague Tribunal was a political instrument against the Serbs (OHRB, 1997A). The SRT apologised and rebroadcast the programme with an introduction provided by the Tribunal two days later; however, the High Representative described the compliance as 'too little, too late' and invoked the power to close down the Pale transmissions completely, handing full control to the Banja Luka supporters of

President Plavsic (OHRB, 1997A). On 17 October, the Contact Group meeting in Rome instructed that the SRT governing board be restructured and a new General Manager instated (OHRB, 1997C). This resulted in the appointment of an international administrator to oversee editorial content (OHRB, 1998b).

International support for President Plavsic and attempts to undermine the power of the Pale-based SDS leadership did not end with the transference of media control. The United States delivered US $700,000 in equipment to SRT Banja Luka and offered media training and the services of a US government media expert to assist Plavsic in her campaign (Wilkinson, 1997b). The United States' government also ploughed reconstruction aid into Plavsic's base in Banja Luka and handed out small-business loans to her supporters in western Bosnia (Hedges, 1997). However, this was not enough to undermine the hold of the SDS, which was the largest party with 24 seats and had the support of the Serb Radical Party (SRS) with 15 seats. Plavsic's SNS gained 15 seats, leaving the hard-liners a comfortable mandate but short of a majority due to the 18 seats won by absentee Muslim and Croat candidates. As one European diplomat noted: 'The move to use the assembly as a wedge ... has failed. Plavsic has much less support than even we imagined' (Hedges, 1997). Initially, international pressure was applied to encourage the MPs to accept a government of experts led by Mladen Ivanic, and the High Representative went as far as to threaten that if a suitable candidate could not be agreed by the Assembly he would appoint the Prime Minister himself (*RFE/RL Newsline*, 1998b). This proved unnecessary as the second session of the Assembly elected a moderate government headed by Milorad Dodik, after the SDS and SRS MPs had adjourned for the night.

THE SUCCESS OF INTERNATIONAL REGULATION IN CHALLENGING NATIONAL PARTIES

The direct intervention by the OSCE and the Office of the High Representative in the regulation of electoral competition and media coverage has been regarded as having had a marked success in undermining the hold of the leading nationalist party in Republika Srpska, although it could be argued that the dismissal of the SDS from power in the Assembly had more to do with the mobilisation of absentee Croat and Muslim voters than with a shift in Serb support.[3] In any case, there is little disagreement that in both entities there has been little success in creating support for non-nationalist parties or demand for non-nationalist media output. It is quite possible that the starting assumptions that nationalist support was a product of a lack of a 'fair playing field' ignored the social and economic climate in which Bosnian voters acted and made electoral decisions.

A leading justification for external intervention in Bosnian elections was the need to stop the governing authorities from restricting the operations of the independent media or non-national parties. However, the use of intimidation or political power to prevent alternative voices has not been a major barrier in this respect. Examples of intimidation by political parties had been recorded in the 1996 elections (see OHRB, 1996i) but the US State Department noted 'few reports of politically motivated harassment or violence' in 1997 (USDoS, 1998b, section 3). Equally, there was little evidence of media sources being hampered by the Bosnian authorities. It was only in Republika Srpska that this was a problem to any extent, particularly after the September 1996 elections gave the SDS political control, but even in this case state regulation proved to be counterproductive and short-lived. In October, journalists from *Alternativa* were put on trial for libel, *Radio Krajina* was closed and Glas Srpski, the state-owned printing press, and the only one suitable for newspapers, refused to print *Nezavisne novine*, by far the most influential of the opposition press. The clampdown on the opposition press backfired as *Nezavisne novine* switched printing to Belgrade and continued to print controversial material, Glas Srpski relented and agreed to print it again (ICG, 1997a, pp. 3–5).

The fact that the independent media, the media sources which were opposed to the main nationalist parties, remained fairly marginal did not prove that they were being restricted by the regional authorities. In fact, it could be argued that state and regional authorities had less influence over the media in Bosnia than in other European states. The close links between the media and elections enabled the OSCE's Provisional Election Commission to play a direct role in establishing media facilities without the consent of Bosnian authorities. In July 1996, the PEC amended its *Rules and Regulations* in order to force the governing authorities to:

> … ensure that licences and frequencies for electronic and print media are granted expeditiously, on the basis of objective non-political criteria … In particular, in accordance with the Geneva Agreed Statement of 2 June 1996, the Governments will grant without delay to the Open Broadcast Network all necessary licences, including the right to broadcast and feed via satellite, frequencies, permissions to use and develop sites, and any other broadcast-related permits and authorisations, local or international. (OSCE PEC, 1997, par. 127)

As international media advisor Michael Maclay noted: 'In order to make the [OBN] Network a reality, the OHR had to get tough: we imposed a draconian regulation under the OSCE's election rules, which overrode all state and local laws' (Maclay, 1997, p. 32). The limitation of Bosnian authorities' rights over the media were demonstrated, for example, in April 1997 when ATV, the Banja Luka affiliate of the international community-run Open Broadcast Network, was inspected and told to cease broadcasting as it did not have a licence. The OHR and OSCE appealed that the application had been submitted and that, under Article 27 of the PEC *Rules and Regulations*, they were entitled to broadcast whilst the application was being processed. As it turned out this was irrelevant as the premises, property and equipment were also protected by SFOR designation as having special status (OHRB, 1997n).

Far from nationalist Bosnian elites restricting media and political pluralism, it would appear that Bosnian citizens had a wide and varied choice of media sources and political parties. In this respect the pattern was similar for both Muslim, Croat and Serb-dominated areas of Bosnia. At the end of the war, there were 272 media organisations active in Bosnia; 203 in the Federation, 69 in Republika Srpska. By the spring of 1998 this number had doubled to 270 media organisations in the Federation and 220 in Republika Srpska. Bosnia has 156 radio stations and 52 television stations on air, 5 daily papers (3 in the Federation, 2 in RS) and 20 periodicals (SAFAX, 1998b). In fact, rather than an inadequate choice, media analysts have stressed that 'there are more media than the market can realistically sustain' (SAFAX, 1998b). An authoritative report from the International Crisis Group (ICG) similarly found that 'the scale of the alternative media and the number of journalists is out of proportion to the size of the population' (1997a, p. 5). In this situation, only the media sources capable of attracting an audience could survive, the problem faced by the non-nationalist media was not one of political pressure but economics, as the ICG noted: 'circulations are generally small and most of the industry would collapse if the [international] donations dried up' (1997a, p. 5).

As the ICG *Media Report* highlighted, funding and supporting media organisations without links to the nationalist parties or regional authorities did not guarantee their success. The plethora of media was not indicative of the health of the media scene in Bosnia, but in fact the opposite: 'it is indicative of the level of outside support and the artificial nature of the market' (1997a, p. 18). The ICG's concern was that the proliferation of funding for alternative media projects meant that there was too much division which weakened the strength of the non-nationalist alternative, that, in effect, the international community had done too much to help the Bosnian media.

A similar situation would appear to have been created by the OSCE's financial support for political parties. For the 1996 elections, funding of over US $4.5 million was shared initially between all the political groups; this was changed in 1997 to deny funding for the three main nationalist parties. Funding for small parties was readily available, with up to DM 4000, given partly up-front in cash, available to single independent candidates (ICG, 1997c, p. 21). This led to the creation of many small parties which otherwise would have not been able to stand in elections or would have been forced to collaborate with others in order to muster enough political and financial support.[4] The result was that there were 90 parties competing in the 1997 municipal elections, many of them with very similar programmes, which meant they were so fragmented it was difficult for them to win much support.

The OSCE Democratisation Branch Political Party Development Co-ordinator, Adrien Marti, felt that another major problem was the lack of support for the political alternatives on offer from the small independent parties. He stated that after the elections he would be pressurising many to give up their status as political parties because groups arguing for non-national politics 'would have much more influence as pressure groups, NGOs and lobby groups than as political parties with only 0.001 per cent of the vote'.[5] Consideration of the failure of internationally funded parties and media outlets as due to a lack of demand for the ideas they presented, as opposed to a technical problem of aid distribution, adds another dimension to the problems facing external initiatives in this area.

International community media

The question of a lack of demand for the political alternatives on offer from the international funders is again raised by the take-up for the biggest media experiments in democratisation that have yet been tried – the international community's own radio and TV stations, Radio FERN and TV-IN, which were not lacking in financial resources or trained staff. By far and away the two largest media projects in Bosnia, they were set up by the international community in preparation for the September 1996 elections.

Free Elections Radio Network (FERN) was financed by Switzerland with two million Deutschmarks and started broadcasting in July 1996. The station was originally scheduled to be on air only until the September 1996 elections. In less than two months and with no advertising campaign to announce its appearance it had little chance of influencing the election outcome. The postponement of the municipal elections enabled it build up the quality of its programmes and to pay regular salaries to its journalists, allowing it to attract Bosnia's better reporters. Its signal now covers 81 per cent of Federation territory and 66 per cent of Republika Srpska, reaching a majority of the population in both entities.

Despite the wide reach of the station, and the generous funding for its journalistic objectivity, audience figures are still disappointing. The ICG explain this as down to two reasons: first, that there still is not enough funding, arguing that the station's structure is 'fundamentally flawed' because it is based in Sarajevo and relies excessively on freelance contributions to cover Republika Srpska and Croat-controlled Federation territory; and, second, that it does not reach the whole of both entities (1997a, p. 12).

TV-IN, also known as the Open Broadcast Network (OBN), was established with US $10.5 million sponsorship from the Office of the High Representative and went on air in September 1996, less than a week before the elections. After the elections, and extension of the international mandates, the project was strengthened with the creation of a Steering Committee including the OHR, OSCE, the European Commission, the United States and the Soros Foundation (OHRB, 1997c). TV-IN suffered a similar experience, failing to establish a strong audience, even with the help of an IFOR transmitter to beam coverage to Banja Luka.

There seems to be little support within Bosnia for what was called 'Bildt media' and one of the initial five networked TV stations, Sarajevo-based NTV 99, capable of generating its own audience, left the project in the early stages and has been one of its fiercest critics. When the satellite link failed, in January 1997, and TV-IN went off the air for a week, few Bosnians even noticed (ICG, 1997a, p. 12). According to the ICG: 'A major shortcoming of TV-IN is that it was put together by the Office of the High Representative and not by Bosnians. It is thus generally viewed as a foreign creation and treated with suspicion' (1997a, p. 12).

It is undoubtedly true that external management of the project has created a low morale amongst the Bosnian staff who 'complain that they do not know themselves where the station stands, who is running it or where it is heading' (ICG, 1997a, p. 13). The project's main focus has been on OHR-produced material, a central news programme broadcast at 8.00 p.m., lasting for 30 minutes, and a weekly programme on refugee issues as well as a programme on women's issues that started in March

1997. Apart from this it has relied on programmes, such as soaps, imported from abroad, and programmes produced by the four small independent Bosnian network stations that are funded by the Office of the High Representative and are based in Sarajevo, Zenica, Tuzla and Mostar.

The ICG report expressed well the perspective of the international media planners, instead of asking why the internationally produced and 'objective' programming had difficulties generating an audience, it focused on the output of the local networked stations as the cause of the stations' shortcomings. It was ironic that the ICG found fault with the programming that the local network stations used to try to establish an audience for themselves and condemned, for example, Sarajevo-based TV Hayat, for its decision to broadcast hours of religious programming a day during Ramadan. According to the ICG:

> The little stations are a major embarrassment. They fail to contribute much in the way of news reports to the hub, as originally anticipated, and what they do contribute is often amateurish and/or as biased as the state broadcaster. Worse still, some of their practices bring the entire network into disrepute. (ICG, 1997a, p. 13)

It could be argued that the real problems stemmed from the fact that there was little demand for the cross-entity perspective promoted by the internationally funded and externally established media outlets. The US State Department annual human rights report for 1997 noted that 'the OBN fares extremely poorly in the competition for viewers with party-controlled media in the two entities' (USDoS, 1998b, section 2A). One credible survey of media audiences, limited to Banja Luka, found that fewer than 0.5 per cent of people watched OBN or listened to FERN regularly (ICG, 1997c, p. 20). Regardless of the popularity of the Open Broadcast Network, its viewers have often been seen as representative of Bosnian democratic opinion *vis-à-vis* the main parties, and OBN phone-in polls have been used by the OHR to argue that there is majority support for internationally-imposed policy, such as the High Representative's edicts on passports, the national flag and licence-plates (OHRB, 1998a).

CONCLUSION

Despite the concerted work of the international community in challenging nationalism through political regulation and media controls there has been only limited success in creating support for a non-nationalist outlook. This would fit other analyses of externally-led democratisation practice. For example, Carothers' study of democratisation in Romania similarly found that external intervention aimed at 'levelling the playing field' and creating a more plural political process was largely ineffectual (1996). One reason for this could be the questionable starting assumption that political parties or media sources create an audience rather than responding to one. For example, studies of the development of the Bosnian media demonstrate that the fragmentation of the media into serving three different markets with three different political perspectives reflected the disintegration of the Bosnian state rather than being itself a causal factor (Thompson, 1994). It would appear therefore that non-national politics could emerge easier if this reflected changing circumstances. As long as Bosnia remains divided and minorities feel insecure, it may prove difficult for external regulation to win majority support for political alternatives.

There is even a danger that the level of external interference in the Bosnian political process could institutionalise national standpoints as opposed to overcoming them. Principal Deputy High Representative Jacques Klein argues that minority fears are understandable but that: 'they have to co-operate with the international community. They have to realise that only then will they be completely protected and safe. Isolation is not the solution' (Klein, 1998b). However, some international officials have openly expressed fears that silencing media broadcasts could provide support for nationalists, such as the Serb authorities who have portrayed NATO as an occupying army (O'Connor, 1997). There are also concerns that international community threats to remove candidates from election lists can increase the level of tensions and insecurities as international intervention may be seen to work to the detriment of one party or to the benefit of another. In a context where there is little security about political control over policy, this level of regulation can easily increase people's fear that they might be losing out. It would seem that external intervention to undermine the control of popular politicians over the selection of candidates or to regulate media editorial policy can just as easily ratchet up tensions as reconcile them.

While the effectiveness of this approach is certainly open to discussion, international community regulation in this area has raised broader questions about the 'top-down' democratisation strategy. This strategy is justified by the High Representative, who argues: 'It is ugly to democratise a country using force, but where you have such abnormal mentality in the leadership, then you have to do this' (Westendorp, 1997b). However, the banning of political candidates for statements made in election campaigns and the censorship of media outlets in the name of democratisation has struck many commentators as contradictory and has been seen by some commentators as being at the cost of traditionally held liberal democratic values, Bosnian self-government and autonomy.

The proposals for media and election regulation being instituted in 1998 would seem to add weight to this perspective. In December 1997, the Peace Implementation Council announced the intention of forming a new regulatory commission, responsible for the restructuring and licensing of all broadcast media in Bosnia (OHRB, 1997B). The Intermediate Media Standards and Licensing Commission (IMSLC) is intended to prevent local media from coming under the control of national parties and is responsible for media restructuring, the licensing body having the power to sanction media for non-compliance with internationally-set editorial standards (OHRB, 1998b). The powers to close down television and radio stations that challenge the international administration have been described by the OHR spokesman Simon Haselock as 'ground-breaking' (Shenon, 1998). Media organisations such as the Vienna-based International Press Institute and the International Federation of Journalists have questioned these new powers of censorship (RFE/RL BR, 1998b; Shenon, 1998). The *New York Times* editorialised that:

> The commission should not venture further into regulating the content of broadcasting, and should stick to its plan not to regulate the print media. If the commission appears to be imposing Western-backed censorship, it will violate democratic principles, enrage Bosnian citizens and encourage neighbouring dictators to strengthen their hold on the media. (*NYT*, 1998)

In relation to the political parties, the OSCE is considering changing the regulations again after the September 1998 elections in order to impose non-nationalist candidates. High Representative Carlos Westendorp stated: 'I wouldn't consider elections to be free, fair and fully democratic until all political parties, even the most important political parties, are really pluralistic, and include all the ethnic groups in this country' (OHRB, 1997z). This stipulation was given international support when the PIC Steering Board confirmed that 'the main parties could no longer be only mono-ethnic parties' (OHRB, 1997B). Even commentators supportive of this approach accept that it 'may seem a shocking affront to liberalism' (Spencer, 1998). Removing the democratic mandate from the leading national parties through new forms of electoral regulation would further disenfranchise Bosnian electors with little guarantee that the political climate would be transformed.

6 Building civil society

For the Dayton Peace Agreement to hold, international community institutions and many commentators have seen the development of civil society as essential for democratisation and peace-building. Civil society development is generally viewed to involve support for the associational sphere of interest groups which stand between the private sphere, of the family and market economy, and the public sphere, of the state and government. A richly pluralistic civil society, generating a wide range of interests, is held to mitigate polarities of political conflict and develop a democratic culture of tolerance, moderation and compromise (see for example, Diamond, 1994; Seligman, 1992; Cohen and Arato, 1992; Keane, 1988). The main focus of civil society-building has often been local non-governmental organisations (NGOs) seen as capable of articulating needs independently of vested political interests and involving grass-roots community 'voices'. Ian Smillie, author of an influential CARE Canada report on NGOs and civil society-building in Bosnia, argues:

> Rebuilding tolerance and pluralism in Bosnia and Herzegovina is perhaps more important than anywhere else in the former Yugoslavia. It is important because without it, the Dayton Accord ... and the hope of a united Bosnia and Herzegovina will be lost ... Accountability, legitimacy and competence in public life are the key, and these can only be achieved through the active participation of the electorate, buoyed by a strong, plural, associational base, by a web of social, cultural and functional relationships which can act as a 'societal glue' and as counterbalance to the market and the state. The alternative for Bosnia and Herzegovina ... is paternalism, exploitation, corruption, and war. (Smillie, 1996, p. 13)

Dialogue Development, preparing the 1998 European Union PHARE Civil Society Development Programme for Bosnia, state:

> The strong emergence of a Third Sector in the form of civil society in Bosnia will be instrumental in the gradual emergence of a pluralistic and democratic society ... NGOs are ... destined to play an important role in this post-conflict situation as they have a vast potential for transcending the fault-lines of

> society through the creation of new partnerships and alliances. They can moderate and mediate in addressing the relevant needs of society, not always within the realm of the state. (Dialogue Development, 1997, Annex 1, p. 1)

Without civil society, international economic reconstruction aid is held to have little impact on political and social division within Bosnia. Smillie argues that 'democracy is more than economy' and other NGO analysts, such as Bob Deacon and Paul Stubbs from Leeds Metropolitan University, note that 'aid is unlikely to challenge feudalist tendencies', and argue that European Union funding of over US $2500 per head to the residents of Mostar, more than EU aid to the whole of Poland, has had little appreciable impact on reducing tensions between Muslims and Croats (Deacon and Stubbs, 1998, p. 103; see also Kenney, 1997c).

There is similar disillusionment with international assistance in the political sphere (see Chapter 5). There is a growing consensus today that elections without civil society do not produce democracy. This link between purely formal democracy and ethnic conflict and human rights abuse has been regularly raised in opposition to the Clinton administration's pursuit of a new 'ethical' foreign policy with an emphasis on democratisation abroad (for example, Zakaria, 1997; Kaplan, 1997). As considered in Chapter 1, in the Bosnian context these criticisms have been sharpest. Bogdan Denitch, a leading authority on ethnicity and democracy, argues that 'elections without a strong civil society will not produce democracy'. He favours 'a temporary UN protectorate' on the grounds that 'Western "outsiders" are far better representatives of the genuine interests of the Croatian, Serbian, and Bosnian peoples and states than their patriotic leaders' (Denitch, 1996, pp. 210; 228–9). Tom Gallagher reflects the general view that elections in Bosnia are 'deeply flawed', merely allowing the three nationalist parties to legitimise their political control (Gallagher, 1997). Robert Kaplan goes further, stating: 'in Bosnia democracy legitimised the worst war crimes in Europe since the Nazi era' (Kaplan, 1997, p. 58).

While intervention in the spheres of economics and politics is often seen to merely perpetuate social segmentation and ethnic nationalism, international support for Bosnian NGOs and civil society-building is held to have an empowering and transformative content. As Jasna Malkoc, the Senior Co-ordinator for Democratisation/NGO Development explained: 'Establishing NGOs is a first principle for democratisation. NGOs are vital for the reconstruction of civil society.'[1] This chapter assesses international community strategy for civil society construction and its relationship to the democratisation process. First, the OSCE approach is considered and, in following sections, the relationship between civil society and democratisation is looked at more closely, highlighting potential pitfalls with the approach of 'democratisation from below'.

BUILDING CIVIL SOCIETY

The Democratisation Branch of the OSCE seeks to encourage the voice and activity of ordinary citizens who support civil society:

> Bosnian citizens as a whole will have to overcome democratisation's challenges if they want their country to develop into a tolerant and democratic state. OSCE Democratisation staff will attempt to help them find the tools to do so. Staff will facilitate local efforts, offer support and guidance. In the end however there is a limit to what international personnel can do – it is for the citizens themselves to participate and take responsibility in the democratic grassroots project. (OSCE DB, 1997j, p. 2)

Although the Democratisation Branch sees that only the Bosnian people can create a civil society, it also believes that Bosnian people themselves are at present not confident enough, or skilled enough, to initiate their own 'grass-roots' projects:

> Throughout Bosnia, but in Eastern RS in particular, democratisation staff recognise that ordinary people are dissatisfied and disillusioned; they thus tend to withdraw from all segments of civic and political life. The aim of the Democratisation Strategy is to overcome this and assist citizens [to] become more participatory to effect change. NGOs have developed in areas of Bosnia where people realise that there are tools available to them to influence their communities. At this stage democratisation staff [are] engaged in facilitating contacts between those who have gained these tools, and those who are only now seeing the importance of organising in civic groups. (OSCE DB, 1997k, p. 5)

This approach is supported by Dialogue Development and other international organisations concerned with the Bosnian NGO sector:

> The breaking down of mental barriers, which will allow people to establish public organisations creating alternatives to solutions proposed by governments and local authorities, is a key task of the European Union and international organisations supporting NGOs in Bosnia and Herzegovina. (Marchlewski, 1997, p. 5)

The OSCE Mission in Bosnia was restructured at the end of 1996 to enable it to carry out a more long-term approach to democratisation, focusing on the challenges of creating or restoring civil society in the region. This perspective was informed by the consensus that peace and stability in Bosnia was 'still very much dependent on the development of a democratic civil society' (OSCE DB, 1997j, p. 3). The focus on civil society, going beyond the governing institutions of the country, gave the international community a much broader remit of involvement in Bosnian affairs by extending the role of the OSCE under Dayton. Annex 3 of the Dayton Peace Agreement, the *Agreement on Elections*, gave the OSCE the authority to 'lay the foundation for representative government and ensure the progressive achievement of democratic goals throughout Bosnia and Herzegovina' (GFA, 1995). This was now seen to include the promotion of civil society through support for the work of Bosnian NGOs.

This broader remit facilitated the development of a separate Democratisation Branch, a unique step for an international institution. The branch was formed as an offshoot from the Human Rights Branch, which had previously formed the closest working relationship with local and international NGOs. Prior to this point, the focus of the Dayton-empowered international bodies had been on the operations of the Bosnian authorities and their compliance with international mandates. Although international and local NGOs had been involved in this process, particularly in human rights monitoring, the development of the political role of local NGOs in civil society-building had not been considered as a priority. Due to the perceived centrality of local NGO work in reconstructing civil society, many NGO analysts had been critical that international support for local Bosnian NGOs seemed more focused on humanitarian aid and service provision than on civil society-building (Deacon and Stubbs, 1997; Duffield, 1996a, 1996b; Stubbs, 1996, 1997; Smillie, 1996). The OSCE Democratisation Branch follows the strategy recommended by these commentators, focusing on participatory grass-roots involvement and on giving NGOs greater weight in policy-making (OSCE DB, 1997f).

The OSCE Democratisation Programme for 1997 was designed to bring the international community into a closer relationship with grass-roots groups and associations which could provide a counterpoint to the politics of the governing authorities and nationalist parties and, through this, to open up political debate and create new opportunities for alternative voices to be heard (OSCE DB, 1997a). Unlike the European Union PHARE programme and similar schemes, the OSCE did not hand out funding to selected projects by local partners and then end the process with a monitoring report on how the money was spent. The OSCE's intervention into the Bosnian NGO sphere operated on a broader level, through a long-term developmental approach, which sought to facilitate the establishment of local partners, NGOs and civic groups, and enable them to approach funders, network with other providers, and to raise their political profile within Bosnia and in the international community.

The OSCE strategy for encouraging political participation has involved a three-stage process: first, identifying targeted individuals or groups who are open to external support and influence and then beginning to network them with local NGOs and external providers; second, providing training and building a civil society agenda within these groups; third, mobilising active NGOs as political voices in the domestic and international environment.

Targeting

The Democratisation Branch works through the extensive OSCE field presence covering the whole of Bosnia, and co-ordinated through five regional centres of operation, based in Mostar, Tuzla, Bihac, Banja Luka and Sokolac. This means that they are strategically placed to play a key role in identifying individuals and groups for democratisation initiatives.[2] Based in the field, the Democratisation Officers have the role of assessing which groups are most open to OSCE influence and to develop strategies in relation to them.

OSCE strategy has a regional approach because the receptivity to external intervention and support is dependent on the local political situation. In the Federation there are many active NGOs, partly because of the influx of foreign donors and partly because the political climate is more receptive to external influence. The OSCE feels that in many urban areas in the Federation there is a 'diverse and vibrant NGO community' (OSCE DB, 1997j, p. 5). The climate has been less receptive in RS, with the Banja Luka area being the centre for NGO activities and parts of Eastern RS having virtually no NGOs.

The strategy is to integrate the 'more developed', politically active, NGOs into the broader OSCE perspective, and under OSCE 'facilitation' for them to link up with groups and individuals in areas with 'less developed' NGOs and a low NGO presence. For example, in the Tuzla region, experienced local NGOs are encouraged to expand their networks to give the OSCE new areas of influence (OSCE DB, 1997e, p. 4). In areas with little organised NGO presence the OSCE has to trawl for prospective partners. For example, the staff in Banja Luka created a workshop on proposal-drafting for NGOs with plans to travel outside the city to the surrounding areas. In Velika Kladusa, a targeted area where the OSCE was concerned about the 'clear dearth of local initiatives', the OSCE organised a one-day seminar *How to Establish an NGO*, which targeted teachers, students, political party representatives, women, intellectuals and local journalists, to enable them to 'form a clearer idea of what fields NGOs work in, their legal status, and funding possibilities' (OSCE DB, 1997l, p. 6).

The target groups for developing networking and community-building initiatives are essentially those that the OSCE feels it can influence. Within this, the more social weight a group has, the better it is. Elite groups, such as lawyers, journalists, religious leaders, teachers, academics and intellectuals are therefore of great importance. Outside this, the OSCE has been able to establish links with groups that are either excluded from the mainstream political processes, in need of funding and resources, or unhappy with their current situation, such as self-help initiatives including women's groups, youth associations, and displaced persons' associations.

In areas where there are no existing NGOs, the Democratisation Branch has a more difficult job to find avenues of influence, making the establishment of initial contacts important. For example, in the Sokolac area of operations, particularly around Visegrad, Democratisation Officers are instructed to 'identify groups and individuals who are interested in increasing their participation in their communities, in some cases by forming NGOs' (OSCE DB, 1997d, p. 4). Once groups or individuals are located, 'advice on how to organise, fund-raise [and develop a] programme might then be given to them by the Democratisation Officer, Senior Democratisation Officer, or local partners' (OSCE DB, 1997e, p. 5).

Any activity that can be undertaken in a cross-entity form, and thereby constitute a potential challenge to ethnic segmentation and division, is likely to be supported. The OSCE's interest is not so much in the activity itself but in locating people who are willing to organise around alternative political focus points to the majority parties. However, the OSCE fears that being up-front about its aims may put off potential supporters: 'When groups focus on non-political matters they have an optimal chance of making gains' (OSCE DB, 1997j, p. 4). The Democratisation Branch monthly report, for March 1997, demonstrates this in relation to sponsorship and other information: 'While promoting inter-ethnic tolerance and responsibility is the main goal of confidence building, events this month show how this is sometimes easiest done when it is not an activity's explicit goal' (OSCE DB, 1997k, p. 4).

Agenda setting

Regardless of the needs the NGO was established to meet, it was expected to participate in cross-entity forums and training and to become part of the NGO lobbying network dominated by the more openly political 'civic groups'. The OSCE involvement with local NGOs (LNGOs) has a directly political goal:

> The goal of the NGO Development work is to assist LNGOs [to] become self-sufficient, participatory, and actively involved in working on behalf of their communities. The kind of LNGO projects which most closely reach this aim, offering a new political voice to citizens, are those which focus on advocacy and are willing to tackle actual political or social issues. As more and more LNGOs accept the responsibility of implementing these kinds of programmes, they gradually strengthen Bosnia's civil society. (OSCE DB, 1997j, p. 5)

There is no hiding the feelings of frustration that the officers of the OSCE have for the local NGOs which they see as 'less developed' because they are concentrating on needs, as opposed to becoming part of a political opposition, or their willingness to use their influence to alter the approaches and goals of local NGOs. The following extract, from one of the Democratisation Branch's monthly reports, illustrates the support and guidance available from the OSCE:

> In areas where LNGOs are barely developed, as a start they implement humanitarian-type programmes which seek to satisfy basic needs. Over the past month, local groups identified in Eastern Republika Srpska (excluding Bijeljina) correspond to this. As true civil actors however, LNGOs must do more; otherwise they will be providing temporary solutions to what remain long term problems. An early step was taken [when] the Helsinki Committee Bijeljina started monitoring and investigating human rights abuses in mid-1996 ... In the Bihac area [of operations], the Centre for Civic Co-operation (CCC) in Livno has gradually gone with OSCE support from a humanitarian LNGO working with children to one which seeks to increase awareness about human rights and democracy. (OSCE DB, 1997j, p. 6)

The OSCE women's development work demonstrates how this process works. Reporting on the OSCE-organised Mostar Women's Conference, in March 1997, it is noted that nine women currently living as displaced persons in Republika Srpska attended. The OSCE was disappointed that while the Federation women were willing to organise politically, the women from RS clearly had not grasped the OSCE's agenda:

> ... while the Federation women appeared poised to work on joint activities, those from the RS seemed more keen on fulfilling their immediate personal wish of visiting Mostar. Whether the RS participants recognise that working with other Mostar women they have a chance of addressing some of the deeper underlying obstacles to freedom of movement and return, is thus likely to determine future conferences' success. (OSCE DB, 1997k, p. 3)

However, the work with women's organisations seems to be having some success as the OSCE has noted that 'women are increasingly finding ways to take on political roles, even though frequently outside of political parties' (OSCE DB, 1997k, p. 5). The report notes that in Bihac a women's NGO is reportedly keen to organise a radio broadcast on elections-related issues with OSCE support and that women's groups in Mostar are considering a similar initiative. The women's groups most active in political activity have so impressed the OSCE that: 'In the coming months OSCE staff may consider encouraging these women to become electoral monitors ... This is a step towards preparing civic groups to take on bigger responsibilities in the political process' (OSCE DB, 1997k, p. 5).

The OSCE also runs the election process (see Chapter 5) and the regulations of the OSCE-chaired Provisional Election Commission allow for citizens' organisations as well as political party representatives to monitor the electoral process, after receiving accreditation from a Local Election Committee. From the OSCE's perspective this is 'an important chance to involve a greater number of actors in the political process' (OSCE DB, 1997d, p. 3). Of course, the new actors involved in this process are those that have already been carefully hand-picked by the OSCE itself. As a Mostar strategy report advises: 'Field Officers and the Regional Centre should begin identifying local partners who could benefit from poll watching training' (OSCE DB, 1997c, section II, B). Democratisation Officers have been instructed by the OSCE Democratisation Branch to facilitate training for these groups with the assistance of the US-funded National Democratic Initiative and the Council of Europe (OSCE DB, 1997d, p. 3).

For the OSCE, the sign of successful civil society-building is when the new local NGOs begin to develop as political actors in their own right. The third monthly report of the Democratisation Branch celebrates the success of their work in northern Republika Srpska, where 'local NGOs are independently addressing more and more sensitive political subjects' (OSCE DB, 1997l, p. 6). Examples include an internationally-financed inter-entity round table, initiated by the Forum of Citizens of Banja Luka, entitled

The Legal Aspects of Return for Refugees and Displaced Persons, and the establishment of preliminary contacts between a new Doboj NGO and displaced persons in Zenica. The OSCE is full of praise for the two NGOs which are raising an issue that it sees as a major part of its own agenda: 'The fact that the two groups are addressing the politically sensitive issue of return points to their ability to take on the kind of independent stance necessary in any democratic society' (OSCE DB, 1997l, p. 6).

The voice of civil society

The OSCE's NGO Development Programme is geared to giving these organisations a coherent political voice of opposition to the nationalist parties. This is made clear in the Semi-Annual Report, which highlights the success of the citizens' group NGOs:

> In the first half of 1997, NGOs have continued to debate the scope and specificities of their *political responsibilities* in Bosnian society. Several local NGOs have become heavily involved in legal aid in the past six months. Both the Serb Civic Council and the Helsinki Committee (Sarajevo and Bijeljina offices especially) play a major role in monitoring and investigating human rights violations. Other organisations such as the Citizens' Alternative Parliament, the Forum of Tuzla Citizens, the Helsinki Citizens' Assembly (HCA) and the Coalition for Return see their role in advocacy and political involvement. (OSCE DB, 1997m, p. 13, original emphasis)

In order to give greater coherence to these voices of civil society, and to ensure that they can spread their influence outside the major urban areas, the OSCE and other international organisations supported the establishment of an NGO Support Centre in April 1997. Based in Sarajevo, its first priority was the creation of an NGO database to begin to develop a network of local NGOs. The long-term OSCE strategy is for this network to organise so that local groups can 'work together on the legal issues, funding problems, and political matters which are of common concern' (OSCE DB, 1997m, pp. 13–14).

The directly political impact of this NGO work can be seen in initiatives like the Citizens' Alternative Parliament and the Coalition for Return, actively supported by the OSCE-backed NGOs. The Citizens' Alternative Parliament (CAP) is a network of Bosnian NGOs which the OSCE sees as strengthening and co-ordinating the work of NGOs in Bosnia. To strengthen the impact of the CAP the OSCE intends to focus on developing the 'member organisations' commitment and capabilities of taking action in their regions' (OSCE DB, 1997j, p. 6). The OSCE's work with displaced persons' groups is designed to feed in with the activities of the Coalition for Return (CFR). The CFR is an association of refugee and displaced persons groups from Bosnia, Croatia, Serbia and Germany.

In advance of the September 1996 elections, Deputy High Representative Steiner had already raised the prospect of refugee associations being used to put pressure on political parties 'from below'. In July he promised that: 'In the future we will aim to include representatives of refugee associations in our meetings in order to speed up the work of the authorities on both sides which has so far been very slow' (OHRB, 1996g). The decision to form the CFR was taken at the Office of the High Representative, following the nationalist parties' success in the September 1996 polls (ICG, 1997b, p. 9). Steiner discussed plans to establish the association with representatives from associations of displaced persons and refugees and gave full support for the formation of a strategy planning group to liase directly with international organisations and the relevant authorities (OHRB, 1996u). The CFR, meeting under the chair of the Office of the High Representative, then worked to encourage return and to raise the profile of the issue with international organisations. In December 1996, the CFR decided to extend its remit to the directly political questions related to the issue of return and to develop an integrated approach to reconstruction and economic recovery.

By February 1997, this political role had extended to developing information and aid networks calling on displaced persons and refugees to vote for candidates committed to the issue of return in the forthcoming municipal elections (OHRB, 1997g). Deputy High Representative Steiner then sought to promote the CFR as a popular 'grass-roots movement' and, in July 1997, at its first meeting not organised and chaired by the OHR, the CFR finally came of age, as an independent organ of civil society (OHRB, 1997l; OHRB, 1997q). It then requested observer status for the municipal elections and equal partnership with elected political representatives in negotiations on donations and reconstruction implementation projects (OHRB, 1997u).

CIVIL SOCIETY BEFORE DEMOCRACY?

The impetus behind the reorganisation of the OSCE Bosnia Mission and the establishment of the OSCE Democratisation Branch was the international community's plans to extend the role of international institutions over the new state. It was only after the elections that the creation of civil society became a central issue in Bosnia. During 1996 many international officials were still referring to the establishment of joint institutions with the elections as the birth of Bosnian democracy (USDoS, 1996b; PIC, 1996a, par. 27).

The focus on civil society legitimated a unique situation. The September 1996 elections were held to have been democratic, and to have met the standards set by the OSCE for the recognition of the results, yet they were also declared to be not democratic enough to allow self-rule. A Democratisation Branch information document explains this apparent contradiction:

> In the biggest event since the signing of the Dayton Accords, Bosnia's citizens chose for themselves a legitimate democratically elected system of government in September, 1996 ... Accordingly the first foundations have been laid for Bosnia to become a democracy. Yet even though elections are essential for the creation of a legitimate democratic state, they are not enough to ensure that democracy in Bosnia prevails. It is a mistake to see elections as the endpoint of democratisation. They are in fact an early stage of what remains by definition a long term process. (OSCE DB, 1997b, p. 1)

Many commentators would agree that elections can only be part of the broader democratisation process, however there would appear to be a problem in asserting that democracy must be consolidated or democratisation completed *before* self-government and electoral accountability are permitted.

This new grass-roots approach has been welcomed as a long-term international commitment to democratic transition, but it could also be seen as expressing a more disillusioned approach to the prospects of democracy in Bosnia. The success of the nationalist parties came as a shock to many of the international human rights groups and NGOs who had been arguing that ordinary people supported a multicultural Bosnia. Before the September 1996 elections, most international agencies had assumed that tighter international regulation over the political process would enable popular opposition groups to gain a hold on power. Their universally poor showing created a strong air of pessimism about the future of a united Bosnia (see Chapter 3 for discussion of the election results). This disillusionment with the choice expressed through the ballot box, resulted in a much more negative view of the capacities of the Bosnian people themselves.

For leading officers at the Democratisation Branch, the problem with international pressure on the elected representatives was that it had only limited effectiveness because it underestimated the problems of trying to democratise Bosnia. The essence of the community-orientated work within the Democratisation Branch is that unlike the UN High Representative's office, which focuses on the practices of the governing institutions, the key to democratisation lies with the grass-roots of Bosnian society. Now that it seemed clear that the problems went much deeper, forcing the elected authorities to toe the line appeared to be just window-dressing. As the Senior Co-ordinator for Democratisation/NGOs explained:

> The most important thing is working at ground level. Carl Bildt and Robert Frowick [the then UN High Representative and Head of the OSCE Mission] can threaten more intervention, and wave the carrot and the stick, and if they don't behave they won't get the carrot. This means that they will do these approaches, for example, having democratic programmes, but they don't believe in it. Nothing will change.[3]

The first monthly report of the new Democratisation Branch identified the obstacles to the development of democratic civil society. Naturally the fact that the international community was, in effect, running the country was not under consideration. All the obstacles were connected to the incapacity of the Bosnian people in general, or specific sections of them, to act and think in a manner suited to meet the 'challenges of democratisation'. For the Bosnian elites, the problem was seen to be a lack of technical and organisational abilities. These incapacities were highlighted by the people involved in building local NGOs in Republika Srpska, who 'continue to struggle for funding, programme ideas and the acquisition of administrative skills', and in leaders of opposition parties more broadly, because 'even though the number of political parties is increasing, they are only now beginning to receive training on how to enlarge their popular appeal' (OSCE DB, 1997j, p. 3). Political problems of gathering support around an alternative programme are here reinterpreted as technical problems that the well-educated Bosnian elites are seemingly unable to grapple with.

While the skills of the elites could be overcome by training and aid, the other obstacles located at the level of Bosnian society in general, were seen to be more long term: first, the problem of an ethnic mentality: 'the passive acceptance of prejudices [which] must be overcome for real and psychological barriers to inter-ethnic reconciliation to be dismantled' (OSCE DB, 1997j, p. 3). Second, there were the problems stemming from a lack of awareness of the workings of a democratic society, which meant that it was difficult to make informed choices at elections: 'The elections served as the basis for the establishment of democratic institutions, yet more efforts are required to increase citizens' awareness of the working and roles of their authorities, the rule of law, and democratic rules and procedures' (OSCE DB, 1997j, p. 3).

The clear intimation is that the international community has provided the democratic institutional framework but that the Bosnian people are not familiar enough with the workings of democracy to ensure their functioning. This view was supported by a Senior Democratisation Co-ordinator: 'Political parties are a new appearance. People don't know how to cope and neither do their leaders, they have no political programme. People just follow the flock. It is the same with the independent parties, people vote for them just because they are the alternative.'[4]

The disparaging attitude towards ordinary people, 'the flock', was not even diminished when they voted for opposition parties because it was assumed that they were not capable of making an independent judgement. The widespread acceptance of this perspective amongst the NGO-building community was illustrated by the Helsinki Citizens' Assembly organiser in Sarajevo, who explained that the people had no democratic experience and were used to 'living under a strong hand', and that this lack of democratic education had to be challenged through NGOs 'teaching people how to behave and to know right from wrong'. She told a joke to illustrate the problem her NGO faced: 'The opposition party leader asks the peasant why he is not going to vote for him. The peasant says that he will vote for him. The opposition leader asks, "When?" The peasant says, "When you get in power."'[5]

Often the analogies about democracy tend to involve uneducated peasants as the symbol of ordinary people. One of the leading officers of the Democratisation Branch went further, to the extent of seeing Bosnian people not supportive of civil society initiatives as still caught up in the backward ideology of feudalism. At the OSCE in Sarajevo, Jasna Malkoc, one of the activists whose ideas lay behind the initiation of the Democratisation Branch, explained that democratisation would be a long process of changing the culture of the majority of the Bosnian people in order to 'implement the concept of individualism':

> The lack of democratic values stems from the divisions of the Austro-Hungarian Empire which instilled individualistic ideas. Areas outside the Empire had feudalist systems which continued as communist structures. Serbia is feudalist, Croatia is individualist. Bosnia is inbetween and the division is between urban, individualist areas and peasant, feudal areas. For example, Banja Luka [in Republika Srpska] is urban and is influenced by the West and Croatia.[6]

A similar perspective which emphasises the long-term problems of civil society construction is the psycho-social approach, also pursued by the Democratisation Branch. Using this framework, one of the main barriers to building civil society in Bosnia is seen to be psycho-social problems. Much or even most of the population is adjudged by many democratisers to be unable to see the gains of a civil society approach due to the impact of their part as victims or as passive supporters of human rights violations during the war (Mimica, 1995, p. 22). This approach puts psycho-social work at the centre of strategies for democratisation because:

> These persons may offer special resistance to confidence-building, dialogue and reconciliation efforts due to the victims' mistrust, isolation, demoralisation and anger. Due to symptoms of victimisation, they are also less likely to be willing to take on new responsibilities as active members of civil society. (OSCE DB, 1997j, pp. 7–8)

Even its advocates admit that this work is 'entering new territory' where 'not much theory exists' in relation to psycho-social projects (Agger and Mimica, 1996, pp. 27–8). However, these doubts do not figure highly for the Democratisation Branch, their Semi-Annual Report states categorically that 'trauma symptoms have become an obstacle to the implementation of the General Framework Agreement for Peace and the development of pluralistic society in Bosnia' (OSCE DB, 1997m, p. 15). As the OSCE itself observes: 'This connection between psycho-social therapy and confidence-building is novel – however, it underlines the links between human rights, democratisation and psycho-social activities' (OSCE DB, 1997l, p. 7).

Central to the OSCE Democratisation Branch's approach is the understanding that the Bosnian population, 'damaged' or 'traumatised' by the war and the transition from one-party state regulation, are not capable of acting independently or making choices between 'right and wrong'. This approach was not universally popular with the OSCE Democratisation Officers, some of whom mentioned in confidence the dangers of a gap between democratisation in theory and in practice: 'It is easy to get patronising. Bosnian society pre-war was highly developed, it was not the civil society of the West, but these people were not illiterate, or not cultured, or not developed, just different'; 'Democratisation is not a good term – it is like teaching them how to behave – naturally people are sensitive to this. A lot of people are educated, they know theory, and they know right and wrong'; 'Civil society and democratic values existed – Bosnia had a multi-cultural society, good nationalities policy and progressive policies regarding women.'[7] However, those that felt awkward with the approach of their superiors did not feel it was possible to express this easily within the organisation: 'There is no discussion about what democracy is'; 'big principled questions you have to leave out and try to find a corner, an area where you can do good work'.[8]

Taking over the language of empowerment from the psychosocial counselling work being developed in the war, the new focus is on the capacity of individuals for democracy as opposed to that of governments. This means that the broader framework of political and economic regulation is ignored. If anything, the Democratisation Branch work of civil society-building from the bottom up is more invidious to democracy than the enforced international administration because it implicitly assumes that Bosnian people are 'damaged' and incapable of rational choice. Once the capacity of Bosnian people as rational political actors is negated, whether this is understood as due to feudalism, to ethnic identity or to war trauma, there is no reason for international administration of the new state to be seen as merely a set of temporary 'transitional' measures, or for democracy to be seen as preferable.

CIVIL SOCIETY AND DEMOCRACY IN BOSNIA

International attempts to ensure that the 'different voices' in Bosnia are heard by the outside world have involved giving support to a variety of groups and organisations within Bosnia which attempt to challenge the political domination of the main political parties. Groups such as Circle 99, the Tuzla Citizens' Forum, the Citizens' Alternative Parliament and the Coalition for Return have been actively supported by many international funders and have logistical and training support from the OSCE Democratisation Branch.

However, as the OSCE Reporting Officer, Sabine Freizer, explained: 'The central problem we have is how to encourage participation.'[9] It may seem surprising that these groups with an international reputation should have problems involving Bosnian people in their work, especially as they are held to represent a grassroots movement for a different voice to be heard. Adrien Marti, the Co-ordinator for Political Party Development, explained the problem of the lack of popular support for the citizens' groups:

> The Citizens' Alternative Parliament, the Shadow Government and the Coalition for Return are basically the same twenty people when you scratch the surface a little. There is really no depth to this. The nationalist parties have a lot of good and respected people, they play on people's fears but also deliver security and a feeling that you can live normally. They are also much closer to the average person than the elitist Sarajevans. The overqualified Yugoslavs are seen as elitist, whereas the HDZ, SDS and the SDA [the leading political parties] have members and supporters on the ground facing the same problems as you.[10]

When asked why, if there was so little support within Bosnia for the approach of these groups, the OSCE considered it a priority to assist their development, Marti's response was: 'They need the money to make them more efficient. But it should be up to the public at the end of the day. I think there is a balance, the public wants the nationalist parties for security, but they also want an opposition.'[11]

The problem with this approach is that the opposition is in this case one that has not been chosen by the electorate but the OSCE and other international agencies. Jens Sorenson notes that:

> The local NGO sector is primarily the creation of an urban middle class, which has been squeezed in the social transformation in the new republics. With polarisation increasing ... as the ethnic states reward supporters of the ruling party, what remains of the politicised middle class can find a new niche in NGOs. Here the distinction between NGOs as social movements or as service providers becomes unclear. (Sorenson, 1997, p. 35)

Zoran Jorgakieski, the OSCE Democratisation Branch Co-ordinator for Dialogue and Reconciliation, expanded on the problem:

> These groups are all run by intellectuals but they have very little influence. During the war they stayed aside and withdrew from politics. These are the people we have to focus upon. They are a minority, but the best, the cream of Bosnian intellectual society. They have good relations with their colleagues across the Inter-Entity Boundary Line. They are top intellectuals, you can't expect ordinary people to understand them. The language they use is too complicated. People doubt they are good patriots.[12]

There seems to be a large gap between the civil society associations funded and supported by the OSCE, and other international institutions, and Bosnian people. For the OSCE and other institutions, this gap demonstrates the lack of a democratic culture in Bosnia. While few people are actively involved in civil society associations, leaving them predominantly middle-class based, the main nationalist parties still easily attain the majority of the votes in elections. In response to this gap, Adrien Marti is advising some of the new civil society groups, which became established as political parties before the September 1997 municipal elections, to abandon electoral competition after the local polls and become NGOs instead.[13] As a piece of tactical advice to aspiring opposition groups wanting to curry favour with the international community, Marti's point may well be right. But it does raise questions over how you can have a strategy for 'democratisation' that depends upon building small, elitist groups of non-elected people into an opposition against parties supported by majorities with distinct political aims.

Furthermore, there is little evidence that this strategy is helping to challenge support for the nationalist parties or to overcome ethnic segmentation and division in Bosnia. The OSCE Democratisation Branch, in its attempts to celebrate cross-community co-operation and turn this into an alternative political voice, unfortunately tends to politicise, and consequently problematise, everyday activity which organically contributes to confidence building. While thousands of people cross the Inter-Entity Boundary Line every day, to work, shop, see relatives, or go to school, this is seen as everyday life going on and making the best of the situation (USDoS, 1997, section 2D). The people whose lives involve cross-entity co-operation do not necessarily want to turn everyday survival into a political movement. The moment these actions become politicised they become an implicit threat to the status quo and create a backlash to a perceived threat that did not exist previously. As an experienced Senior Democratisation Officer related: 'I'm surprised they tell us anything anymore. Inter-entity contacts are very common with businesses, etc. If I was a businessman I wouldn't report it, not just for tax reasons – no one pays tax anyway – but because it just creates problems.'[14] The OSCE Youth and Education Co-ordinator explained that the teachers she worked with had not wanted attention to be drawn to them and had told her not to park her OSCE car near to their houses.[15] Similarly, people were much more willing to use the cross-entity bus-line once the OSCE licence plates were removed (USDoS, 1998b, section 2D). People want to cross the Inter-Entity Boundary Line, and in some cases to return to their pre-war homes, but without drawing attention to themselves and without their actions being seen as threatening the security of others. Returns that have been organised spontaneously have had much more success than internationally enforced return under the threat of sanctions which have both angered and raised the fears of current residents (Amnesty, 1996, section V, A; ICG, 1997b, p. 13).

Ironically, the more support given to the 'grass-roots' civil associations by the OSCE, the less effective they tend to be. The unintended consequence of creating civil society NGOs which are reliant on external support has been that they are never forced to build their own base of popular support or take on the arguments or political programmes of the nationalists. Guaranteed funding and the ear of international policy-makers, the Citizens' Parliament and other favoured groups are in fact more likely to prevent or impede the development of an opposition with roots in society.

As Jens Sorensen notes, the reliance on external funders can tend to fragment society rather than create a pluralistic exchange of political opinions. His criticism is that because the funding of civil society NGOs is portrayed as apolitical assistance to democratisation, this has led to a variety of projects and NGOs being funded with no overall strategy. Instead of building bridges within a society, as political parties who have to argue for their political programme would have to, these NGOs relying on outside funding have no need to engage in discussion or create broader links to society:

> [Democratisation] a highly political and sensitive business has thus become depoliticised and technicalised ... The financing of private bodies, as representatives of democracy and development, without a clear policy may in fact encourage the fragmentation of societies under political breakdown rather than encourage pluralism ...The model of NGO assistance to democracy can serve only to complement; it cannot be the leading edge. (Sorensen, 1997, p. 35)

CONCLUSION

This chapter has suggested that there is a link between the low level of support for civil society alternatives to the leading political parties and a lack of democracy in Bosnia. However the relationship between civil society and democracy is not necessarily the one suggested by the advocates of greater international support for NGO-led civil society-building strategies.

It appears that the assumption of democratisation strategy that civil society non-national associations are a precondition for Bosnian self-government is open to question. It could perhaps be more cogently argued that the extent of international regulation over Bosnian life, the denial of self-government at local and state level, and with this the inability for Bosnian political representatives to give their constituents a level of accountability for policy-making, is perpetuating a political climate ill-conducive to the development of broader voluntary associational ties. The fact that the strategy pursued ignored this broader context of international regulation in Bosnia could well explain the lack of success on the ground, particularly as the citizens of Bosnia and the former Yugoslavia had extensive higher education provision, and a relatively high level of involvement in local political and civic life prior to the war (Heath, 1981; Ignatieff, 1998, p. 40; McFarlane, 1988; Seroka, 1988; 1989).

Lack of success aside, the focus on civil society as a key indicator of the level of democratisation has meant that the consequences of this approach have been of substantial importance. Once Democratisation Branch officers ignored political power and relations between political elites and the international community, instead focusing on ethnic segmentation and civil society, democracy assessment became a subjective exercise in the measurement of attitudes and culture. The lack of progress has only reinforced the idea that the people are too backward or traumatised to be able to cope with political choices. The solution has not been to question the theoretical framework which informed the approach of top-down imposition and bottom-up empowerment, but to tinker with the programmes and call for more resources. As the process has continued a vicious circle has been created in which the Bosnian people are seen to be less capable of political autonomy and the international community appear ever more necessary to guarantee democratic development.

7 Assessments

In the preceding chapters, it was concluded that democratisation strategy had done little to facilitate democracy and self-government in Bosnia. The opening section of this chapter summarises these conclusions and highlights the trend towards greater external regulation of policy-making in Bosnia and the marginalisation of Bosnian representatives from this process. The following section then considers the response of the leading international institutions, involved in democratisation, to this trend, this constitutes the 'official' assessment. Further sections consider the alternative assessments of democratisation practice, grouping the critics of Dayton into two broad categories: the 'liberals', who argue for greater international intervention to democratise Bosnia; and the 'conservatives', who argue that there is little that the international community can do to bring democracy to the region.

In the British press, the criticisms have come predominantly from the liberal perspective, led by international NGOs, such as Human Rights Watch, the Helsinki Citizens' Assembly, and the Brussels-based International Crisis Group, and the campaigning journalism of the *Guardian* and *Observer*. Liberal critics feel that the international institutions lack commitment to democratisation and that the lack of success is, to a certain extent, self-created, through the Dayton Agreement's acceptance of the division of Bosnia into two separate entities. They argue that this problem has been accentuated by the international community's use of electoral accountability, believed to heighten political divisions and give authority and legitimacy to the nationalist leaders responsible for war and division in the first place.

The conservative critique radically dissents from this position and argues that democratisation is unlikely to bring about change because of the strength of ethnic segmentation. In the opinion columns of the American press, there has been increasingly strident debate provoked by the conservative critics of Dayton who assert that American lives are being put at risk through an unnecessary and ill-considered entanglement in Balkan affairs.

After outlining the 'official', 'liberal' and 'conservative' assessments of democratisation in Bosnia, there is a consideration of some of the contradictions raised over the rationale for the extension of international mandates and the high-level international focus given to the Bosnian situation. This chapter concludes by highlighting the high degree of consensus at the centre of the democratisation discussion which has enabled accountability for the extension of democratisation to be shifted away from the international institutions and on to internal Bosnian factors.

MORE DEMOCRATISATION BUT LESS DEMOCRACY

The chapters which investigated specific democratisation strategies concluded that their implementation tended to restrict democratic accountability rather than develop mechanisms which could allow a transition away from international administration towards self-government. In Chapter 3, it was noted that elected Bosnian institutions of government at state, entity, city and municipal levels had a largely formal existence with little capacity to develop or implement policy independently of the international community and that minority ethnic groups lacked the protection and security of a degree of political autonomy. Chapter 4 considered how the framework of human rights protection further weakened the peace-building and integrative capacity of Bosnian political and judicial institutions through placing decision-making in the hands of international institutions. International regulation of political competition and media output, analysed in Chapter 5, restricted the democratic mandates of elected politicians and limited political debate while having a marginal impact on support for the nationalist parties. Chapter 6 considered the approach of 'democratisation from below' through support for civil society-building; support given to small unrepresentative civic groups tended to downplay the importance of democratic debate and competition for cohering support, fragmenting the political opposition while doing little to encourage popular involvement in the political process.

The empirical findings that democratisation practices operated in ways which limited the sphere of democracy are not necessarily surprising or unexpected. The proponents of democratisation argue that it is the failure of democracy to produce stable, legitimate government that necessitates an external process of democratisation. Rule by external administrators, political conditionality, electoral and media regulation, and civil society-building are seen as preconditions for a functioning liberal democracy in the future. As with the broader discussion of transition in the region, the more specific discussion of democratisation presupposes liberal democracy as the end point of international policy practices. Restrictions on democracy in the short term are designed to be temporary and to gradually prepare the people so that they can eventually take on the responsibilities of democratic citizenship.

International practice to date, however, indicates not only that democratisation limits accountability and autonomy but also that there is little tendency towards rolling back external regulation over the process. Over the first three years of Dayton implementation, the powers of the international community, already uniquely extensive, had grown consistently. As High Representative Westendorp declared in December 1997: 'We shall never be as strong in Bosnia as we are today' (OHRS, 1997a, par. 21). As of December 1997, after two years of international administration, talk in terms of 'exit strategies' was replaced by that of 'long-term engagement' and the mandates of the OHR, OSCE, IPTF and NATO were all extended indefinitely. Yet, the High Representative, in his speech to the Peace Implementation Council (PIC), played down this accumulation of power and emphasised that this indefinite time-extension and the use of greater powers to impose international policy did not mean an altered mandate:

> Let there be no misunderstanding. I am not seeking from this Council a new or revised mandate. Not yet. But what I will need from you is your full support in the more vigorous exercise of my existing mandate … I intend to exercise to the full the final authority in theatre, given to me under Annex 10 of the Peace Agreement. (OHRS, 1997a, pars 22 & 23)

The 'vigorous exercise' of the mandate giving Westendorp's office 'final authority', makes the distinction between an international protectorate and the situation in Bosnia a fine one. Westendorp stated his intention of breaking the 'log-jam', caused by the lack of political support within Bosnia for international policy proposals, by resorting to decisions on the following:

- The timing, location and chairmanship of meetings of the common institutions.
- Interim measures to take effect when parties are unable to reach agreement, which will remain in force until the Presidency or Council of Ministers has adopted a decision on the issue concerned, consistent with the Peace Agreement.
- Measures to suspend enforcement of legislation which does not comply with the Peace Agreement.
- Other measures to ensure implementation of the Peace Agreement throughout Bosnia and Herzegovina and its Entities, as well as the smooth running of the common institutions. Such measures may include dismissal from office of

officials who are absent from meetings without good cause or persistently block the implementation of the Peace Agreement. (OHRS, 1997a, pars 22 & 23)

The PIC Bonn Conference issued an extensive 26-page list of internationally prepared legislative measures that were required to be passed by certain deadlines (PIC, 1997b). These measures covered policy-making powers at both state, entity and municipal level; intervening in order to regulate policy on housing, education, the legal system, citizenship, travel, the constitution, refugee return, policing, the media, electoral regulation, economic reconstruction and regional relations. The extent of regulation held necessary to enforce Dayton extended right down to requirements for the Bosnian sports teams at the Winter Olympics in Nagano, Japan (PIC, 1997b, section II, 3).

In December 1997, High Representative Westendorp began enacting law in Bosnia, starting with the disputed law on citizenship (*RFE/RL Newsline*, 1997h). Although it was assumed that this law would be later adopted by the Bosnian Parliament, Westendorp made clear that this would be purely formal as it would have to be assented to without comments or conditions (OHR SRT, 1997d). The same month Senior Deputy High Representative Schumacher attended the Council of Ministers meeting to announce that the High Representative had decided to enact the disputed Customs Tariff Schedule and impose other decisions that the CoM had not ratified by the PIC deadline (OHRPS, 1997). At the end of the year, he presented two sets of policy proposals with deadlines to the inaugural meeting of the new Republika Srpska Assembly (OHRS, 1997b).

The German Foreign Minister, Klaus Kinkel, openly confirmed the same month that the international community had little hesitation in moving to make decisions contrary to the will of the Bosnian people (OHR SRT, 1997c). Carlos Westendorp declared in his 1998 New Year Message: 'As High Representative, I have to take decisions now and in the future with your best interests in mind, should your leaders fail to take them' (OHRS, 1997c). As Bosnian opposition SDP party leader, Lagumdzija, stated on Sarajevo TV: '[These proposals mean] we will be left to play consideration and deciding, and when we are unable to adopt, someone else will adopt it. If that is called a protectorate, that is a matter of speaking, someone else decides for us' (OHR BiH, 1997).

After the extensions of the international community's powers, ratified at the PIC conferences in Sintra and Bonn in 1997, and Luxembourg in 1998, the elected institutions of Bosnia have even less of a formal say in their own affairs. As the Dayton democratisation process continues, the token nature of the elected assemblies at both state and entity level becomes increasingly exposed. Following the September 1998 RS Assembly elections, Carlos Westendorp had no qualms about overriding the democratic mandate by threatening to end international financial aid to the entity if the leading nationalist parties were included in the new government (*RFE/RL Newsline*, 1998h). Even the presence of Bosnian representatives is now openly seen as superfluous, Robert Gelbard, Special American Envoy for the Balkans, stating that should the High Representative remove any Bosnian official for a failure to co-operate, and the party affected fails to appoint a replacement, the institution concerned will continue to operate normally (OHR SRT, 1997c). The Bonn and Luxembourg PIC conferences may not have declared an international protectorate, but this is surely semantic given the indefinite time-span of international mandates and that failure to ratify policy within set deadlines will lead to the dismissal of elected representatives and policy being enacted regardless by the High Representative.

Democratisation in Bosnia would appear to have little to do with democracy as traditionally understood. It seems contradictory that the process of democratisation has taken Bosnia through a series of stages leading further away from democratic accountability:

- Stage one – the Dayton Agreement, in December 1995, which established a one-year transitory regime of international peace-building preparatory to elections, which were declared to be free and fair.
- Stage two – the announcement of a two-year regime of 'consolidation', in December 1996, with the High Representative having increased powers of economic regulation.
- Stage three – an indefinite regime of international regulation announced a year later, in December 1997, with the High Representative empowered to overrule and dismiss elected representatives and directly impose policy.

Along with the increase in international authority, political discussion has been marginalised through the clamping down on criticism of international policy-making. As Ted Galen Carpenter of the Cato Institute noted in the *Washington Times*:

> The US-led democracy mission in Bosnia has become a grotesque parody of democratic principles ... we are teaching ... the virtues of democracy by showing ... that an outside power, if it possesses enough military clout, has the right to overrule court decisions, establish political purity tests for candidates for public office and suppress media outlets that transmit politically incorrect views. (Carpenter, 1997)

From the evidence of three years of externally imposed democratisation, it would seem that far from just limiting democracy in the short term, an argument could be made to demonstrate that democratisation has a dynamic towards the limitation of representative democracy *per se*. If Bosnia is more democratic after three years of internationally managed transition to democracy, then democracy has been redefined out of recognition. If Bosnia is less democratic then this raises *prima facie* evidence to suggest that democratisation implementation, or the initial assumptions about its effectiveness, seems to be flawed.

Noting an empirical trend away from democracy and the developing gap between policy aims and outcomes does little to provide an explanation for the extension of the democratisation process. The following sections discuss 'official', 'liberal' and 'conservative' assessments of the democratisation process in Bosnia and highlight the nature of the ideological consensus which makes democratisation a low-risk policy option with little accountability for success or failure.

OFFICIAL ASSESSMENTS

Despite the exhaustive monitoring mechanisms, put in place in Bosnia by international institutions and NGOs, to ensure the compliance of Bosnian parties with international requirements under the Dayton Agreement, there has been little monitoring of how effective international policy has been in giving greater accountability to the Bosnian people over the political process.[1]

Considering the alleged centrality of success in Bosnia to the international community and the experimental and unique nature of many of the democratisation initiatives, it is perhaps surprising that there is very little critical evaluation of international practice in Bosnia. The international regulation of Bosnia is accountable to the Peace Implementation Council through the reports of the UN High Representative, but there is little analysis beyond the short-term impact of international policy on compliance with Dayton. The fact that many of these international policy initiatives depend on enforcing compliance on the Bosnian leadership, as opposed to building support for international policy within Bosnian society itself, seems not to be considered. The policy aim would appear to be the acceptance of the Dayton framework, with little thought of the impact that reducing the capacity and accountability of elected representatives may have for the long-term consequences of the democratisation process.

The high-level biannual international conferences of the Peace Implementation Council present a peculiar assessment of democratisation strategy. If the extension of the Dayton mandates is a sign of failure, then it is a failure which seems to have little effect on the nature of policy-making in Bosnia, and a failure which is in danger of being replicated on a broader scale as international mandates are extended. If three years of international regulation by the most powerful institutions in the world, such as NATO, the UN, the World Bank and the International Monetary Fund, in co-operation with the world's most powerful states, including the United States, Russia, Germany and Japan, cannot make a serious impact in a small, weak and economically and politically fragmented state with little internal or external sources of alternative support, then it would seem that either there is something seriously wrong with the policies being pursued or that no external intervention is going to make much of a difference. The fact that all the institutions and states seem to be content with sticking to the Dayton mandates and extending them would indicate that something was happening in Bosnia that was seen as useful and important enough to merit not just the uncritical continuation of the policy but also the continued high-level attention of the world's most powerful statesmen and policy advisers.

If the extension of the mandates is a sign of success, then this makes little difference to the question posed above. If it is a success then what is successful about it? There would seem to be little evidence of success on the ground in Bosnia beyond traditional peace-enforcement stabilisation. For the last three years there has been a stand-off between the three politically- and ethnically-cohered groups, little different to the pre-war situation, and there is little tendency either towards conflict or greater co-operation. Political insecurities are still rife as to the political autonomy of the Serb entity and Croat areas of the Federation, and the central political authority of the state remains very weak with state authority as reliant on outside support as when Bosnian recognition was called for in 1991. The fighting has stopped, but many commentators argue that war may not have broken out, and the conflict been so prolonged, if a negotiated power-sharing solution had been acceptable to the United States, either when recognition was being considered by the international community or during the European- and UN-led peace negotiations (Boyd, 1995; Petras and Vieux, 1996; Woodward, 1995, pp. 302–32; 1996b, pp. 164–72).

It could be argued that the remit of the Peace Implementation Council is not primarily that of ensuring democracy, but the broader task of preventing conflict and ensuring stability. The Dayton Agreement itself mandates the OSCE 'to lay the foundation for representative government and ensure the progressive achievement of democratic goals' (GFA, 1995, Annex 3,

Preamble). However, the OSCE Democratisation Branch similarly appeared to place little emphasis on Bosnian self-government and democratic accountability. As Siri Rustad, Deputy to the Head of Mission for Democratisation, stated:

> It is difficult to measure the overall democratic level of the country. We measure different levels – the running of institutions, the role of NGOs, the views of the Peace Implementation Conference, etc. We don't have a broader theoretical approach at all. That's how the Mission works – it's concerned with practical results.[2]

She expanded on these three levels, first, the democratic functioning of the state institutions, suggesting that the Constitution should be universally in force and a legal framework, up to European standards, clearly established. She stated that 'political institutions should follow the rules, as long as they are not following the rules – then it is not democratic'. However, the institutional framework and the rules governing it have never been approved by the Bosnian people, a legitimate test of a democracy, but are set down and interpreted by the international community. Second, she proposed 'gaining an impression of how much power is distributed through informal channels'. In many democracies, the distribution of power through 'informal' and unaccountable mechanisms would be seen as anti-democratic. However, for Rustad, the influence of citizens' groups and NGOs, 'independent sections of civil society', on political decisions through the lobbying process was indicative of a free society. The third level highlights the shift in accountability from the Bosnian people to the international community, already implicit in her approach: 'There is also the level of the Peace Implementation Conference and the fulfilment of the Dayton Peace Accords. If they are satisfied it is a way of saying it is a democracy or a society that can, by itself, develop democracy further.'

None of these indicators refer to the accountability of the Bosnian government to the electorate. Christian Ahlund, the OSCE Director General for Human Rights, similarly saw democracy as residing in the international institutions.[3] He stated that the OSCE's role was a 'pedagogic' one of informing Bosnian people about international standards and 'telling them what democratisation is all about'. For him it was impossible to imagine the Dayton process as a barrier to democracy as it guaranteed the same rights and freedoms as the best states in the world and therefore any democratic activity would be in accordance with the constitution. Political parties which did not agree with the international community did so because they were not democratic. As he stated: 'Elections are just the first primitive stage of democracy. Political parties are still a pretty blunt form.'[4] OSCE Chairman-in-Office, Niels Helveg Peterson, has condemned Bosnian voters, describing their 'political level' as 'not very high' which has led to elections, such as those in September 1997, that 'fell far short of normal democratic standards' (*RFE/RL Newsline*, 1997f).

This negative view of representative democracy in Bosnia was shared by the Office of the High Representative. Spokesman for the High Representative, Duncan Bullivant, has publicly stated that 'Bosnia is a deeply sick society, ill at ease with even the most basic principles of democracy' (*Washington Post*, 1997). High Representative Carlos Westendorp's critique of democratic accountability has a distinct ring of Rudyard Kipling's 'White Man's Burden':

> They [Bosnian representatives] have a wrong perspective. They are not serving their population properly, the real interest of the population, which is to co-operate with the international community, because the interest of the international community is that the country is prosperous and democratic. (Coleman, 1997)

It is this view of Bosnian people and their representatives as lacking democratic capacities that has legitimated the extension of policy-making by international institutions. The implication of this approach is the end of formal democracy, of legitimacy through accountability to the electorate. Democracy is redefined as its opposite, adherence to outside standards not autonomy and accountability. This approach is also pursued in official statements of world leaders such as US President Bill Clinton, who has successfully pushed for the 'exit strategy' to be replaced by a series of vaguely defined externally-set goals for civilian and economic management, such as rooting out corruption, reforming and retraining the police, restructuring the media, increasing refugee return and indicting more war criminals (*RFE/RL Newsline*, 1997i). The indeterminate nature of the number, let alone the content, of these benchmarks for NATO and UN withdrawal was illustrated in July 1998 when Clinton stated there were ten while US Ambassador Robert Gelbard referred to twelve (Clinton, 1998).[5] The decision on what the required standards of democracy are and whether they are met is without question assumed to be a matter for international agencies, not the Bosnian electorate or their representatives.

The explanation for the ease with which international administrative powers can be legitimised as facilitating democracy has been the redefinition of democracy within the democratisation framework. As considered in Chapter 1, democracy is no longer defined as the outcome of popular decision-making but as an adherence to democratic ethics and values. Because these ethics and values are held to reside in Western governments and international institutions, it has been easy to transform democracy-building – democratisation – into a process of meeting external targets prescribed by the international community. It is this 'de-politicisation' of democracy that makes the view, expressed by the most senior OSCE Democratisation Supervisor, next to the OSCE Head of Mission himself, that there was no 'broader theoretical approach at all' unsurprising. The official assessment of democratisation indicates that there is little conception of Bosnian self-government as a priority for the democratisation process nor any assumption of a merely temporary role for the OSCE, NATO, UN Office of the High Representative and other international community bodies.

The power of this consensus and lack of critical assessment of democratisation practice in Bosnia appears to be unexceptional. Thomas Carothers draws similar conclusions from his analysis of US democracy assistance programmes (1997b). He makes the point that US democratisation strategy is not drawn from historical Western experience or from academic writings about transition processes, but is focused on reforming institutions to make them compatible with an idealised Western model. He concludes that US democracy assistance:

> ... tends to ignore the power relations that underlie and in many ways determine a country's political life ... with little reference to the social, political and economic forces that actually shape those sectors. Democracy assistance providers operate as though it is possible to change the basic functioning of key institutions ... without grappling with the deep-seated interests of the actors involved. (Carothers, 1997b, p. 122)

Carothers sees the 'artificial technical quality' of democracy assistance as a central problem, which can mean that democratisation practice tends to ignore 'the stubborn reality that politics involves competing interests, struggles over power, conflicting ideologies and clashing values' (Carothers, 1997b, p. 123). The overview of the democratisation approach in Chapter 1 and the analysis of its operation in Bosnia in the following chapters would seem to reinforce Carothers' view that 'stubborn realities' can easily be interpreted, from within the democratisation approach, as cultural 'incapacities' and thereby as barriers to democracy.

As seen in Chapter 6, the response of the official democratisers in the UN and OSCE to the lack of success in imposing an external framework which pays little heed to Bosnian concerns, has not been to question the theoretical framework which informs the approach of top-down imposition and bottom-up empowerment, but to tinker with the programmes and call for greater mandates and more resources.

THE LIBERAL ASSESSMENT

Liberal assessment of the democratisation strategy is critical of the official institutions, however their critique does not highlight the lack of democratic accountability or political autonomy. Liberal critics, in fact, take the opposite approach and argue that the goals set for external accountability to international institutions are too low. They argue that this unwillingness to impose policy on the Bosnian parties has led to the problems of civilian implementation. The main source of criticism is the belief that the three-way division of Bosnia is not a product of the wishes of the Bosnian people, but the actions of the international community. While the international institutions see Dayton as the yardstick for democratisation and above question, the liberal critics see Dayton as a compromise with the nationalist elites seen to be responsible for the war and division:

> The West's mistake was to set too much store by holding elections in Bosnia long before the conditions were ripe ... The West allowed Bosnia's politicians too much power over the last three years. As a result the very nationalists who started the war were not challenged firmly. Now is the time to rectify the error. (*Guardian*, 1998)

The reasons for this international failure of purpose in acting to impose a unitary multicultural Bosnia are usually explained to be either a product of a racially biased approach to the region, which has generated a fatalist perspective that nothing can be done to overcome 'ethnic rivalries', or the placing of self-interest above justice for Bosnia. Liberal critics argue that imposing democracy is seen as either too costly or too dangerous and therefore the major powers are willing to compromise with nationalist leaders pursuing divisive strategies. For example, Bradford University Peace Studies author Tom Gallagher writes:

> Western policy-makers have been adverse to acting as organisers, leaders, or peace-makers in the region because they are imbued with a sense of fatalism about the potentialities of its local elites and their populations to aspire to good government and modern forms of conduct. There is plenty of evidence to suggest that the problems of the Balkans are seen as culturally determined and historically recurring and therefore beyond capable solution. (Gallagher, 1997, pp. 32–3)

Perversely, the lack of success of democratisation initiatives is often put down to the Bosnian politicians having too much power in relation to the international institutions. According to Mary Kaldor a stronger mandate is required by the international community because 'the relationship between the International Community and the Parties is changed, because the International Community has become too dependent on the Parties for the implementation of the Dayton-agreement, which makes itself foolish' (Kaldor, 1997, p. 27). Mient Jan Faber, Helsinki Citizens' Assembly (HCA) co-ordinator in The Hague, believes that: 'The International Community has made itself dependent on the "manipulations", "tricks" and "demands" of the Parties. It is not in charge, it does not even control its own activities in Bosnia' (HCA, 1997, p. 16).

Many international commentators feel that the leading Bosniak, Serb and Croat politicians should not be allowed to play a role in Bosnia's future. Kaldor explains the lack of progress of Dayton as due to the fact that 'those responsible for implementing the agreement were the parties to the agreement, i.e. those nationalists who favoured separation' (Kaldor, 1997, p. 29). The *Guardian*'s Martin Woollacott writes that Western pressure on Milosevic and Tudjman to police the Bosnian Serbs and Croats is perpetuating resistance to Dayton and avoiding the 'confrontation' he sees as necessary to force through a solution: 'America and Europe still base their policy on accommodating to the strength of the local actors ... it remains the case that the West still shields itself from the cost and confrontation by working with rather than *against* the lines of strength in the Balkans' (Woollacott, 1997b).

The OSCE and the Office of the UN High Representative have generally taken an ambiguous approach to elections, setting them up as democratic enough to legitimise the governing institutions, but not legitimate enough to allow the dominant parties to challenge the OHR's right to shape policy. However, the liberal critics see elections as highly problematic and have been much more vocal about the necessity of distancing the holding of elections from democratisation. For these critics of the OSCE, elections merely provide nationalist politicians with legitimacy which is then used by the international institutions to justify compromise solutions.

Nearly all the liberal critics argue that elections are not just an unreliable indicator of democracy but bad for democracy in Bosnia *per se*. Woodward writes: 'In fact, by declaring elections the precondition for the exit of US military forces, the Dayton negotiators determined that all aspects of the implementation process in the first year would be dominated, and in some ways distorted, by the electoral motives of the three political parties' (Woodward, 1996a, p. 34).

Calling elections gave credibility to the leading parties and the opportunity to acquire resources and use them for partisan gain. Woodward puts the political disagreements over Dayton implementation down to the fact that the political parties were competing in what was in effect a year-long election campaign. This competition for potential votes exacerbated conflict as 'territorial demarcations, humanitarian aid, economic assistance, electoral laws, government ministries, and population resettlements all provide resources for winning elections' (1996a, p. 34). In fact, merely holding elections, on this logic, contributed to an undemocratic climate:

> The goal of winning at the polls has thus had the opposite effect of the conditions that foreign monitors identify as necessary to elections and to peaceful implementation. It has created a climate less open to dissent and fairness, poorer conditions for independent alternatives, and increasing restrictions on freedom of movement and resettlement. (Woodward, 1996a, p. 35)

If even calling elections was considered to be anti-democratic, it was little surprise to see that their outcomes were roundly condemned by the liberal critics. The September 1996 state-level elections were judged to be 'deeply flawed', merely ratifying the consequences of the war, legitimising the three nationalist leaderships and allowing them to consolidate their hold over power (Gallagher, 1997, pp. 19–20). Their ratification by the OSCE as 'free and fair' was written off as dictated by the US agenda of achieving a foreign policy success before the US Presidential elections (Gallagher, 1997, p. 20; Williams, 1996, p. 13). Liberal critics on the ground in Bosnia nicknamed the OSCE the 'Organisation to Secure Clinton's Election' and sought to downplay the significance of the elections.[6]

After the September 1996 elections, some commentators, such as Mary Kaldor, argued that the only reason for the success of the nationalists was the shortcomings of formal democracy:

> Elections were held in September without meeting the basic preconditions laid down in the Dayton Agreement ... While the conduct of the elections, although not the preceding campaign, was largely peaceful, thousands of people were unable to vote because so few were able to return to their places of origin and where they did there were problems with voter lists, and because absentee polling stations were inadequate. The consequence of all this was that the nationalist parties won the elections. (Kaldor, 1997, p. 28)

However, the facts of the matter invalidated Kaldor's assertion. While it was true that up to 30,000 displaced people from the Federation did not take the opportunity to vote in person in Republika Srpska, it is difficult to establish the exact reasons why. Certainly there were problems with the organisation of the polling stations and problems with the voter lists; also, many of those entitled to vote did not cross the IEBL from fear of intimidation, a lessening of interest after the postponement of the municipal elections, lack of information about transportation arrangements and the realisation they would not be allowed to visit their previous homes. However, those 30,000 votes would have made little impact on the success of the nationalist parties, in this case the Serbian SDS. The winners of the Serb seats for the Bosnian and the Republika Srpska Presidencies received 350,000 and 400,000 votes over their nearest rivals and to gain a fourth seat in the Republika Srpska House of Representatives the Bosnian Muslim SDA would have needed 40,000 additional votes. According to the OSCE the maximum impact of the 30,000 displaced persons-vote would have been to give an additional three seats in the 83-seat Republika Srpska National Assembly to the SDA or another opposition party (OSCE PEC, 1996b, pp. 167–72).

Once the claim that the election results were invalid for procedural reasons no longer held, the liberal critics followed the official view that the success of the nationalist parties was a product of ethnic division accentuated by patronage relations, media misinformation and the lack of political awareness of Bosnian voters. Under these conditions, most commentators argued the elections could not result in democratic outcomes and the OSCE was generally criticised for a failure to challenge the domination of nationalist parties. The International Crisis Group, for example, have suggested an alternative system of weighted voting, that maintains the ethnic key but weakens the attraction of nationalist politicians. They suggest that the ethnic results of all elections should be set in advance and the Bosnian electorate divided into Serb, Croat and Muslim electoral rolls with every elector having a weighted vote for all three ethnic categories in order to promote moderate candidates (ICG, 1998a, pp. 3–4).

The liberal approach to democracy was illustrated in the discussion at the round table seminar 'Dayton Continued', organised by the Law Centre and the HCA in Sarajevo at the end of 1996. It was attended by international institutions, political parties and citizen group NGOs whose dominant response to the state-level election results was a call for an international protectorate to be enforced. Mient Jan Faber argued for a new mandate 'close to that of a Transitional Authority' (HCA, 1997, p. 16);

Vehid Sehic, President of the Tuzla Civic Forum, and Mujo Kafedzic, Vice President of MBO, both called for a protectorate, Kafedzic suggesting:

> ... the international community should introduce a protectorate in Bosnia Herzegovina, by suspending all governments, and taking power for the next two years ... De facto we have a semi-protectorate already. The international community does what it likes to do, and restricts what it does not like. Why doesn't it take over completely, appoint a governor and remove everybody spreading the germs of hatred, particularly from the media. (HCA, 1997, pp. 25–6)

As noted above, the international institutions and leading Western states involved in democratisation are wary of presenting their policy enforcement as a new form of international protectorate, stressing that the Dayton mandates have not been changed and that at the end of the day the success of Dayton depends on the Bosnian leaders and their constituents. However, the liberal critics of Dayton have few qualms about using language previously associated with the colonial past and many have openly called for a protectorate as the best way of safeguarding democracy. *Guardian* leader-writers and columnists have consistently called for the end to elections and instead an 'open-ended occupation' or 'benign colonial regime' (Woollacott, 1996; Borger, 1996). The less formal democracy there is, the more positive liberal critics are about internationally-led democratisation. One striking example of this dynamic was the *Guardian*'s response to the OSCE ratification of the municipal elections in September 1997. Jonathan Steele, noting the 'imperial nature of the international presence' and Ambassador Frowick's ability to decertify winning candidates, complained not about the powers but Frowick's possible lack of use of them, raising the danger that he may 'cede to the nationalist majorities' (Steele, 1997a).

The International Crisis Group (ICG) at least formally acknowledge the gap between democratisation and democracy; however, their response to this serves to highlight the diminished nature of the liberal critics' view of democracy in Bosnia. The ICG argue that:

> Respect for Bosnian authorities and basic notions of reciprocity argue for at least the degree of transparency necessary for the Bosnian authorities and people to understand the basis for decisions, and the decision-making processes, that so affect them. If the point of the international encampment in Bosnia is to 'teach' democracy, tolerance and good governance to the Bosnians then there is no better way to start than by example. (ICG, 1996c, p. 17)

In this case democratic accountability is reduced to 'transparency'. 'Teaching democracy' ends up as a call for international institutions to make widely available their future plans and policy goals for the region. The Bosnian people have no active role in decision-making and instead are reduced to passive onlookers.

These critics of democratisation strategy in Bosnia do not argue that there is too little autonomy but that there is too much. Deacon and Stubbs, for example, argue that even local government questions of social policy should be 'implemented by non-elected impartial authorities appointed from outside [Bosnia]' (Deacon and Stubbs, 1998, p. 107). The barriers to democracy appear to be the Bosnian voters and their representatives and the democratic solution appears to be that of an international protectorate. International withdrawal from Bosnia is raised as a sign of failure and the product of a negative and prejudicial view of the region while the extension of the international mandates is seen as a sign of commitment and as making a positive statement about the role and values of the international community.

THE CONSERVATIVE ASSESSMENT

Like the liberals, the conservatives are highly critical of democratisation policy in Bosnia, in this case, not because the external goals are too low but because they are too high. The conservative critique centres on the view that ethnic division makes democracy promotion an unwise policy guide. They tend to see liberal democracy as an impossible short-term goal in an ethnically segmented society, making international attempts at 'nation-building' dangerous and destabilising.

The conservative critics, like the liberal ones, stress the failure of the civilian side of Dayton (Johnson, 1997; Kenney, 1997a; 1997b; Kissinger, 1997; Mearsheimer, 1997). They highlight that the Croatian areas of Bosnia are *de facto* part of Croatia and that the common institutions imposed on the Federation and the Bosnian state are sham external constructs. Former US Foreign Secretary Henry Kissinger, a leading conservative critic, flags up ethnic division within the US-engineered Federation, with no Muslim or Croat officials outside their own areas and few Croats in Sarajevo itself (1997). John Mearsheimer alleges that the positive assessments of international regulation, especially when it comes to the central institutions and refugee return, 'are based on theology, not on the facts on the ground' (1997). Writing in October 1997, he notes that, in terms of ethnic integration, since Dayton 30,000 refugees had returned to areas in which they were a minority group but 80,000 had left, making Bosnia less integrated after two years of Dayton (Mearsheimer, 1997).

The difference between conservatives and liberals is that the failure is not put down to the lack of international commitment but the nature of Bosnia itself. The conservative critics argue that democratisation policy is unrealistic. It is criticised as a pretence that three hostile ethnic groups can live together within a single country; Michael O'Hanlon, from the Brookings Institution, for example, asks: 'Where is the precedent – or the logic – for that arrangement' (O'Hanlon, 1997). Kissinger writes:

> … for the Bosnians, the overwhelming reality is their historical memory, which has sustained their ineradicable and unquenchable aspirations for centuries … Throughout their histories, the Serbs and Croats have considered themselves defenders of religions, first against a Muslim tide, then against each other … The deep-seated hatred of each party for all of the others exists because their conflict is more akin to the Thirty Years War over religion than it is to political conflict. (Kissinger, 1997)

For conservatives, the failure to recognise the importance of ethnicity has meant that international intervention in Bosnia has been flawed from the start. The West's desire in 1992 to create a single independent nation, is seen as 'Western arrogance and insensitivity about Bosnian reality [which] resulted in a war among three ethnic groups' (Rosenthal, 1997). The Dayton process is seen as an extension of this mistaken policy in attempting to create a federation composed of three warring parties. According to Charles Krauthammer: 'Everyone with an ounce of sense knows this is an impossible objective' (1997). John Mearsheimer writes:

> American forces are stuck in Bosnia because they are there to carry out an untenable accord, the 1995 Dayton agreement. That agreement calls for unifying Bosnia's three hate-filled ethnic groups in a single state. But that goal is infeasible. The Croats and the Serbs want no part of a multi-ethnic Bosnia – that is why they fought the war in the first place. They want partition. Even the Muslims, who favoured integration only because they would dominate a united Bosnia, now talk openly of partition. (Mearsheimer, 1997)

For these commentators, every intervention taken by the international community to enforce the central state authorities means risking instability and opposition, to the extent of possibly reigniting the war:

> The same flaw that attended the birth of the Bosnian state lies at the heart of the dilemmas of the Dayton accords … Its military provisions separate the parties substantially along the

> lines of the ethnic enclaves that emerged as hostilities ceased. But the political provisions do the opposite: They seek to unite these enclaves under the banner of a multiethnic state that caused the explosion in the first place. (Kissinger, 1997)

Because of the depth of division, conservatives, like Charles Krauthammer, argue that democratisation is not a neutral policy. Without any consensus on the legitimacy of the new Bosnian state, democratisation policy only antagonises groups and plays on divisions instead of attempting to build bridges and reconcile them. Under these circumstances, international interference means the risk of involving the US in a new war, one provoked by the international community. He concludes that democratisation policy 'may assuage the conscience of armchair moralists living 4,500 miles away, but it will kill a lot of people on the ground' (1997).

O'Hanlon agrees that Dayton is perpetuating ethnic tensions: '[Dayton] keeps Muslim hopes for resettlement of refugees and ultimate reintegration of the country unsustainably high and therefore keeps the Serbs on edge and paranoid about losing wartime gains' (1997). The conservative critique directly challenges the positive gains for Bosnian society alleged to flow from democratisation. Considering the depth of ethnic segmentation, the conservatives hold that elections can play no role in solving ethnic division. Kissinger, for example, writes: 'elections are not about alterations in office but about dominance determining life, death and religion'. For this reason, he sees the OSCE strategy of using absentee voting in municipal elections to encourage multi-ethnic rule, in areas that are currently mono-ethnic, as a waste of time or generating renewed conflict; either the current ethnic division is consolidated or there is the risk of conflict as absentee voters regain the right to rule (Kissinger, 1997).

The conservative critics fear that US commitment to democratisation is symbolic of a loss of direction in foreign policy. This would seem to be warranted when the justification for the extended mandates is compared to the statements made by policy-makers at the outset of the Dayton mandate for a one-year external international administration. Dayton negotiator Richard Holbrooke at that time stated: 'We are not going to leave behind a force [after this] ... If a year doesn't work, two, three, or five years won't do either' (G. Rose, 1998, p. 65). Even the Joint Chiefs of Staff chairman John Shalikashvili said, at the time, that 'I cannot imagine circumstances changing in such a way that we would remain in Bosnia [beyond a year]' and, after the two-year extension was decided, in December 1996, admitted 'everyone I've talked to has been unable to explain to me what it is that is going to happen during the period of time that would make the conditions at the end of [the SFOR deployment] worth taking the risk of bringing in a new force' (G. Rose, 1998, pp. 65–6).

Conservatives express concern that unrealistic expectations will draw the US increasingly into the sphere of Balkan rivalries with no achievements to show for it. For the critics, extending the international regulation beyond keeping the peace is dangerous 'mission creep' and they see no strategic interest in staying. For Henry Kissinger: 'America has no national interest for which to risk lives to produce a multiethnic state in Bosnia. The creation of a multiethnic state should be left to negotiations among the parties' (1997). The *Chicago Tribune* has editorialised in similar vein:

> The United States has no vital national interests at stake in Bosnia. There is no fundamental need for a US military involvement that threatens to drag on indefinitely. If our European allies believe there is a need for armed peacekeepers in Bosnia beyond next spring, they are capable of handling the job on their own. (*Chicago Tribune*, 1997)

In a rare voice of conservative dissent from Britain, Simon Jenkins argues in *The Times* that American policy has sucked Britain into a 'morass' where there is no clear military objective, no exit strategy and no national interest, yet it appears that British troops will be stuck for ever (1997). Charles Krauthammer complains that despite promises of withdrawal, the US government will:

> ... as is our custom, proclaim the great success of our expeditionary force, change its name and essentially leave it in place. It started as IFOR (implementation force). It then became SFOR (stabilisation force). SFOR will surely be retired, too – and then remain in Bosnia renamed ... My suggestion is BFOR, baby-sitting force. What is the new mission? No one really knows. (Krauthammer, 1997)

General George Jatras and General Charles Boyd, among other leading former US military commanders, have denounced US policy in the belief that this mistaken intervention is a product of media portrayal of the conflict as an external Serb invasion of a mythically multicultural Bosnia (Jatras, 1997; Boyd, 1995; 1998). George Kenney, who resigned from the US State Department Yugoslavia Desk in protest at US policy ignoring the 'genocide' in Bosnia, later felt that US policy-makers had been influenced by Muslim 'black propaganda' and came to see this as the explanation for the irrational extension of US engagement, in an attempt to support Muslim war-aims against the Serbs (1997a).

Other conservatives view US meddling as the result of the White House falling prey to 'political correctness'. Ted Galen Carpenter, criticising the US entanglement in complex political rivalries, sees democratisation policy as driven by a 'Frankenstinian experiment' in 'politically correct micro-management' (1997). For many, the intervention on the side of Plavsic in the November 1997 Republika Srpska Parliamentary Assembly elections, when there was little to choose between her and Krajisnik, and even less to be gained by interfering, was the last straw. Republican Senator Kay Bailey Hutchison wrote: 'The Clinton Administration has decided, without Congressional consultation, to change our role in the Balkans. Beyond serving as neutral peacekeepers ... We have become partisans in a local struggle' (1997).

Conservatives often seem to be at a loss to understand what the international community is doing or why it is there. Ernest Blazar, in the *Washington Times*, asked why, with universal agreement on the success of the military aspects of Dayton, the NATO forces were not being withdrawn in line with previously set deadlines. The reason given for extended NATO mandates, the need for troop enforcement of the civilian implementation of Dayton, he thought was weak. The seizure of the Serb TV transmitters, for example, was justified on the grounds of protecting NATO from hostility within Bosnia; however, Blazar commented:

> Talk like that borders on the elliptical; that US troops are in Bosnia to defend themselves. It's surely not what Pentagon leaders privately think ... But absent more candour on what US troops are doing in Bosnia and for how much longer, it's nearly all the American people are getting lately. (Blazar, 1997)

Other conservative critics have compared the Bosnia deployment to the moon landings, with the principal objective appearing to be to send men far away and bring them back safely (G. Rose, 1998, p. 66).

At the heart of the conservative critique is the question of why so many international resources are going into Bosnia when it seems unlikely that the policy will result in any qualitative improvement and quite likely make matters worse. George Kenney sums up this approach in the *Washington Times*, saying that the two intelligent options would be either the 'full-scale occupation and administration of Bosnia' or the 'Cyprus-like partition solution', democratisation just 'pours resources down a bottomless black hole' (1997b).

THE CONTRADICTIONS OF THE EXTENDED DEMOCRATISATION MANDATES

The official response to the conservative critique has been a contradictory one. On the one hand, the international community is said to be making headway and have majority support for the new state; on the other, there are so many barriers that the international missions have to be extended into the indefinite future with stronger mandates and no fixed exit goals. It is this fine balance between success and failure that keeps the democratisation bandwagon on the road and understanding this process is the key to unravelling the source of the contradictions involved in democratisation.

The conservative critique draws out the contradictory dynamic at the heart of democratisation. When conservatives argue that most people oppose Dayton and the international community are wasting resources to change little, they are met with the response that international policy is a good use of resources and achieving a lot with the support of most of the population. Against the conservative doomsday scenarios of the potential instability and cost of intervention, US Dayton architect Richard Holbrooke responds that it is the conservatives who are out of touch with 'reality on the ground', stating: 'We can well afford the costs, and there have been no US or NATO fatalities from hostile action in 21 months – an astonishing record' (1997). Holbrooke astutely points out that 'the clash of civilisations can be much overstated' (1997).

The observation by Holbrooke about the 'overstatement' of the dangers of ethnic violence seems to be well grounded in practice as over the last three years the threat of nationalist extremism has seemed constantly to be on the other side of the horizon. The lack of such opposition to Dayton recalls the late Bill Hicks' observation about Saddam Hussein's feared elite Republican Guard, during the 1991 Gulf War, which after several weeks of US carpet-bombing, and not one response, went from being described as 'the elite Republican Guard' to 'the Republican Guard' to 'the Republicans made this all up' (Hicks, 1992). Like the alleged threat posed by the Iraqi leader, the power of hard-line Serb nationalists to use intimidation and Nazi-style propaganda to undermine the international community seems to be more State Department invention than considered analysis.

While it is an open question whether the majority of the Bosnian electorate support the Dayton Agreement, the lack of viable alternatives is also striking. For most Bosnian citizens the most pressing concerns are mundane issues of work and security and there is little desire to see further instability (see Boyd, 1998, p. 51). Neither the feared backlash amongst Serbs and Croats, nor attempts by the Muslims to make use of their military superiority to make further gains have materialised. Instead of greater division and renewed conflict, expected by both liberal and conservative critics, passive acceptance has been the underlying response by Bosnians of all ethnic groups, and even those factions expected to be most antagonistic towards it increasingly see the Bosnian state as a non-negotiable institution.

Biljana Plavsic, the President of Republika Srpska, argues that only the international community can maintain the autonomy of the Serb entity and that as Dayton guarantees the Serbs one-third of all positions in joint Bosnian institutions this is the best way of ensuring Serb interests will be protected (RFE/RL BR, 1997). Plavsic has also, on various occasions, called for the RS army to be involved in the US 'train and equip' programme; these calls have been welcomed by the Bosnian Muslims as a first step to creating a joint army and qualifying for NATO's Partnership for Peace programme, but have been rejected by Washington (*RFE/RL Newsline*, 1997b; *RFE/RL Newsline*, 1997e). Plavsic represents a growing view among Bosnian Serbs, fearful of the consequences of international isolation. As she told the SRNA news agency: 'integration processes have started and whoever rejects them has no sense of reality' (*RFE/RL Newsline*, 1997d).

Among Bosnian Croats, there is also a realisation that Dayton and their formal separation from the Republic of Croatia is beyond contestation. According to the UN High Commissioner for Refugees, nearly 30 per cent of Bosnian Croats have left Bosnia since the Dayton Accords were signed, many resettling in the formerly Serb-inhabited Croatian Krajina (Boyd, 1998, p. 44). The perpetuation of the Croat para-state as the 'Croatian Community of Herceg-Bosna' has been more an attempt to shore up the domination of the HDZ in the region than an expression of opposition to Dayton. Meetings of this body have been held without the participation of the opposition Croatian Peasants' Party which has argued that attempts to re-establish the organisation are counterproductive (*RFE/RL Newsline*, 1997a). In June 1998 the Croatian HDZ split, with the Croat member of the Bosnian Presidency, Kresimir Zubak, establishing a new pro-Dayton party to compete in the September elections (SAFAX, 1998d; *RFE/RL Newsline*, 1998d; AFP, 1998a).

In all three communities there is little hostility to the international community or sense of alternatives. This is reflected in the fact that even those political parties with most support are commonly seen to be self-serving elites. The dominant sense is disillusionment, quite the opposite of the image of fervent ethnic nationalism. In November 1997, an RFE/RL correspondent asked people in the 'hard-line' SDS stronghold of Pale what they expected from the elections and noted: 'Almost all respondents said that they expect nothing, and that they are apathetic about Bosnian Serb politics. One woman concluded that none of the politicians offer a real vision for the future' (RFE/RL BR, 1997). A *Times* journalist reflected this pessimism in Prijedor in November 1997, a young local journalist telling him: 'We have reached the point where we no longer care about issues like war criminals ... There is a desperation among young people to leave this environment ... to improve their living standards. Whether Muslims come back is a minor issue' (T. Walker, 1997b).

At no point in the democratisation process has it been suggested that there is a danger of formal democracy being undermined by Bosnian opponents, by the cancellation of elections or the interference of the military in the political sphere. At the Joint Military Commission, held in August 1997, SFOR reported that the situation remained 'calm' and the commanders were congratulated on keeping the military out of the political tensions (OHRB, 1997y). Apart from displaying Karadzic posters in defiance of international edict and a few incidents of stone-throwing, there has been little sign of any popular opposition to the international community. In September 1997, when the SDS held an election rally in Banja Luka to oppose President Plavsic, this was alleged in some Western media reports to have been an attempted coup. The reality was rather different: NATO troops stopped buses of SDS supporters from attending and eventually had to rescue the SDS leadership, described by Jacques Klein later as a 'pretty sorry bunch', from angry crowds outside the Bosna Hotel (T. Walker, 1997a).

Attempts to talk up the media threat to IFOR appear similarly forced. What these 'extremists' allege in the Bosnian Serb media is little different to what some prominent conservative American critics have argued in relation to war crimes, the Hague tribunal and NATO policy (OHR SRT, 1997a; ONASA, 1997). Western officials' interpretation of these criticisms as a call for Serbs to 'take up arms' implied that criticism was on the same par as physical violence. This was supported by a NATO official, who stated: 'It was a direct attempt to demonise SFOR, which is a direct threat' (Dinmore, 1997). Media analyst William Woodger directly questions whether it was the international community's concerns about violence which led to them seizing Bosnian Serb transmitters in the run-up to the RS Parliamentary elections: 'With 35,000 heavily armed troops in Bosnia, is NATO worried about "violence" which has so far only been provoked by NATO action – and amounts to verbal abuse, stone and bottle throwing and a couple of Molotov Cocktails?' (Woodger, 1997).

Momcilo Krajisnik, the Serb member of the Bosnian presidency, often held up as the main opponent of Dayton, seems to have little power *vis-à-vis* the international community. As the *Washington Post* reported, Principal Deputy High Representative, Jacques Klein could gloat after the NATO seizure of the SRT transmitters: 'He [Krajisnik] wasn't happy. But all he can say is, "I don't like this". Well, I'm sorry ... Before, if they had their hand in the cookie jar it was just slapped. This time someone took the cookie jar away' (Hockstader, 1997b). Apart from being treated as a naughty child, Krajisnik suffered the further indignity of being punished after displaying good behaviour. As one European official commented: 'The irony is, they were co-operating in general. The Americans were looking for one misstep, and when they finally got one, it was a whopper' (Hockstader, 1997a).

The contradiction at the heart of the democratisation process is that if there is not much resistance to it and the international community are in control, why has it been necessary to devote so many resources to Bosnia? Similar sentiments were expressed by Boutros Boutros-Ghali, the UN Secretary-General, when he stated that Bosnia had 'dominated the [UN] Organisation's peace-keeping agenda and distorted its peace-making efforts at the expense of other parts of the world' (UN, 1995b).

It could be argued that the biggest problem facing the international community in Bosnia is what to do with the power that they have accumulated. One example, picked up on by commentators, was the seizure of the Bosnian Serb TV transmitters. William Drodziak noted that 'NATO commanders found themselves in the uncomfortable role of television programmers' and Lee Hockstader that 'officials conceded privately that they have no firm idea of exactly how to proceed' (Drodziak, 1997; Hockstader, 1997a). Chris Hedges, in the *New York Times*, noted in early 1997 that boredom was the main problem for the US forces, that 'there was no clear enemy; the mission is difficult to define; there is no conflict looming to motivate troops through the period of routine and drill' (Hedges, 1997).

On the other hand it seems that the conservative argument that the tensions will be so severe as to necessitate a permanent presence are fully agreed with when it comes to arguing for the mandates to be extended. The response of the liberal democratisers to withdrawal and the termination of the externally-led democratisation process is always to find some reason or threat that necessitates international involvement. In order to justify the extension of international mandates, the institutions involved in democratisation have been forced to contradict themselves and talk up the opposition from within Bosnia. Holbrooke, for example, argued that pulling back would mean: 'surrender … to the worst elements in Bosnian society, those that preach and practice ethnic hatred, using techniques Goebbels would have admired' (Holbrooke, 1997). The International Commission on the Balkans argue: 'Without an indefinite international military presence – IFOR II, or IFOR "light" – the Dayton framework and the process of peace-building might fall apart as soon as the more obstreperous local actors felt free of the constraints inherent in the presence of foreign forces on the ground' (ICoB, 1996, p. 3).

High Representative Bildt felt that the risk that uncertainties about withdrawal would influence political developments in the present meant that structures of long-term regulation were necessary to prevent a renewal of hostilities (OHRB, 1997n). *Guardian* journalist Jonathan Steele argued that: 'Annual arguments about whether to leave create uncertainty from which the wrong people benefit. Europe's government[s] should have the sense to say we are in Bosnia to stay' (Steele, 1997b, p. 17). Before the extension of the NATO presence beyond June 1998 was confirmed, High Representative Westendorp argued for an extension 'to keep former warring factions in check and to give people a clear message that there will be no new war'. He asserted that only a military presence in Bosnia would be adequate:

> Over the horizon is not a good solution for Bosnia's security ... [this] would lead to an over the horizon international community and Dayton cannot be implemented from such a position ... The international community needs to be on the spot, in a secure environment, giving immediate treatment to Bosnia's pains. (OHRB, 1997B)

The deep feeling that the Bosnian people cannot really be trusted with democracy, and that once the international community has left they will re-start hostilities, has allowed international agreements to be overridden before the ink has dried; this includes pre-Dayton agreements between the US and Croatia over the Federation and aspects of Dayton itself, such as the Brcko arbitration time limits and agreements on international withdrawal (for example, see OHR BiH, 1997). As the conservatives point out, the original goals of international involvement seem to have disappeared into the background as 'mission creep' has transformed a humanitarian and military mission into a highly politicised one. Over the last three years the liberal interventionists have rewritten Dayton in flexible terms. The dynamic of external democratisation, and the shifting policy goals, was illustrated by High Representative Bildt's statement that: 'each step forward we have taken has also demonstrated how many more are the steps which must be taken for the peace process to be self-sustaining and stable' (OHRR, 1996d, par. 100).

The experience of the High Representative, that the more international involvement there is, the greater are the calls for this involvement to be extended, has been constantly played out in practice. At the start of 1998, the OHR's office secured the election of a Republika Srpska parliament that excluded the dominant nationalist parties, this then created a new set of tasks as the priority became the support of the weak sectional government through stepped-up military and police patrols and economic support. In Brussels, the High Representative reiterated how the multitude of new tasks extended to paying government salaries, help in housing and refugee resettlement, and restoring water and sewage systems (M. Walker, 1998a). Once one election had finished it was time for the OHR to prepare for the next one and ensure the new government retained power.

It was not just in RS that external regulation was extended. As Deputy High Representative Schumacher indicated, success in one area became the justification for new goals being set in others: 'If this democratisation process really continues, and if [RS Prime Minister] Dodik only delivers even a few of the promises he's made, then very quickly the political emphasis will have to shift to the Muslim-Croat Federation' (Wilkinson, 1998). With increased success in undermining resistance to international policy-making in the RS there has been growing pressure on the Muslim and Croat Federation partners to, in Robert Gelbard's words, 'retain their "moral authority"', if they want to secure international funding (R. J. Smith, 1998b). This has involved opening up their policy-making further to international supervision under pressure of claims that 'now the Muslim side of Bosnia is less pluralistic, less open, less democratic than [Republika] Srpska' (*Washington Post*, 1998). In a joint declaration, in February 1998, the US, OHR and European Commission issued deadlines for refugee return and measures on the distribution of job and school placements in Sarajevo with the threat of unspecified 'non-compliance' measures (R. J. Smith, 1998b). As William Woodger has noted, the Dayton Agreement has become increasingly irrelevant as new tasks are built in under the 'spirit of Dayton' (Woodger, 1997).

CONCLUSION

Although the assessments of democratisation practice vary widely with critics arguing a range of perspectives from a full protectorate to international withdrawal and partition between three separate entities, there is little challenge to the democratisation approach that international regulation is necessary and little consideration of the impact of the international administration on the Bosnian political sphere.

The liberal critics essentially argue for more of the same and view the only limitation to internationally imposed democratisation as the lack of will of the international community itself. The conservative critics argue that the problem with international policy is that Bosnian culture and ethnic divisions make it an idealistic proposal which could entail international embroilment in Balkan affairs with little possibility of a solution to the complex questions of ethnic division.

The common ground across all these assessments is that the Bosnian people, or Bosnian 'culture' itself, are perceived to be the barrier to international community attempts to bring democracy, to the new state. In relation to the historic or cultural roots of Bosnian resistance to democracy the international institutions appear to be powerless. As Michael Ignatieff notes: 'A very great deal of exculpatory moral disgust circulates around the failures of the new world order, a self-excusing sense that "we" tried and "they" failed' (Ignatieff, 1998, p. 99). This perception of powerlessness means that the international community never sees its own role in institutionalising divisions or preventing compromise solutions. NATO Secretary-General Javier Solana has declared that the struggle between the international community and nationalist Bosnian elites is so balanced that criticism of international policy could be dangerous and encourage resistance to Dayton (Solana, 1997).

With powerlessness also comes the lack of responsibility. This was starkly demonstrated when former US Secretary of State Warren Christopher declared Bosnia 'a test case of America's ability to nurture democracy in the post-Cold War world' and the following month argued that Bosnia was 'an intractable "problem from hell" that no one can be expected to solve ... less as a moral tragedy ... and more as a tribal feud that no outsider could hope to settle' (Woodward, 1995, p. 307). A similar lack of responsibility was voiced by Clinton at the beginning of the international administration over Bosnia: 'If we leave after a year, and they decide they don't like the benefits of peace and they're going to start fighting again, that does not mean NATO failed. It means we gave them a chance to make their peace and they blew it' (G. Rose, 1998, p. 65).

As will be considered in the following chapter, the democratisation approach's facilitation of an international co-operative project where there is little accounting for success or failure has made intervention in Bosnia highly attractive for institutions of the international community looking to project themselves on a world stage.

8 The external dynamic of democratisation

The international mandates continue to be extended despite the lack of clear objectives or quantifiable success in meeting them. The ideology of democratisation, considered in the previous chapter, begins to explain why there is little critique of this process but does not indicate the dynamic behind it. The consensus on democratisation may well be a necessary condition for the extension of international regulation over Bosnia, but this does not make it a sufficient explanation for it. The empirical findings of this work and the contradictory assessments of the democratisation process from its leading proponents suggest that the prolongation of this process provides a flexible form through which international institutions have extended their capacity to accommodate to and to influence new East/West and West/West international relations without the framework of the Cold War.

This chapter reconsiders the debate between conservative critics and official proponents of democratisation within the US foreign policy establishment, locating this in the broader context of US foreign policy and in particular the expansion of the US-led NATO alliance to the 'new democracies' of Eastern Europe. It is suggested that the close linking of success in Bosnia with the development of new forms of international co-operation, through the UN, NATO and the OSCE, reflects attempts to use the international consensus on democratisation in Bosnia to overcome problems of cohering and legitimating these international institutions. It would appear that the more contradictory aspects of the democratisation process, such as the growing restrictions on self-government at all levels, result more from the external pressures on this process than the exigencies of the situation within Bosnia itself.

DEMOCRATISATION AND THE INTERNATIONAL ORDER

Support for democratisation has little to do with attitudes towards democracy. The official, liberal and conservative assessments of democratisation practice all concur that democracy is a good thing, but not in Bosnia. The debate as it is summed up by Fareed Zakaria, in *Foreign Affairs*, is between those who want 'to make the world safe for democracy' and those who want 'to make democracy safe for the world' (1997, p. 43). The difference between these perspectives has little to do with the history or reality of Bosnia, there is general agreement among international actors that Bosnia lacks the cultural prerequisites for democracy and that international regulation of some form is a necessity. The difference lies in the strategic and political importance of Bosnia and the need for concerted high-level international action.

The existence of the democratisation consensus, reconsidered in the previous chapter, cannot explain the practice of democratisation. While the democratisation approach legitimises the extension of international regulation and problematises the capacities and institutional practices of the objects of democratisation, in this case the Bosnian people and their representatives, the content of that regulation and its application and extension would appear to depend on factors unrelated to this. To answer the question of why Dayton and democratisation in Bosnia has attracted the attention, support and resources of the international community, and to shed light on the extension of the democratisation process itself, it is necessary to begin by reconstructing the debate between the conservative critics and the defenders of democratisation within US government circles.

It can be argued that the debate about democratisation in Bosnia has been about the priorities for US foreign policy. The heart of the conservative critique is the question of what the 'pay-off' is. Predominantly from the pre-Clinton foreign policy establishment, the conservatives argue that the US has no security interest in Bosnia and that getting drawn into Balkan politics with no strategic objectives is a high-risk strategy. In answering the 'pay-off' question, the leading US policy-makers, supported by European governments and heads of international institutions, provide a set of answers which enable us to begin to relocate the democratisation dynamic away from the situation in Bosnia itself.

Richard Holbrooke took up Henry Kissinger's September 1997 opinion-piece in the *Washington Post* arguing that Kissinger, above all people, should be able to see the larger issue at stake in Bosnia – US leadership:

> One of the most consistent themes in Dr. Kissinger's career has been the need for America to remain engaged in Europe. At the end of the Cold War, he opposed calls to withdraw from the field of European security, argued that NATO should remain an indispensable instrument of American policy and called for its enlargement – all views with which the Clinton administration agrees. (Holbrooke, 1997)

Pulling back from democratisation would 'undermine America's commitment to European security just on the eve of the event he [Kissinger] has so eloquently supported: the enlargement of NATO' (Holbrooke, 1997). For Holbrooke, the US partnership with its European allies in Bosnia 'has defined our post-Cold War American security commitment to Europe'. He concludes his article with a call to action, stating: 'The United States should not sacrifice its dual role as a central part of the European security system and a leading advocate of universal human values' (Holbrooke, 1997).

Charles Kupchan (1997), on the National Security Council staff at the start of the Clinton administration, believes that 'also at stake in Bosnia is the future of European integration' as the EU would be paralysed in the face of renewed conflict. According to NATO Secretary-General, Javier Solana (1997), retreating from democratisation in Bosnia would be 'highly destabilising for wider Europe ... thus it would run against the strategic interests of all NATO allies'.

Kupchan argues that retreating from Bosnia makes a mockery of US plans for enlarging NATO. He argues that the Senate cannot ratify treaty-based defence guarantees to Poland, Hungary and the Czech Republic and withdraw from Bosnia, 'peace in Europe's centre is either worth American lives or it is not' (Kupchan, 1997). Warren Zimmerman, former US ambassador to Yugoslavia, also argues NATO's credibility is at stake in Bosnia and that if it fails 'not only will NATO's expansion look ludicrous, but serious roles for NATO anywhere will be hard to imagine' (cited in Wilson, 1998, p. 148). Anthony Lewis (1997) makes the same point, in the *New York Times*, that the message US withdrawal from Bosnia would send out to NATO, when it is expanding its membership and enlarging its promise of security and freedom, is 'Don't believe us.' Lewis (1997) insists that America must not abandon 'our leadership role in carrying out Dayton'. In order to demonstrate US leadership, Kupchan (1997) is not worried about a little blood being spilt and argues that, instead of a fear of US casualties holding back intervention, Clinton should 'prepare the public for the prospect of US casualties' and 'up the ante' by arresting war criminals and shutting down more broadcasts and, in the case of retaliation, use 'overwhelming force'.

The view that international intervention in Bosnia is essential for the coherence of US relations with Europe and also for European Union cohesion has been widely voiced across the international community prior and during the Dayton process. In Britain, Will Hutton argued that failure in Bosnia could lead to a repeat of the inter-war period when US withdrawal from the

League of Nations led to the breakdown of the international diplomatic order: '[Withdrawal] will be the clearest signal yet that there is no will or capacity to resist aggression motivated by territorial aggrandisement and ethnic tribalism. The spell will have been broken; international law will have been flouted; and we will live in a lawless, orderless world' (Hutton, 1995). Tom Gallagher, a leading British democratisation proponent, sees European Union involvement in Bosnia as an expression of European identity and purpose which, as he notes, seems to have been lost in the late 1990s:

> Perhaps one of the most useful functions of the Balkans in the 1990s is to be a mirror to the face of a West European nearly-union which has lost belief in the federalist idea and the policies of a economic and social consensus that fuelled its progress. If Europe was now a vital political concept rather than a geographical expression, then the problems of South-Eastern Europe, far from being a nightmare from hell, might instead be viewed as a marvellous preparatory ground for diplomats, administrators, politicians and NGOs imbued with the need to promote a post-nationalist agenda across the continent. (Gallagher, 1997, p. 34)

The question then follows of why Bosnia should be so crucial to international security, to NATO's existence and to European unity? Surely this says more about NATO and European unity than about Bosnia itself. If there was a rationale for the existence of NATO after the Cold War, or a greater consensus on what Europe stood for in the late 1990s, it is doubtful that Bosnia would have assumed the international importance that it has.

Many commentators have emphasised the importance of Bosnia for international relations after the Cold War. Susan Woodward, for example, argues that Dayton was 'a turning point … in American leadership in the post-Cold War era' and argues that, through intervention in Bosnia, NATO and European security mechanisms have been transformed (1996a, p. 1). As she describes elsewhere, Bosnia has been the focus through which the international institutional framework of international relations has been reconstituted after the Cold War: political restrictions on German military actions were removed, allowing involvement outside NATO frontiers for the first time since the defeat of Nazism; NATO's strike against the Bosnian Serbs was the first NATO combat action since its founding; the WEU also took its first military and policing actions; the UN sent troops to Europe for the first time and mounted the largest, most complex and most expensive operation in its history, and Russia became re-integrated into the international community through the five-power Contact Group (Woodward, 1995, p. 2; 1996b, p. 173).

Despite the column-space given to the importance of Bosnia to post-Cold War international institutional arrangements, there has been little clarification of this relationship. For example, Woodward argues that the importance of the democratisation process is that a failure to secure a democratic and stable solution in Bosnia will then discredit American leadership in the world and question the new institutional arrangements. Along similar lines, the *Guardian*'s Martin Woollacott argues: '[The arrest of war criminals] could turn out to be a turning point for Bosnia and for NATO. All the agonising over whether or not the expansion of NATO is a good thing has tended to obscure the fact that if the NATO intervention in Bosnia ends in failure ... it could break the alliance' (Woollacott, 1997a).

It is the suggestion of this book that it is not failure in Bosnia which might then question the new international security arrangements but the weakness of the new security arrangements that has necessitated a continued high-level involvement in Bosnia. NATO is a high-profile example of the problem that confronts the international institution-builders today. Simon Jenkins (1997) unintentionally pinpoints the problem when he argues that withdrawal from Bosnia would not risk British security or that of the alliance and in the same article describes NATO as 'an alliance whose obscurity of purpose is now complete'. If it was not for Bosnia as a vital post-Cold War focus of organisation it is doubtful that NATO's existence, which otherwise involves international conferences around self-established targets of expansion, would appear relevant. NATO plays a new role today, that of a political forum for managing the integration of the former communist bloc, but without the focus on Bosnia there would have been little coherence to this process (Burgess, 1997, pp. 19–20). As Woollacott notes, it has been through co-ordinated international action in Bosnia that NATO's new relationship with the East has been formalised:

> NATO deployment, enlargement, and the relationship with Russia intertwine in Bosnia. Poland and the Czech Republic, as an earnest of their seriousness about membership, sent peace-keeping contingents. Hungary became, effectively, a forward NATO base ... the Hungarians and Romanians moved into a new better relationship. Russia joined the NATO force on special terms of its own, which prefigured the NATO-Russia charter. (Woollacott, 1997a)

As Carl Bildt noted, in May 1997, Bosnia has been at the cutting edge of a transition in European security and stability. In 1991 there had been no foreign troops in South-East Europe; now there were deployments in southern Hungary, Croatia, Montenegro, Macedonia and Albania, apart from Bosnia. A new regional security arrangement was being established on this basis and 'Bosnia and the region might be as important for the overall effort to create stability in Europe in the future as Berlin was in the past' (OHRB, 1997m). Later that month, Bildt expanded on the need to develop the military capacity of the WEU and co-operation with the US for a new long-term framework in the region, stating that short-term military exit strategies were not possible without risking a political collapse:

> What we must do is shape a coherent security structure for the region as a whole, which includes the stationing of outside forces at key positions in order to be able to deter any attempt – by anyone in the region – to resort to aggression, war or large-scale violence ... Politically the European Union would need to be ready to act and to assume responsibility, possibly through the active political presence of Special or High Representatives who would be the face and voice of Europe in specific areas and on specific issues. (OHRB, 1997q)

The importance of Bosnia has been that in a period of international transition after the Cold War it became a focus for international institutions that could enable them to redefine their political and strategic objectives and transform themselves organisationally in the new post-Cold War environment. Democratisation has been central to this process of transition from anti-communism to human rights promotion, enabling a level of constancy whilst redefining the role of the international community and reorganising international co-operation. As Robin Cook stated in his first public statement on Bosnia: 'The basic political rights of democratic pluralism are now needed in Eastern Europe to combat totalitarian nationalism as much as they ever were to challenge communism' (Cook, 1994).

The fact that it is not Bosnia that is important but the international co-operation symbolised by the democratisation process is starkly revealed by the later actions of the British Foreign Secretary. Cook has not been slow to make political capital out of strident demands for the Bosnian parties and regional leaders to accede to international priorities, taking the lead on issues such as political corruption, war criminals and a free media (Black, 1997). However, despite the priority Bosnia has in terms of British foreign policy, there is no possibility of unilateral British action in Bosnia as he made clear on his first official visit to Washington: 'I do not want anyone in the US to be under any misapprehension: the principle is one out, all out. We were there before US troops arrived, and it was an uncomfortable and lonely place to be' (Maddox, 1997).

For the British establishment, as Cook explained, the highest priority is 'to signal that we want to have a strong working relationship with one of our oldest allies' (Maddox, 1997). The importance of Bosnia for Britain is primarily that of cementing a relationship with the US and the fact that political capital can be made is a welcome bonus. Central to the international support for democratisation is that it provides a focus for 'strong working relationships' at a time when there appears to be few other examples of untainted political goals.

International democratisation policy practice and the vast sums invested in the democratisation process in Bosnia, may not make sense in terms of Bosnia, but they are understandable in relation to these broader policy needs. To fill in the final piece of the puzzle we must retrace our steps and reanalyse democratisation practice in Bosnia to understand that the importance of democratisation is in its form, as a process of relationship management, rather than its end goals.

THE EXTERNAL DRIVE TO DEMOCRATISE

Once the dynamic behind democratisation is grasped, as the desire to unify an international agenda and set a new framework of integration into the international community, then democratisation policy in Bosnia becomes explainable. Democratisation is a process that involves the main international powers around a common agenda under US leadership and sets new standards of legitimacy for international institutions.

Woodward and others have correctly indicated that it has been through Bosnia that international relations of the post-Cold War order have been worked out. However, the analysis of this process has generally been restricted to that of great power relations, especially the new relations between the US, Europe and Russia. James Petras and Steve Vieux, in the *New Left Review*, exemplify this approach in their article 'Bosnia and the Revival of US Hegemony' (1996). The problem is that, in Carl Bildt's words, 'there is no quick fix' – not for Bosnian rivalries, but for the new mechanisms of international regulation. The experience of Bosnia would indicate the perceived instability of that process. Bosnia may have given new life to NATO, the WEU and other international forms of co-operation, but the forced nature of international calls for their perpetual extension in Bosnia indicates that the question of legitimacy needs more than a new language of democracy and human rights but also an active and interventionist role.

Bosnia is one of the few international policy interventions that has drawn universal support from all the major international powers. As soon as other international issues appear on the agenda, it is clear that the unity over Bosnia is a superficial or at least transient one. The unique aspect about democratisation in Bosnia has been the ability to match a moral high ground over democracy, human rights and civil society with concerted international organisation. Raising the same issues of democracy in other parts of the world is much more difficult, and conflicting domestic and international interests come into play. In relation to China and South-East Asia, for example, US and British attempts to play the democracy card have only opened up divisions between major Western powers and revealed the fact that economic interests can easily blunt new 'ethical' foreign policies (Cumming-Bruce, 1997).

The unique nature of the Bosnian involvement has had such a cohesive impact on the international institutions involved that there is a great reluctance to stop the co-operative project. Democratisation is the key to extending this co-operative relationship, not merely because the language of democratisation allows involvement to be seen as taking the high moral ground, nor because it provides a flexible framework for self-flattery while denigrating the 'ethnic rivalries' of the less civilised Bosnians. These aspects are important for legitimising a relationship of domination but the same could be said for other issues high on the international agenda, such as the rights of children, women or minorities. What distinguishes democratisation from other themes of concern is the fact that it is a process; a cohering co-operative project with no fixed definitions and time limits, a cohering mechanism that can last as long as its practitioners require. As Javier Solana, NATO's Secretary-General, stated in July 1998 on the occasion of NATO's first seminar about democracy, held in Sarajevo, the significance of international community activity in Bosnia goes beyond Bosnia itself because 'the reconstruction of Bosnia shows perhaps the most powerful co-operative momentum in Europe's recent history' (AP, 1998b).

The international consensus around democratisation in Bosnia has little to do with either democracy or Bosnia itself. The key to understanding the dynamic of democratisation is that the process is the most important aspect. Already in July 1996, the High Representative noted the pressure put on his office by the 'continuous widening of the scope of OHR activities' (OHRR, 1996b, par. 6). The pressure to widen the remit has not come from popular Bosnian demand, but from the institutions themselves (*RFE/RL Newsline*, 1997g; Boyd, 1998, p. 51).

This is why, according to the democratising institutions, Bosnia is always on a knife-edge and the progress could be undermined by one lapse of control, or one sign of weakness from the international community. To withdraw or to bring in an international protectorate, Kenney's suggestions cited in the previous chapter, would end the dynamic of democratisation. The nature of Bosnia as an ongoing process of international co-operation explains why, even though the powers of Carlos Westendorp amount to an international protectorate, this can never be openly admitted. This may not be purely because there is some reluctance to appear colonial or, more importantly, a reluctance to take responsibility for what happens in Bosnia. Installing a formal protectorate would remove the relationship process whereby mechanisms of international community co-operation continually have to be re-energised as new issues arise that generate opportunities for united action.

Although democratisation has necessitated increased international powers over Bosnia and set new standards of intervention, this may well be a by-product of Bosnia being a focus for international co-operation and the necessity of 'upping the ante'. This does not necessarily indicate that international protectorates are going to be established in such a direct form over other states in the region. In fact, this analysis would suggest that the opposite is the case, if Bosnia is the fulcrum for international co-operation, there is less necessity to talk up the problems of other states such as Macedonia and Albania, or to intervene more directly in the question of Kosovo.

It would appear that Bosnia has been an experiment, not primarily in new forms of international protectorate, but in new frameworks of international co-operation. It has been difficult for Bosnia to bear the brunt of this responsibility; it has not been easy to keep the democratisation process going with very little opposition to international community policy proposals. This is why democratisation has been forced to problematise aspects of political life that could have been resolved between the parties, and why there has been a growing tendency to problematise the Muslim leadership as well as the Croats and Serbs.

The problem faced by the Bosnian people is one that is not of their own making. The democratisation process, through linking democratisation to international institutional mechanisms, has ensured that the international administration will be prolonged for as long as it is in the interests of the major international powers to use Bosnia as a focus for international co-operation. There are always new problems and new institutional involvements. Corruption, for example, became an issue in July 1997 when Robin Cook accused leaders on all sides of a failure to tackle customs irregularities and the black market (Binyon, 1997). This new level of interference in relation to problems hardly unique to Bosnia was justified by Cook in the terminology of democratisation and defending 'the ordinary peoples of Bosnia['s] ... right to accountability' (OHRB, 1997w). Within a month, the international approach to the issue was transformed, the Contact Group found that corruption was pervasive throughout Bosnia and instructed the High Representative to formulate action to be taken in this hitherto neglected area (OHRB, 1997y).

Every international institution, policy analyst and NGO involved in Bosnia, appears to have their own list of additional demands they would like to see fulfilled before international withdrawal. In July 1998, for example, additional demands raised by Hrair Balian, the former Balkan Director of the ICG, included, amongst others, the establishment of a South African-style Truth and Reconciliation Commission, to be established after the Hague Tribunal had finished its work.[1] The prior completion of these two lengthy processes would take Bosnian self-government off the agenda for the foreseeable future. With so many organisations arguing for support for the extension within Bosnia of their pet projects and concerns, unaccountable international bodies are then free to choose which demands, if any, they pursue. This enables US government representatives to force the pace, with leading actors, such as US Special Adviser Robert Gelbard, emphasising the need for European powers to support the US over new demands for action which range from concerns that the Bosnian police be community-based to the ethnic constitution of Bosnian political parties.[2]

The by-product of continually raising new needs for international community co-operation in Bosnia has been to make the small state, as Simon Jenkins (1997) states, 'the world capital of interventionism'. As George Kenney (1997c) points out, the amount of resources going into reconstruction in Bosnia, a third of the total US foreign policy budget, in per capita terms about US $1200 a head, compared to US $3 a head in Africa, is symptomatic of the lack of relationship between resources invested in the state and relative need of the Bosnian people. As some commentators have observed; the powers and authority taken on by the international institutions have been breathtaking. Ted Galen Carpenter, of the Cato Institute, writing in the *Washington Times*, notes:

> US and NATO meddling ... [has] taken the form of actions that make a mockery of any meaningful concept of democracy. Those actions reflect the vision of democracy that advocates of speech codes and other forms of political correctness would love to impose in the United States – if only they had unchal-

lenged power. The Bosnian Serb republic has become a laboratory for their experiments in Frankenstinian democracy. (Carpenter, 1997)

This work suggests that the dynamic for democratisation does not stem from a desire to foist a 'politically correct' policy nightmare on the Bosnian people, but that this has, in effect, been the unintended consequence of attempting to build international co-operation around democratisation. Inevitably more and more barriers to international withdrawal have been flagged-up and in the process Bosnian people and politicians portrayed in an increasingly unflattering light. The extension of democratisation has necessitated the continual postponement of self-government. The postponements of the municipal elections, the extension of EU control in Mostar, the two-year 'consolidation period' and its indefinite extension, and extensions to direct international administration over Brcko, have all been legitimated on the basis that international management is the best method of democratisation. The expansion of the democratic preconditions necessary before Bosnian institutions can be democratically accountable to the citizens of Bosnia has developed with a speed and confidence that has left little room for discussion.

CONCLUSION

Bosnia has become a parody of democratisation because international action in Bosnia appears to be geared towards the democratisation process as opposed to democracy. The process would seem to be the primary concern of international actors and the outcome largely secondary. As one leading democratisation theorist expressed: 'Paradoxically enough, the case for democracy assistance, and in fact for foreign assistance generally, may at times depend less on the specific impact of the assistance on others than on what the assistance says and means about ourselves' (Carothers, 1996, p. 132).

It would appear that democratisation strategy has been determined less by Bosnian problems than by the developing process of international co-operation. The international community has created a new cohering framework whereby states operating through the UN, NATO and OSCE can develop their democratic credentials and moral standing through pledging their allegiance to international US-led policy in Bosnia. The Dayton process has been one of international target-setting in which the coherence and legitimacy of international institutions have had to be constantly affirmed. As soon as the original targets are met new ones have been constantly placed on the agenda as new mission statements for these institutions. This is why the UN High Representative's office has constantly expanded its powers at the expense of Bosnian self-government, NATO have been compelled to play a civilian role and the OSCE have acquired unique powers to ratify elections on the basis of post-election policy-making.

9 Conclusion

This analysis of the strategy of externally imposed democratisation in Bosnia indicates that the claims made for the democratisation process are not as compelling as they would appear from mainstream academic and journalistic assessments of the Dayton process. This work concludes that the international consensus behind the current democratisation strategy in Bosnia cannot be explained by analysis of its impact on the ground in Bosnia itself. Instead, it is suggested that the drive behind democratisation can be located in the needs of international institutional actors for new forms of co-operation and new ways of legitimating their international regulatory role.

The democratisation process in Bosnia has been central to the reshaping of international institutions in the post-Cold War period. The international consensus that developed through the Bosnian war tied European and US interests together and reshaped international co-operation under US leadership through the NATO alliance. NATO has also been the key institution for reintegrating the former Soviet bloc states into the international community. Bosnia was not just NATO's defining post-Cold War success, but also remains a central focus for cohering the alliance. It would appear that for this reason the international community has been reluctant to see the process of engagement come to an end.

Democratisation provides the perfect form for this ongoing process of international co-operation because there is no fixed end-point. This is due to the circular nature of the democratisation approach itself which tends towards the problematisation of recipients of democratisation assistance, making self-government increasingly less likely. Critics of the consequence of this process, international entanglement in the affairs of other countries with no 'exit strategy', have inadvertently reinforced it by stressing the problems as due to the inevitable nature of Bosnian culture rather than analysing the impact of external regulation itself. This has reinforced the pre-existing attractiveness of external democratisation to international institutions as a 'win-win' strategy. If external regulation is not successful this is merely evidence of the deep-seated nature of the problems.

The fact that democratisation is driven by external needs tells us little about the impact of the process itself. The previous chapters have demonstrated that there is little question that, in the case of Bosnia, democratisation has undermined autonomy and self-government on the assumption that external assistance is necessary for building an alternative that will more effectively bridge segmented political divisions. The case for this assumption about the effectiveness of third-party mediation appears to be unsubstantiated from the experience of democratisation in Bosnia. The findings in this respect differ little from those of Carothers (1996) in his analysis of democratisation programmes in Romania. As Carothers notes, the limited success of democratisation practice was met with the near universal response from international democratisers that 'at least we're not doing any harm' (1996, p. 94). Carothers' study challenged this assumption, and was highly critical of 'top-down' externally imposed democratisation, on the basis that third-party intervention in the political process tended to fragment rather than unite the political elite. Western sponsorship of a pliant section of the Romanian elite created dependency relations in this group while excluding other sections of the elite. This worked against the possibility of negotiated solutions because favoured parties were encouraged not to compromise while excluded ones retreated into a 'siege mentality' (1996, p. 94).

The results of democratisation in Bosnia, where interference has been more direct and had a much greater impact, would appear to be more divisive. As has been demonstrated, through the consideration of international policy-making powers and their application in the spheres of human rights, multi-ethnic administrations, and election and media regulation, in Chapters 2, 3, 4, and 5, negotiation and compromise solutions between the Bosnian elites have been virtually precluded from the outset by the imposition of a finalised external policy agenda. This, in effect, has made the elected representatives superfluous to policy development and implementation. Instead of strengthening the central institutions of the new state, and facilitating compromise and negotiation, the democratisation process has removed policy-making capacity from both the state and the entities. The First Councillor to the Bosnian President Izetbegovic, Mirza Hajric, has astutely noted the contradiction between strengthening the cohering institutions and the High Representative's post-Bonn role in enacting policy blocked by the parties: 'A protectorate is not good, because the international community would bring all the decisions which would decrease all the functions of Bosnia-Herzegovina institutions. The High Representative's mandate is, actually, an opposite one, to strengthen the Bosnia-Herzegovina institutions' (OHR BiH, 1997).

The frailty of Bosnian institutions has perpetuated the fragmentation of political power and reliance on personal and local networks of support which were prevalent during the Bosnian war. Both Susan Woodward and Katherine Verdery provide useful analyses of the impact on Bosnian society of the external undermining of state and entity centres of political power and security (Woodward, 1995, pp. 236–7; Verdery, 1996, pp. 82–3). The lack of cohering political structures has meant that Bosnian people are forced to rely on more narrow and parochial survival mechanisms, which has meant that ethnicity has maintained its wartime relevance as a political resource.

It would appear that the removal of mechanisms of political accountability has done little to broaden Bosnian people's political outlook. The removal of sites and relations of political power has in fact reinforced general insecurity and atomisation which has in turn led to the institutionalisation of this narrowing of the political sphere as security is sought in more individual links to those with influence and power. This narrowing of the political sphere and search for individual survival strategies assumes a generalised pattern across society. The 'new feudalism', acutely observed by Stubbs and Deacon, and the continued existence of weak para-state structures in Muslim and Croat areas of the Federation are symptomatic of the vacuum of integrative institutional power at state and entity level rather than some disintegrative dynamic (PIC, 1997c; Deacon and Stubbs, 1998).

The overwhelming concern for Bosnian people is security, the two entities and the state itself have been established on very weak foundations and there is little guarantee that current arrangements, as they stand, will last past international withdrawal. The lack of political security has, in effect, guaranteed continuing support for the three main nationalist parties despite disillusionment with their leaderships. As the International Crisis Group note, the lack of security has meant that in elections 'Bosnians vote for candidates and parties which promise the most robust defence against the perceived threat of the communities to which they do not belong, that is for their own ethnically-based parties' (ICG, 1998a, p. 2). Fear of losing out in future developments over which people have little control has discouraged refugee return and perpetuated a similar 'siege mentality' of disempowerment to that noted by Carothers in Romania.

There is little disagreement that concerns about a lack of security have been central to Bosnian life since Dayton (see, for example, OHRB, 1997r). This book suggests that international democratisation strategy has done little to alleviate these concerns. As former USAF General Charles Boyd has noted in *Foreign Affairs*:

> There is no reason three ethnic sub-states cannot live within the borders of one state, self-governing in all but the few elements of government it is in everyone's interest to have handled centrally. But that can only happen if all parties are convinced they are autonomous, secure, and not disadvantaged relative to the others. Travelling around Bosnia today, it is clear that several aspects of Western policy are having the opposite effect. (Boyd, 1998, p. 46)

The dynamic of the Dayton process has been to institutionalise fears and insecurities through disempowering Bosnian people and their representatives. The logic of democratisation, that power cannot be given to Bosnian institutions until there is greater political security, has led to a vicious circle. It is suggested here that this is a problem of the international community's own making and that this circle could be broken by allowing greater levels of political autonomy – more democracy. By allowing more independent decision-making power for Bosnian institutions at both state and entity level, there would be less dependency on the international community and less concern over international withdrawal.

Support for greater autonomy for regional minorities within Bosnia should not be seen as cohering support for the nationalist parties or their programmes nor as giving up on a united Bosnian state. As many actors in the region and commentators have argued, the fragmentation of Yugoslavia made little sense in terms of the realities of trade and economic development (Bildt, 1996e; ICoB, 1996, pp. 140–2). It makes even less sense for the tiny and economically struggling Bosnian state to fragment into two or three mini-states or para-states.

As Susan Woodward notes, the economy of Bosnia does not segment ethnically (1996a). The economy of Banja Luka relies heavily on the ability to trade with Croatia. Tuzla cannot prosper without its road and rail network and markets in Serb-held areas and Serbia proper. The economy of Bihac equally relies on alliances between Muslims, Croats and Serbs and, although politically within Federation control, is dependent on economic links with Croatia and to a certain extent Banja Luka. Pale, the wartime capital of Republika Srpska, relies heavily on Croat-controlled Kiseljak, and Muslim-controlled Gorazde needs its economic links with the surrounding Serb-controlled areas, such as Visegrad. The political divisions between Pale and Banja Luka are at least in part economically driven as business leaders in Banja Luka need open borders and access to markets in the Federation. She concludes:

> ... economic relations and communal survival in Bosnia and Herzegovina require cross-ethnic alliances and freedom of

> movement across its space and to the outside. As in much of Europe, economic regions cross political boundaries, and they both require and engender co-operation. None of the three units of Bosnia as currently constituted are economically viable. (Woodward, 1996a, p. 74)

In fact, as discussed above, the use of economic sanctions and political conditionality for reconstruction aid has contributed to undermining the non-political links which could have been, and still could be, central to cohering Bosnia as an increasingly efficient economic state unit. Leaving the market to its own devices is likely to be more efficient in rebuilding economic bridges between communities than politically conditioned aid, sanctions and the new measures of international regulation through the anti-corruption drive, which combined seem set to further restrict the informal economy (see also Boyd, 1998, pp. 52–3).

The politics of nationalism and ethnic exclusivity are without doubt a limitation on the possibilities of progress in Bosnia, not a solution. The question posed by the situation in Bosnia today is who is best placed to take society beyond the divisions of ethnicity and exclusion. The experience of international democratisation has demonstrated that it is not possible to impose a common bond on the people of Bosnia merely by administrative fiat. As long as Bosnian people have little relationship to decision-making processes, it is unlikely that any broader sense of common interest will emerge. Although it is easy to argue that division and segmentation is not a way forward for the Bosnian people, external attempts to overcome this division appear only to have institutionalised these insecurities. The extended mandates of the international implementation of the Dayton settlement, which have undermined all the main parties, have not created a political basis for a unitary Bosnia, except in so far as it is one artificially imposed by the international community.

There seems to be little indication that democratisation strategies have contributed to developing mechanisms which can facilitate cross-ethnic political cohesion. It seems unlikely that further coercive measures which have been suggested, such as openly declaring a UN protectorate or banning mono-ethnic political parties, can secure greater political stability or more support for the Dayton settlement. This analysis indicates that in imposing an external framework of integration instead of facilitating the autonomous development of political forces, the democratisation strategy prevents the possibility of long-term solutions generated by Bosnian people themselves. As Boyd notes: ‘Once people’s sense of national identity is secured, the appeal of radical nationalist politicians will evaporate and a reasonable politics and economics can emerge’ (Boyd, 1998, p. 53). The marginalisation of the main political parties and attempts to weaken their institutional influence has created political insecurities and tensions from which, as illustrated in the material on alternative non-nationalist parties, civic groups, NGOs and media sources, in Chapters 5 and 6, the cross-ethnic alternatives have lost out. The democratisation strategy has, in fact, run counter to its stated aim of overcoming the insecurities and tensions of the war, encouraging cross-ethnic political, social and economic co-operation, and the creation of active, politically responsible citizens in civil society.

At present, effective political legitimacy in Bosnia, if not effective political power, is exercised over three separate regions under Serb, Muslim and Croat control. This is not a situation that the people in those regions resent, in elections there is consistent support for the dominant nationalist parties. With the mutual insecurities generated under the Dayton conditions, it makes a lot of sense to people to vote for strong nationalist parties. For the Bosnian Croats it is entirely rational to shore up their position in Bosnia through protecting and extending their links to richer, Westward-looking Croatia. The Croatian government currently subsidises the welfare payments and pensions of Bosnian Croats who also have voting rights in Croatia and have been a central bastion of support to Tudjman's HDZ. For the Bosnian Serbs, given little grounds for affinity or allegiance to the new state, the desire for a measure of autonomy stems from a fear of losing out to an alliance of Muslim and Croat interests which would have the backing of Germany and the US. All the Serb parties share a similar outlook in this regard. The Bosnian Muslims naturally want to defend their status and position in the state which they have gained through support from the international community.

The current international policy direction taken under the Dayton framework has demonstrated little power to resolve the political divides in Bosnia. The one solution that has not been advocated by the international community and those who want to regulate Bosnian society, or educate Bosnian people about democracy and co-operation, is that of letting the Bosnian people begin to work out their own way forward. It would appear that organic compromises, which pass responsibility and accountability on to Bosnian actors and thereby could have a greater chance of guaranteeing long-term stability, will only be possible once greater autonomy to negotiate is available.

For some commentators this may seem a step back from the standpoint of unifying Bosnia around central joint institutions (see Johnson, 1997). However, as Susan Woodward has noted:

> A single Bosnia comprised of three national units is a compromise for all three parties that awaits political forces to make it

> one country. This evolutionary process would be comprised of stages, beginning with an end to the uncertainty about political end states and rights of self-determination ... Reassurances to citizens who currently feel that the only protection is with their own national community and who fear that they will be forced to live in a minority position will have to be firmer. But by removing this uncertainty, radical nationalists will also lose influence and non-political processes of integration can begin. (Woodward, 1996a, p. 83)

It is feasible that granting people greater autonomy may be the only way for Bosnians to overcome the divisions on their own terms. Allowing Croat-governed areas of Bosnia to have closer links with Croatia and allowing greater independence for Republika Srpska would take away a lot of the insecurities felt by ordinary Bosnian people. Once the return of refugees and displaced people did not implicitly question the borders and political allegiances of the regions, then cross-border movement would face fewer obstacles and people would begin to have a real choice about where they wished to live. The support given to the nationalist parties at present stems not so much from the lack of alternatives but the inability of alternative political groups and opinions to gain a broader hearing when the dominant concern is for the security of the entity itself and the jobs and homes that are dependent on a secure political settlement. With greater political security through a more accountable and representative framework, opposition parties would no longer be seen as unpatriotic and a threat to peoples' interests. There could then be a much more open debate about the way forward for the entities and Bosnian society more generally.

It may be that as H. L. Mencken once put it, 'the cure for the evils of democracy is more democracy' (cited in Talbott, 1996, p. 61); to which should now be added, 'and less internationally imposed democratisation'.

Afterword: From Dayton to Rambouillet

This book, completed at the beginning of 1999, set out to critique the democratisation process of extended international institutional intervention and the degrading of state sovereignty in the Balkans. It sought to establish three points. First, that this process resurrected the divisive colonial framework of the 'White Man's Burden' in the liberal language of international 'ethical' rights-based foreign policy. Second, that far from contributing to democracy, ethnic-reconciliation or peace-building, this process of external regulation restricted democratic rights and freedoms, cohered ethnic and regional divisions and prevented any lasting solution based on the needs of the people of the region. Third, that the drive towards extended international intervention had less to do with the problems of the region and more to do with the search for legitimacy and policy-coherence on the part of international institutions and leading Western governments.

Little satisfaction can be taken in seeing these points affirmed as the destructive nature of the international democratisation process and the dangers of the interventionist consensus have become increasingly apparent. That a second edition is now required has much to do with the fact that, over the past year, the Balkans have remained at the centre of the international policy agenda. The Kosovo crisis took international intervention in the affairs of a sovereign state to a qualitatively new level in February 1999, with the Rambouillet proposals that the international regulatory framework of the Dayton settlement should be repeated.

The adage of history repeating itself first as tragedy and then as farce has been reversed on this occasion as the international democratisers turned the Bosnian farce into a Kosovan tragedy. Where Dayton was imposed on the exhausted parties at the end of the Bosnian conflict, Rambouillet was imposed on the Federal Republic of Yugoslavia only after a barbarous 78 day NATO bombing campaign which laid waste much of Kosovo and Serbia (Norton-Taylor, 1999). In the Orwellian world of ethical foreign policy we now not only had protectorates for democracy but also cluster bombing for peace as NATO jets carried out 12,000 bombing raids (many on civilian targets) in the cause of justice and ethnic-reconciliation (Norton-Taylor, 2000; Blair, 1999; Chomsky, 1999, pp.150–57).

While Kosovo understandably made the headlines, the international regulators in Bosnia continued to extend their powers at the expense of representative democracy, affirming the dynamic of democratisation identified in the previous chapters. In the following sections, some of the developments in Bosnia will be briefly considered, and then, in more detail, the structures and problems of the international protectorate in Kosovo.

THE BOSNIAN FARCE

The lack of problems facing the international community in managing the Bosnian state was apparent when, as the High Representative noted, 'not even NATO's campaign in Kosovo could stir the Bosnian Serbs into insurrection' (Petritsch, 1999). Despite having no military role to play, NATO's SFOR operation still has no exit strategy but there are plans to reduce the 32,000 troop commitment to 20,000 by April 2000 (BD, 1999d). However, political stability has not led to a liberalisation of external rule; instead the lack of opposition to international meddling has given the High Representative and the international bureaucracy greater confidence to enhance their regulatory powers.

During his two-year term, the High Representative Carlos Westendorp increasingly imposed his will over the elected representatives, imposing over 45 decisions and laws on the country, dealing with everything from the design of banknotes to the establishment of the courts. In May 1999, before leaving office, Westendorp made clear his views on the Bosnian model of externally imposing democracy, arguing that in Kosovo there should be a full international protectorate, adding: 'Yes, this disregards the principles of sovereignty, but so what? This is not the moment for post-colonial sensitivity .... The problems of the region will only be solved when we have introduced a general respect for democracy and the rule of law' (Westendorp, 1999). In order to impose respect for democracy Westendorp removed 16 high-ranking elected officials from their positions, including, in March 1999, the recently elected President of the Serb entity, Republika Srpska (RS), Nikola Poplasen.

High Representative Westendorp was replaced in the summer of 1999 by Austrian career diplomat Wolfgang Petritsch who has been as willing to override Bosnian institutions as his predecessor. Petritsch's big idea is the 'ownership concept', the High

Representative says he plans to 'give the people the feeling that this is their country' by allowing Bosnian leaders more say (Kaminski and Etz, 1999). The problem is that Petritsch has been very choosy about which leaders he feels should have a say, and seems convinced that Bosnian voters are not up to deciding as they are still 'in the middle of a crash course in democratic accountability' (Petritsch, 1999). Petritsch made his position clear, in October 1999, when he prevented the Vice-President of RS, Mirko Sarovic from the SDS, from taking up the vacant Presidential position. After months of internal debate the SRS and SDS accepted Westendorp's dismissal of Nikola Poplasen and negotiations with moderate Serbian political parties had finally produced an agreement to get a functioning Presidency. However, Petritsch felt that 'this would not serve the interests of the RS' and believed that Sarovic and the SDS 'still have a way to go before they can expect the confidence and support of the international community' (OHRR, 1999). This further interference in the workings of the RS Presidency ensured that Republika Srpska would remain dominated by Milorad Dodik's moderate Sloga coalition in the Parliamentary Assembly (BD, 1999a).

In November, High Representative Petritsch outdid Westendorp's high-handedness and sacked twenty-two elected Bosnian officials, including nine mayors, one governor, two ministers, and several parliamentary deputies and other local or regional officials. Most of the dismissed officials, nine Serbs, seven Muslims and six Croats, also held high-ranking positions within the ruling nationalist parties. Bosnian Serb officials included the Banja Luka mayor Djordje Umicevic, the mayor of Gorazde, Slavko Topalovic, and several leaders of Serb-held towns and municipalities in northern and eastern Bosnia. Bosnian Muslim officials included two influential figures from the Muslim ruling Party of Democratic Action (SDA), Mirsad Veladzic, governor of the Bihac canton, and Dzevad Mlaco, SDA parliamentary deputy and former mayor of Bugojno, as well as Kemal Brodilija, mayor of Kakanj, and Jusuf Zahiragic, Sarajevo cantonal justice minister. Several high-ranking and influential party members were dismissed from the Bosnian Croat Democratic Union (HDZ), including Krunoslav Kordic and Pero Pazin, mayors of Capljina and Stolac, and senior officials from municipalities in southern and central Bosnia, like Mostar, Kiseljak and Prozor. According to OHR spokeswoman Alexandra Stiglmayer: 'The dismissed officials are not the officials that Bosnia needs'. Tanya Domi, the OSCE spokeswoman, confirmed this adding that all of the 22 officials had done 'virtually nothing' to implement the Dayton Peace Accord in the past (BCR, 1999c).

For the municipal elections in April 2000 and the state and entity elections set for August 2000, the OSCE has again drawn up new election rules. The rule changes have little to do with bringing Bosnian election law into line with the rest of Europe and much to do with using OSCE powers for short-term instrumental support for moderate parties in the Federation and Republika Srpska. As the International Crisis Group note:

> [It is] obvious that [the] OSCE was not acting as an impartial international referee envisioned by [the] DPA ... [but] actively involved in the international community's efforts to unseat the SDA, HDZ and the Serb nationalist block, most notably the SDS and SRS. (ICG, 1999a, Annex 3.E)

On 4 October High Representative Petritsch, together with OSCE Bosnia Head of Mission Robert Barry, also the Chairman of the Provisional Election Commission (PEC), sent letters to the Serb Radical Party (SRS) and the smaller Serbian Party of the Republika Srpska (SSRS), warning them that if they did not comply with certain requests by 22 October, they would not be allowed to participate in the municipal elections. The requirements for the SRS were the replacement of party president Nikola Poplasen and two other leading party officials, Ognjen Tadic and Mirko Blagojevic, and the re-registration of the party under new leadership with the courts. The SSRS was instructed to remove its president, Predrag Lazarevic. All the leading party representatives were cited for personal obstruction of the Dayton Peace Accords. The parties challenged the OSCE's attempt to remove their chosen leadership and publicly humiliate them, resulting in the OSCE excluding both parties from the April ballot (BD, 1999b; 1999c). The main Bosnian Croat party, the HDZ, is threatened with being banned from competing in Prozor-Rama, Capljina, Stolac, Kiseljak and Mostar-Jugozapad unless they satisfy the OSCE that the officials dismissed by Petritsch in November are playing no political role in the municipalities (BD, 2000b).

The OSCE began the process of dismissing candidates even before the candidate lists were drawn up, penalising the main parties for attempted fraudulent ballot applications for the out-of-country balloting. For example, after fraudulent applications dealt with by the Bosnian Consulate in New York, the OSCE reserved to itself the right to dismiss up to 15 Muslim SDA candidates, but would only decide which individuals were to be excluded once the complete list of SDA candidates had been received (BD, 2000a). When the party lists were in, the OSCE rapidly declared that around one in six of the election candidates would be barred. According to the Head of the Banja Luka

OSCE, Pierce McCorley, 4,000 candidates appeared to have failed to satisfy the updated OSCE regulations which had recently been amended to include new residency requirements under which candidates could not occupy accommodation owned by a refugee or displaced person (OHR SRT, 2000).

After more than four years of democratisation, Bosnia is further away from democracy than at any point since the war. The Bosnian state and entity institutions exist largely on paper, with policy preparation and implementation in the hands of external agencies. Not one single law put to the state Parliamentary Assembly has been drafted and ratified by Bosnian representatives themselves (ICG, 1999a, Annex 4.I). Even the Council of Europe, heavily involved in this process, concludes that: 'Since the High Representative is effectively the supreme legislative and executive authority in the country, this means in the final analysis that Bosnia and Herzegovina is not a democracy' (ESI, 1999).

THE KOSOVAN TRAGEDY

The international Contact Group proposals for the future of Kosovo were initially forwarded at the Paris/Rambouillet talks, in February 1999. The provisions for the United Nations Mission in Kosovo (UNMIK) closely followed those of the Dayton Peace Agreement. As at Dayton, the US policy-advisers instituted a division of powers between military implementation of the peace agreement under NATO authority and civilian implementation under a UN High Representative, with election and media control under the OSCE. Where Dayton initially specified a one year transitional remit for the civilian powers of the High Representative and the OSCE, under the Rambouillet Agreement international institutions had a three year mandate of regulation in the region, prior to a final settlement, regardless of internationally organised elections to be held within nine months (IAP, 1999).

The international community not only assumed overall power over military and police forces but also the final right of decision-making in all civilian areas of government. Media and election rules, the courts and judicial system, economic policy and the constitutional division of powers were all to be regulated by international appointees. The UN High Representative was to be the *de facto* ruler of the province with the power to remove elected representatives, curtail institutions and close down media organisations, with no right of appeal. Rambouillet was a repetition of the Dayton framework, but updated to include the additional powers awarded to the international institutions since November

1995, under the flexible 'spirit of Dayton' interpretations (IAP, 1999, Chapter 5; Chandler, 1999b).

The provisions of Rambouillet clearly demonstrated that international 'state-builders' in the Balkans were, by now, under little pressure to make policy accountable to the people of the region nor to set a clear time-scale or strategic aims for international withdrawal. The liberal consensus of support for greater international powers in the Balkans became even more fervent as columnists encouraged the extension of NATO war-aims in Kosovo. The *Guardian* boasted that 'we argued from the start ... for a land war to capture Kosovo and turn it into an international protectorate' and its sister paper, the *Observer*, asserted that 'the only viable course is to use the Bosnian precedent and establish a NATO protectorate in Kosovo' (*Guardian*, 1999; *Observer*, 1999).

The Rambouillet Agreement was a detailed 83-page document, drawn up by the US State Department and presented to the KLA and the Yugoslav government, but it was never formally agreed to or signed. UN Security Council Resolution 1244, adopted on 10

Military implementation	*Civilian implementation*
NATO	UN Security Council
KFOR Chief of Staff	UN High Representative
	Deputy High Representative
	Executive Committee:
	UN – Civilian Administration
	UNHCR – Humanitarian Assistance
	OSCE – Democratisation
	European Union – Reconstruction
	UNMIK Administration:
Five regional sectors	*Five regional centres*
North – French	Mitrovica
West – Italian	Pec
South – German	Prizen
Central – British	Pristina
East – American	Gnjilane

Figure 1: The Kosovo Power Structure

June, established a UN mandate to impose 'substantial autonomy and meaningful self-administration of Kosovo' while respecting the 'sovereignty and integrity' of the Federal Republic of Yugoslavia. However, this resolution merely accepted the 'general principles on a political solution' adopted by the G-8 summit of Foreign Ministers on 6 May 1999, and the Belgrade Agreement of 2 June, which both in turn took the Rambouillet accords into account (UN, 1999a). Two days later UN Secretary-General Kofi Annan presented a report to the Security Council outlining the structure of the international administration under the 'four pillar' plan. Under the High Representative, the civil administration would be allocated to the United Nations, humanitarian assistance to the Office of the UN High Commissioner for Refugees, democratisation and institution-building to the OSCE and economic reconstruction to the European Union (UN, 1999b). On 12 July a further, more comprehensive, report on the UN Mission was presented by the Secretary-General to the Security Council (UN, 1999c). It is this 12 July report that establishes the authority and competencies of UNMIK, not the Rambouillet Agreement. The governing responsibilities are mapped in Figure 1.

Events since NATO troops entered the province suggest that the sweeping powers awarded to international agencies have undermined the two pillars of stability on which the administration was to be based, respecting Yugoslav sovereignty while also providing substantial autonomy for the, predominantly ethnic-Albanian, people of Kosovo.

RESPECTING YUGOSLAV SOVEREIGNTY?

It is estimated that some 180,000 Serbs of a pre-war population of 200,000 have left Kosovo, during and since the war, 10 per cent of the population. Barely 1,000 remain in Pristina, so few that NATO troops have resources to provide 24-hour guards, 'granny patrols', for remaining Serbs, mainly the poor and elderly. The majority of the Serbs who have stayed on have been displaced to Serb-majority areas in the north of Kosovo (Gall, 1999; Steele, 1999b). The high-profile attacks and kidnappings of Kosovo Serbs and destruction of religious sites, homes and property, were hardly surprising given the desire for revenge after the war and the fact that the Serbs were easy targets once Yugoslav police and army forces were forced to withdraw from the region. This problem was intensified by the fact that few Serbs felt that the NATO forces, which had been bombing them during the war and working in close contact with KLA ground forces, were likely to protect them. The decision not to give non-NATO

Russian forces a zone in the north of Kosovo, which could have given Serbs more confidence in the neutrality of international peace-keeping, seemed to verify these fears.

Security for Kosovo Serbs was to have been attained through the province remaining within the Federal Republic of Yugoslavia (FRY), however, the UN take-over makes FRY sovereignty over Kosovo meaningless and negates any protection Belgrade could provide. There is no longer any independent Serbo-Croat language television or radio in the province, the German Mark has replaced the Yugoslav Dinar, postal links have been cut, the new cellular network will not retain the '38' Yugoslav country code and the legal system is being reshaped without any Serb or FRY input (Prentice, 1999). The Yugoslav government representative in Pristina, Stanimir Vukicecvic, has argued that Yugoslavia's links with Kosovo have been substantially weakened: 'The customs service employs not even one Serb. There is no Yugoslav flag at border crossings ... or any other symbol that would mark the territory of the state' (R. J. Smith, 1999).

As the *Washington Post* revealed in September, 1999, senior US officials seem privately to have dropped their opposition to Kosovo's independence, seeing the province's secession as inevitable with the prioritisation of self-governing democracy above issues of sovereignty (R. J. Smith, 1999). The end of Serb influence in the running of the province was ratified by the UN's decision to expropriate and put under its direct control 'any movable or immovable property, including monies, bank accounts and any property of or registered in the name of the FRY or Republic of Serbia or any of its organs which is in the territory of Kosovo' (UN, 1999c, IV, par. 37). These include the Trepce mine, several large power plants on the outskirts of Pristina and the cellular phone network, all owned by the Yugoslav state (R. J. Smith, 1999). The UN is even proposing to remove the formal trappings of Yugoslav statehood by issuing travel documents as temporary passports. NATO may have 48,000 troops policing Kosovo, and the promise of more international armed police under UN control in the future, but as long as the Serb community and other minorities have no security even high levels of manpower and resources seem unlikely to be able to prevent Kosovo becoming 'ethnically-pure'.

KOSOVAN AUTONOMY?

The UN has justified its rule in Kosovo on the grounds of restoring autonomy to the region, previously denied by the Serbs. However, far from allowing ethnic-Albanians a say in their affairs, the international community has been busy preventing them from taking greater control over local government, media facilities and even service provision (UN, 1999c, III, par. 24). The original aim of allowing autonomy is being put to one side as the UN establishes a vast bureaucratic machinery of regulation. UNMIK regulations have already been issued covering the appointment and removal of judges, banking, licensing, the establishment of a Central Fiscal Authority, run by foreign appointees, and a Kosovo budget (70 per cent of which is funded by donor grants). UNMIK is also issuing birth, marriage and death certificates, as well as licences for small businesses and construction projects and plans to issue identity cards to everyone over 16 using biometric and fingerprinting techniques to verify the integrity of its database (ICG, 1999b; UN, 1999e).

On 2 July 1999, representatives from the G7 powers and eleven other Western states, meeting under UN auspices, decided Bernard Kouchner, the former French Health Minister, was to be the international governor of the 'autonomous' province. No Kosovo citizens or representatives were involved in the selection process. The Executive Committee running the province similarly has no Kosovan involvement, it is made up from UN international appointees who join Kouchner in the capacities of Principal Deputy Special Representative (from the United States) and four Deputy Special Representatives (from France, New Zealand, the Netherlands and the UK) (UN, 1999c, V, par. 47). This committee will be assisted by the Joint Planning Group, again consisting of international UN appointees and senior planning staff from the UNHCR, OSCE and European Union (UN, 1999c, V, par.48).

As illustrated in Figure 1, the international bureaucracy is not just concerned with the top-level co-ordination of executive, legislative and judicial powers. The UN's writ runs through the establishment of international appointees in control of the five administrative regions, with offices in Pristina, Pec, Prizen, Mitrovica and Gnjilane, and continues down to the 29 municipalities where 'UNMIK public administration staff will oversee the implementation of policy directives' and use executive authority, where necessary' (UN, 1999c, III, par. 23 and VI, par. 58).

This vast international bureaucracy leaves very little room for Kosovan autonomy. There will be no elections for Kosovan government representatives for at least a year, and probably much longer, although a compliant 'Transitional Council' is in the process of being hand-picked by Kouchner himself (Rozen, 1999). The council will not vote on UN decision-making and Kouchner's say is final. As Kouchner explained in his opening remarks at the first meeting: 'There will be no voting; it will be the weight of argument that will count. We will work together to reach agreement, but if we fail to do it, I will have to make a decision' (UN, 1999d). The stated aim of the UN is that this talking shop, or 'sounding board for proposed decisions', will 'restore confidence between the communities' and act 'to ensure participation of the people of Kosovo in the decisions and actions of UNMIK' (UN, 1999c, III, par. 20). The UN is clearly in need of a reality check if it believes that seats on the 'sounding board' is all it takes to overcome ethnic tensions, assuage ethnic-Albanian desires for autonomy and Serb needs for greater security.

Kosovo Albanians are becoming increasingly frustrated at discovering that removing Belgrade appointees from positions of influence is not necessarily a step towards greater autonomy or self-rule. In the harsh reality of post-war Kosovo, ethnic-Albanians find it hard to understand why the departure of the Serbian managers and administrators has meant that the UN has taken over, not the ethnic-Albanian managerial teams (Steele, 1999a; 1999c). There have been protests about high-handed international regulation in the legal system, health, education and the media, as Americans and Europeans have taken on the formerly Serb-held positions. For example, Albanian media staff were unhappy that UNMIK unilaterally created Radio Television Kosovo without consulting or involving local journalists (BCR, 2000). They are also concerned that the OSCE Media Board, overseen by Daan Everts and two other OSCE media affairs staff, will restrict criticism of international decision-making, with the raft of regulation planned by the OSCE-run Media Regulatory Commission and Media Monitoring Divisions (BCR, 1999a). At Pristina hospital the UN appointment of a British management team has resulted in ethnic-Albanian doctors organising a parallel system, similar to that used under the old Serb regime (Price, 1999). Kosovan lawyers and people caught up in the law are frustrated by the imposition of UNMIK legal codes, such as 542 new articles of criminal procedure, which have not been translated or disseminated (ICG, 1999b; BCR, 1999b). UNMIK provoked protests over economic management when Kouchner dismissed the manager of Kosovo Telecom, who lobbied for mobile network construction by German company Siemens, willing to provide more income to its Kosovan partners, rather than French company Alcatel favoured by UNMIK (BCR, 2000).

Autonomy for Kosovo under the UN and NATO is increasingly looking no more democratic than life under the Yugoslav regime. KFOR clashes with ethnic Albanian KLA supporters reinforce the comparisons, not only because they indicate that UN rule over the province will have to be enforced against the ethnic-Albanian majority through military and police security actions, but also because they raise similar human rights concerns. The UN has set up a unique legal system where NATO troops in KFOR are the only recognised police force, with the power to arrest people under their own national laws and bring them before panels of UN-appointed judges with law-making powers (Steele, 1999a). Amnesty International have raised concerns over several KFOR incidents including the British contingent's fatal shooting of two celebrating KLA supporters. There is at present, according to Amnesty, no mechanism to ensure that complaints of KFOR human rights violations against the local population are promptly and independently investigated and effectively dealt with in an impartial manner, or for the victims to receive adequate compensation (Amnesty, 1999).

Apart from the direct regulation of NATO, the UN, OSCE and other institutions, there is international interference in every aspect of life and work through the perceived need to re-educate the population as part of the 'bottom-up' democratisation agenda of 'capacity-building'. Nearly every international institution is involved in implementing programmes of training in democratisation, the rule of law and human rights issues, for, among others, judges, prison officers, civil service administrators, the police, political parties, NGOs, medical staff, media officers and local businesses. As one authoritative study notes, the negative responses caused by this patronising programme indicate that the international community 'must work harder to treat Kosovars less like errant children in want of firm parenting and more like self-respecting, accountable citizens' (ICG, 1999b). It is easy to see how the vast international re-education campaign around 'human dignity' training may seem insulting, particularly bearing in mind the international manoeuvring which prevented a political solution to the crisis and the role of the extensive international bombing campaign in undermining community relations and the rule of law (see Chomsky, 1999; Herman and Hammond, 2000).

The destabilising and fragmentary impact of the international protectorate in Kosovo should not be underestimated. The international community's military intervention to force the province's autonomy led to the destruction of much of the economic basis of Kosovan society and caused widespread damage to community-level facilities of the autonomously-run 'parallel system' (UN, 1999c, II, B, par. 10). These locally-run 'parallel' networks, vital for holding society together under Serb rule, have disintegrated under UN pressure and international NGO activity. The economic and social dislocation has been compounded by the UN's exclusion of Kosovan representatives from decision-making bodies, making it impossible for Albanian institutions to regulate and re-cohere society. This process of external 'top-down' regulation has institutionalised a highly fragmented social and political system. At the political level, this is illustrated by faction-fighting and the creation of a plethora of 'alternative governments' as, without the benefit of elections, competing ethnic-Albanian elites scramble for the patronage of the international administration. At the broader level of society itself political exclusion, this time under international rule, has resulted in even narrower social allegiances, like family and clan connections, emerging to fill the vacuum as people seek some form of security.

CONCLUSION

Having more KFOR troops on the ground or giving the UN greater powers is unlikely to reassure Serbs of their future in the province, these measures are equally unlikely to be able to restore law and order or social stability. In fact, the international administration is contributing to the fragmentation of Kosovo society, rather than cohering it, by giving neither Kosovo Serbs nor ethnic-Albanians any stake in the running of the province. The International Crisis Group similarly sees that 'at the core of the international community's failure to deliver is its refusal to take self-governance by the population of Kosovo as the desired end ... looking outside Kosovo for solutions that could be solved locally' (ICG, 1999b). This explains the apparent contradiction between the vast amount of resources being pumped into Kosovo and the lack of success in restoring order. A police force that excludes Albanians and Serbs and is not familiar with the area or the language was never going to be a serious proposition. Law and order breaks down, not when there are not enough enforcers but when there is no legitimate authority. To achieve some form of legitimacy the UN will need to involve those it is allegedly there to help.

The problem is not that KFOR is under-manned; at 48,000 troops, that is more than one for every thirty adults. The difficulty is that the Kosovo Serbs have been given no stake in the province's future, with *de facto* independence from the FRY, while the ethnic-Albanian community have seen their desire for autonomy crushed by the imposition of a new set of even more powerful overlords. The UN's international protectorate breaks the international commitments made to the Yugoslav government and to the Serb and ethnic-Albanian communities of Kosovo. The Kosovo tragedy affirms the lessons of the on-going Bosnian farce, that any lasting solution will need to be one freely chosen by, and accountable to, the people of the region.

David Chandler, Policy Research Institute, Leeds, February 2000.

Notes

Chapter 3

1. Interview by the author with the assistant to James Ross, OSCE Democratisation Branch Governance Co-ordinator, Sarajevo, 13 June 1997.

Chapter 4

1. Interview by the author with Dieter Wolkewitz, OSCE Democratisation Branch Co-ordinator for the Rule of Law, Sarajevo, 13 June 1997.
2. Ibid.
3. By late 1998 the justification for the focus on war crimes had turned full circle. Instead of reconciliation through convicting the guilty few, leading prosecutors argued that 'no matter how well the tribunal does its job, the scope of history is far broader than proving the guilt of a few specific individuals' (Goldstone, 1998). For Judge Richard Goldstone (1998) it was necessary for all members of a 'damaged society' to go through the reconciliation process so they would not 'transmit to future generations the drive for revenge' and to 'burn away the hatred and lies that have been foisted upon them' by 'their nationalist leaders'.
4. After contacting Human Rights Watch, I managed to speak to the 'anonymous' researcher behind the report, who had since left the organisation, to try to verify the source of the crude box-diagram that was alleged to constitute proof of the Doboj SDS having direct links both to Radovan Karadzic and organised crime. It was alleged to be confidential IFOR information but clearly from the poor English was unlikely to be something that IFOR intelligence had produced themselves. From his new office in Sarajevo, the ex-Human Rights Watch researcher was unconvincing in alleging that it was in fact 'written by military intelligence within IFOR' and stressing that verification was impossible because he was sworn to the utmost secrecy and couldn't possibly reveal who had written it or how he came across it (Confidential interview with the author, Leeds/Sarajevo, 10 February 1997).

5. This policy is in contrast to that of the international community in similar situations; for example, the Georgian refugees who fled the civil war in Abkhazia have been instructed by the UN to be integrated into the receiving communities within Georgia, and Georgian officials have been told to stop treating the refugees as a special population (McMahon, 1998).
6. Confidential interview carried out with a UN Development Project officer, Sarajevo, 16 June 1997.

Chapter 5

1. Interview by the author with Betty Dawson, OSCE Press and Public Affairs Officer, Sarajevo, 17 June 1997.
2. This approach of 'guilt by association' reached new extremes in the run-up to the September 1998 state and entity elections when two SDS candidates were removed merely because a supporter held up a portrait of Radovan Karadzic at an election rally and four HDZ candidates were removed in response to television coverage of the elections in a neighbouring state, Croatia (AFP, 1998b; AP, 1998c).
3. The third Assembly elections, in September 1998, confirmed the decline in votes for the SDS, whose supporters had by then been removed from influential positions in government and business. However, the party which gained most from this process was the Serb Radical Party (SRS). The SDS and SRS combined to take a greater share of the Serb vote than the more openly pro-Dayton national parties in the Sloga coalition led by RS President Biljana Plavsic and Prime Minister Milorad Dodik. The moderate coalition, relying on Muslim and Croat support from displaced voters in the Federation, won the Serb seat on the joint-Presidency and, supported by candidates elected from the Federation, was able to form a majority in the RS Assembly, while the SRS and SDS coalition won the RS Presidency (see Tables 5.1 and 5.2).

Table 5.1 Party Composition of the Republika Srpska Assembly (September 1998)

Party		Seats	%
SDS		19	23
Radical Party		11	13
Plavsic's SNS	Sloga coalition parties	12	14
Socialist Party		10	12
Dodik's SNSD		6	7
Others (Serb)		6	7
SDA-led coalition		15	19
Others (Federation)		4	5

Source: OSCE MBH, 1998d.

Table 5.2 President/Vice President of Republika Srpska (September 1998)

Candidates	No of votes
Nikola Poplasen (SDS/SRS coalition)	324,033
Biljana Plavsic (Sloga coalition)	286,914
Zulfo Nisic (Bosniak candidate)	107,037

Source: OSCE MBH, 1998c.

4. Interview by the author with Adrien Marti, OSCE Co-ordinator for Political Party Development, Sarajevo, 14 June 1997.
5. Ibid.

Chapter 6

1. Interview by the author with Jasna Malkoc, the Senior Co-ordinator for Democratisation/NGO Development, Sarajevo, 16 June 1997.
2. Interview by the author with Sabine Freizer, OSCE Democratisation Branch Reporting Officer, Sarajevo, 16 June 1997.
3. Interview by the author with Jasna Malkoc, OSCE Senior Co-ordinator for Democratisation/NGO Development, Sarajevo, 16 June 1997.
4. Ibid.
5. Interview by the author with Mirjana Malic, Helsinki Citizens' Assembly, Sarajevo, 16 June 1997.
6. Interview by the author with Jasna Malkoc, OSCE Senior Co-ordinator for Democratisation/NGO Development, Sarajevo, 16 June 1997.
7. Confidential interviews by the author with OSCE Democratisation Branch Officers, Sarajevo, June 1997.
8. Ibid.
9. Ibid.
10. Interview by the author with Adrien Marti, OSCE Co-ordinator for Political Party Development, Sarajevo, 14 June 1997.
11. Ibid.
12. Interview by the author with Zoran Jorgakieski, OSCE Democratisation Branch Co-ordinator for Dialogue and Reconciliation, Sarajevo, 16 June 1997.
13. Interview by the author with Adrien Marti, OSCE Co-ordinator for Political Party Development, Sarajevo, 14 June 1997.
14. Confidential interview with the author, Sarajevo, 14 June 1997.

15. Interview by the author with Rannveig Rajendram, OSCE Democratisation Branch Youth and Education Co-ordinator, Sarajevo, 14 June 1997.

Chapter 7

1. A similar point about the lack of monitoring of international institutions was forcefully made by Hrair Balian, former Balkan Director of the International Crisis Group, at the Building Bridges panel discussion, Sarajevo Charter international conference at the Riverside Studios, London, 4–5 July 1998.
2. Interview by the author with Siri Rustad, OSCE Deputy to the Head of Mission for Democratisation, Sarajevo, 14 June 1997.
3. Interview by the author with Christian Ahlund, OSCE Director General for Human Rights, Sarajevo, 16 June 1997.
4. Ibid.
5. Ambassador Robert Gelbard, Opening Address, Sarajevo Charter international conference at the Riverside Studios, London, 4–5 July 1998.
6. Interview by the author with Dr Paul Stubbs, Dubrovnik, 12 June 1997.

Chapter 8

1. Comments made at the Building Bridges panel, Sarajevo Charter international conference, Riverside Studios, London, 4–5 July 1998.
2. Comments made at the Inaugural Lecture, Sarajevo Charter international conference, Riverside Studios, London, 4–5 July 1998.

References and Select Bibliography

AFP (1998a) 'Zubak drops Plans for new Bosnian Croat Party', *Agence France Presse*, Sarajevo, 6 June. Posted on Tribunal Watch e-mail newsgroup, 9 June 1998. Available from: <http://listserv.acsu.buffalo.edu/archives/twatch-l.html>.

AFP (1998b) 'Serb Nationalist Candidates Disqualified', *Agence France Presse*, Sarajevo, 1 September. Posted on Tribunal Watch e-mail newsgroup, 2 September 1998. Available from: <http://listserv.acsu.buffalo.edu/archives/twatch-l.html>.

Agger, I. and Mimica, J. (1996) *Psycho-social Assistance to Victims of War: an Evaluation* (European Community Humanitarian Office).

Allison, L. (1994) 'On the Gap between Theories of Democracy and Theories of Democratization', *Democratization*, vol. 1, no. 1, pp. 8–26.

Amnesty (1996) *Bosnia – the International Community's Responsibility to Ensure Human Rights* (Amnesty International Report). Available from: <http://www.io.org/amnesty/ailib/aipub/1996/EUR/46301496.htm>. [Accessed 5 February 1997].

Amnesty (1999) 'Kosovo: Clarification into police functions undertaken by KFOR crucial', *Amnesty International Press Release*, 16 July.

AP (1998a) 'Bosnia's Muslim President condemned a Top US Diplomat', *Associated Press*, Sarajevo, 8 May. Posted on Tribunal Watch e-mail newsgroup, 9 May 1998. Available from: <http://listserv.acsu.buffalo.edu/archives/twatch-l.html>.

AP (1998b) 'NATO holds First Seminar about Democracy in Sarajevo', *Associated Press*, Sarajevo, 2 July. Posted on Tribunal Watch e-mail newsgroup, 2 July 1998. Available from: <http://listserv.acsu.buffalo.edu/archives/twatch-l.html>.

AP (1998c) 'Tension rises in Bosnia after 15 Croat Candidates Banned', *Associated Press*, Sarajevo, 5 September. Posted on Tribunal Watch e-mail newsgroup, 6 Sept 1998. Available from: <http://listserv.acsu.buffalo.edu/archives/twatch-l.html>.

Barratt Brown, M. (1996) *The Yugoslav Tragedy: Lessons for Socialists* (Nottingham: Spokesman).

Bates, S. (1998) 'EU Applicant faces "Five Years in Hell"', *Guardian*, 20 April.

BBC (1998) 'Bosnian Croat Official Criticises Foreign Efforts to Sideline National Parties', *BBC Summary of World Broadcasts*, 20 February. Posted on Tribunal Watch e-mail newsgroup 20 February 1998. Available from: <http://listserv.acsu. buffalo. edu/archives/twatch-l.html>.

BCR (1999a) 'Kosovo Journalists' Suspicion of OSCE Media Controls', *Balkan Crisis Report*, Institute of War & Peace Reporting, No. 72, 6 September.

BCR (1999b) 'Justice Delayed In Kosovo', *Balkan Crisis Report*, Institute Of War & Peace Reporting, No. 96, 25 November.

BCR (1999c) 'Mass Sackings Hope To Kick-Start Bosnian Peace Process', *Balkan Crisis Report*, Institute of War & Peace Reporting, No. 98, 30 November.

BCR (2000) 'Special Report: Chaos and Complexities in Kouchner's Kosovo', *Balkan Crisis Report*, Institute of War & Peace Reporting, No. 107, 14 January.

BD (1999a) 'High Representative Rejects Sarovic As RS President', *Bosnia Daily*, Network Bosnia, Issue 1.16, 4 October.

BD (1999b) 'Petritsch Orders Radicals To Re-Register', *Bosnia Daily*, Network Bosnia, Issue 1.18, 6 October.

BD (1999c) 'Serbian Radical Party Banned From 2000 Municipal Elections', *Bosnia Daily*, Network Bosnia, Issue 1.30, 25 October.

BD (1999d) 'SFOR To Be Reduced By A Third', *Bosnia Daily*, Network Bosnia, Issue 1.36, 2 November.

BD (2000a) 'OSCE Accuses Bosniak Nationalist SDA Of Vote Fraud', *Bosnia Daily*, Network Bosnia, Issue 2.0, 3 January.

BD (2000b) 'HDZ Warned On Sacked Officials', *Bosnia Daily*, Network Bosnia, Issue 2.6, 11 January.

Beissinger, M. R. (1996) 'How Nationalisms Spread: Eastern Europe Adrift the Tides and Cycles of Nationalist Contention', *Social Research*, vol. 63, no. 1, pp. 97–146.

Bildt, C. (1996a) 'The Important Lessons of Bosnia', *Financial Times*, 3 April. Available from: <http://www.ohr.int/articles/a960403a.htm> [Accessed 29 November 1996].

Bildt, C. (1996b) 'Bosnia: don't Delay the Vote', *Washington Post*, 12 June. Available from: <http://www.ohr.int/articles/a960612a.htm> [Accessed 29 November 1996].

Bildt, C. (1996c) 'Extend the Brief on Bosnia', *Financial Times*, 2 August. Available from: <http://www.ohr.int/articles/a960802a.htm> [Accessed 29 November 1996].

Bildt, C. (1996d) Response to Henry Kissinger's Article in the *Washington Post* of 8 September entitled, 'In the Eye of a Hurricane', OHR Article by the High Representative, 14 September. Available from: <http://www.ohr.int/articles/a960914a.htm> [Accessed 29 November 1996].

Bildt, C. (1996e) 'A Regional Plan for the Balkans', *The European*, 24 October. Available from: <http://www.ohr.int/articles/a961024a.htm> [Accessed 29 November 1996].

Binyon, M. (1997) 'Cook warns Bosnia Aid may be Cut Off', *The Times*, 30 July.

Black, I. (1997) 'Cook reads Bosnia Riot Act', *Guardian*, 25 July.

Blair, T. (1999) 'A New Generation Draws the Line', *Newsweek*, April 19.

Blazar, E. (1997) 'Bosnian Seduction', *Washington Times*, 16 October.

Bogdanor, V. (1995) 'Overcoming the Twentieth Century; Democracy and Nationalism in Central and Eastern Europe', *Political Quarterly*, vol. 66, no. 1, pp. 84–97.

Bonner, R. (1997) 'Belgrade and Moscow stall Bosnia Vote desired by US', *New York Times*, 16 October.

Borger, J. (1996) 'Trials and Error for a Bosnian Solution', *Guardian*, 7 September.

Bougarel, X. (1996) 'Bosnia and Herzegovina – State and Communitarianism', in D. A. Dyker and I. Vejvoda (eds), *Yugoslavia and After: a Study in Fragmentation, Despair and Rebirth* (London: Longman) pp. 87–115.

Boyd, C. G. (1995) 'Making Peace with the Guilty: the Truth about Bosnia', *Foreign Affairs*, vol. 74, no. 5, pp. 22–38.

Boyd, C. G. (1998) 'Making Bosnia Work', *Foreign Affairs*, vol. 77, no. 1, pp. 42–55.

Boyle, K. (1995) 'Stock-taking on Human Rights: the World Conference on Human Rights', Vienna 1993, *Political Studies*, no. XLIII, pp. 79–95.

Brown, J. F. (1994) *Hopes and Shadows: Eastern Europe after Communism* (Essex: Longman).

Burg, S. L. (1997) 'Bosnia Herzegovina: a Case of failed Democratization', in K. Dawisha and B. Parrot (eds), *Politics, Power, and the Struggle for Democracy in South-East Europe* (Cambridge: Cambridge University Press) pp. 122–45.

Burgess, A. (1997) *Divided Europe: The New Domination of the East* (London: Pluto Press).

Carothers, T. (1996) *Assessing Democracy Assistance: The Case of Romania* (Washington DC: Carnegie Endowment).

Carothers, T. (1997a) 'Democracy Without Illusions', *Foreign Affairs*, vol. 76, no. 1, pp. 85–99.

Carothers, T. (1997b) 'Democracy Assistance: the Question of Strategy', *Democratization*, vol. 4, no. 3, pp. 109–32.

Carpenter, T. G. (1997) 'Bringing PC "Democracy" back to Bosnia', *Washington Times*, 24 October.

CFWG (1997) 'Meeting Minutes 6 May'. Community Facilitation Working Group. Unpublished document.

Chandler, D. (1997) 'Globalisation and Minority Rights: how Ethical Foreign Policy recreates the East–West Divide', *Labour Focus on Eastern Europe*, no. 58, pp. 15–34.

Chandler, D. (1998a) 'The OSCE and the Internationalisation of National Minority Rights', in K. Cordell (ed.) *Ethnicity and Democratisation in the New Europe* (London: Routledge) pp. 61–73.

Chandler, D. (1998b) 'Democratization in Bosnia: the Limits of Civil Society Building Strategies', *Democratization*, vol. 5, no. 4, pp. 78–102.

Chandler, D. (1999a) 'The Limits of Peace-building: International Regulation and Civil Society Development in Bosnia', *International Peacekeeping*, vol. 6, no. 1, pp. 109–25.

Chandler, D. (1999b) 'The Bosnian Protectorate and the Implications for Kosovo', *New Left Review*, No. 235, May/June, pp. 124–34.

Chandler, D. (2000) 'Western Intervention and the Disintegration of Yugoslavia, 1989–99', in Herman, E. and Hammond, P. (eds) *Degraded Capability: The Media and the Kosovo Crisis* (London: Pluto Press).

Chicago Tribune (1997) 'No more Extensions in Bosnia', *Chicago Tribune*, editorial, 7 November.

Chomsky, N. (1999) *The New Military Humanism: Lessons From Kosovo* (London: Pluto Press).

Chossudovsky, M. (1997) 'Dismantling Former Yugoslavia, Recolonising Bosnia', *Capital & Class*, no. 62, pp. 1–12.

Clinton, W.J. (1998) *Report to the Congress of the United States, 28 July*, released by the White House Office of the Press Secretary, 29 July. Available from: <http://www.pub.white-house.gov/uri...ma.eop.gov.us/1998/7/30/11.text.1> [Accessed 3 August 1998].

Cohen J. L. and Arato, A. (1992) *Civil Society and Political Theory* (Cambridge, MA: MIT Press).

Cohen, L. J. (1995) *Broken Bonds: Yugoslavia's Disintegration and Balkan Politics in Transition* (2nd edn) (Colorado/Oxford: Westview Press).

Cohen, L. J. (1996) 'Bosnia and Herzegovina: Fragile Peace in a Segmented State', *Current History*, March, pp. 103–12.

Coleman, K. (1997) 'Sceptic Serbs doubt the Plavsic Revolution', *Guardian*, 22 November.

Commission on Global Governance (1995) *Our Global Neighbourhood* (Oxford: Oxford University Press).

Cook, R. (1994) 'Bosnia: What Labour would Do', *Guardian*, 10 December.

Council of Europe (1992) *The Final Declaration of the Third Strasbourg Conference on Parliamentary Democracy, Compendium of Documents* (Strasbourg: Council of Europe).

Council of Europe (1995) *Framework Convention for the Protection of National Minorities and Explanatory Report* (Strasbourg: Council of Europe).

Cumming-Bruce, B. (1997) 'Albright bangs the Democracy Drum', *Guardian*, 28 July.

Dahl, R. (1989) *Democracy and its Critics* (New Haven: Yale University Press).

Dahrendorf, R. (1990) *Reflections on the Revolution in Europe: in a letter intended to have been sent to a gentleman in Warsaw, 1990* (London: Chatto & Windus).

Dawisha, K. (1997) 'Democratization and Political Participation: Research Concepts and Methodologies', in K. Dawisha and B. Parrott (eds) *Politics, Power and the Struggle for Democracy in South-East Europe* (Cambridge: Cambridge University Press) pp. 40–65.

Deacon, B. and Stubbs, P. (1998) 'International Actors and Social Policy Development in Bosnia-Herzegovina: Globalism and the "New Feudalism"', *Journal of European Social Policy*, vol. 8, no. 2, pp. 99–115.

Denitch, B. (1996) *Ethnic Nationalism: the Tragic Death of Yugoslavia* (revised edn) (London: University of Minnesota Press).

Dialogue Development (1997) *Survey of Bosnian Civil Society Organisations: Mapping, Characteristics, and Strategy* (Copenhagen: Dialogue Development).

Diamond, L. (1994) 'Rethinking Civil Society: Toward Democratic Consolidation', *Journal of Democracy*, vol. 5, no. 3, pp. 4–17.

Diamond, L., Linz, J. and Lipset, S. M. (eds) (1989) *Democracy in Developing Countries*. (Boulder, CO: Lynne Rienner).

Dinmore, G. (1997) 'Hardline Serbs hit back through Media', *Financial Times*, 23/24 August.

Drodziak, W. (1997) 'Bosnia TV put through NATO's Hoop', *Guardian*, 22 December.

Duffield, M. (1996a) *The Globalisation of Public Policy* (University of Birmingham, Centre for Urban and Regional Studies).

Duffield, M. (1996b) *The Symphony of the Damned* (School of Public Policy Occasional Paper 2, University of Birmingham).

Dyker, D. A. and Vejvoda, I. (1996) *Yugoslavia and After: a Study in Fragmentation, Despair and Rebirth* (London: Longman).

ECMM (1996) *Comprehensive Survey Report on the Political Environment in the Banja Luka Area* (European Community Monitoring Mission, Banja Luka, 27 March).

Economist (1998a) 'Bosnia, the Protectorate', *The Economist* (US Edition), editorial, 14 February.

Economist (1998b) 'Bosnia, Councils of Despair', *The Economist* (US Edition), editorial, 11 April.

ESI (1999) *Reshaping International Priorities In Bosnia And Herzegovina*. Part One: 'Bosnian Power Structures', European Stability Initiative, 14 October. Available from: <http://www.egroups.com/docvault/balkans/papers> [Accessed 7 January 2000].

Fazlic, M. (1998) 'Interview with Deputy High Representative Hanns Schumacher: Unreal Dreams of Separation of the HDZ Hard-Liners', *Vercernje Novine*, 3 March. Translation posted on the Office of the High Representative e-mail service, 3 March 1998.

Ferdinand, P. (1997) 'Nationalism, Community and Democratic Transition in Czechoslovakia and Yugoslavia', in D. Potter, D. Goldblatt, M. Kiloh and P. Lewis (eds) *Democratization* (Cambridge: Polity Press/Open University) pp. 466–89.

Financial Times (1996) 'Bosnian Vote', *Financial Times*, editorial, 16 May.

Fine, K. S. (1996) 'Fragile Stability and Change: Understanding Conflict during the Transitions in East Central Europe', in, A. Chayes and A. H. Chayes (eds) *Preventing Conflict in the Post-Communist World* (Washington: Brookings Institution) pp. 541–81.

Fleishman, J. (1998) 'Despite NATO presence, violence in Bosnia goes on', *Sunday Gazette Mail*, 8 March.

Fukuyama, F. (1995) 'The Primacy of Culture', *Journal of Democracy*, vol. 6, no. 1, pp. 7–14.

Gall, C. (1999) 'UN May Be Forced to Abandon Idea of Multiethnic Kosovo', *New York Times*, 26 August.

Gallagher, T. (1995) 'Democratization in the Balkans: Challenges and Prospects', *Democratization*, vol. 2, no. 3, pp. 337–61.

Gallagher, T. (1997) 'A Culture of Fatalism towards the Balkans: Long-Term Western Attitudes and Approaches', paper presented at the British International Studies Association, 22nd Annual Conference, Leeds, 15–17 December.

Gellner, E. (1994) *Conditions of Liberty: Civil Society and its Rivals* (London: Hamish Hamilton).

GFA (1995) *The General Framework Agreement for Peace in Bosnia and Herzegovina*. Available from: <http://www.ohr.int/gfa/gfa-home.htm> [Accessed 21 May 1998].

Glenny, M. (1996) *The Fall of Yugoslavia* (3rd edn) (London: Penguin).

Goldstone, R. J. (1998) 'Ethnic Reconciliation Needs the Help of a Truth Commission', *International Herald Tribune*, 24 October.

Gow, J. (1998) 'A Region of Eternal Conflict? The Balkans – Semantics and Security', in W. Park and G. W. Rees (eds) *Rethinking Security in Post-Cold War Europe* (London: Longman) pp. 155–72.

Gow, J. and Tilsey, J. (1996) 'The Strategic Imperative for Media Management', in J. Gow et al. (eds) *Bosnia by Television* (London: British Film Institute).

Graham, B. (1998) 'Ruling again delayed on Control of Brcko', *Washington Post*, 13 March.

Guardian (1998) 'No Retreat: Bosnia must keep Dayton rules', *Guardian*, editorial, 16 September.

Guardian (1999) 'A Choice that cannot wait', *Guardian*, editorial, 7 May.

Guerra, S. (1996) 'The Multi-Faceted role of the ODIHR', *OSCE ODIHR Bulletin*, vol. 4, no. 2, pp. 11–21.

Gunther, R. et al. (1996) 'Debate: Democratic Consolidation: O'Donnell's "Illusions": a Rejoinder', *Journal of Democracy*, vol. 7, no. 4, pp. 151–9.

Halliday, F. (1994) *Rethinking International Relations* (London: Macmillan).

Halliday, F. (1995) 'Interpretations of the New World', *Soundings*, no. 1, pp. 209–22.

HCA (1997) *Dayton continued in Bosnia Herzegovina*, vol. 1. (The Hague: Helsinki Citizens' Assembly).

Heath, R. E. (1981) 'Education', in S. Fischer-Galati (ed.) *Eastern Europe in the 1980s* (London: Croom Helm) pp. 225–55.

Hedges, C. (1997) 'Bosnian Vote fails to end Rivalry', *New York Times*, 8 December.

Hedges, C. (1998) 'A Spaniard rules Bosnia with a strong Hand', *New York Times*, 10 April.

Heitmann, M. (1996) 'Wahlen in Bosnien: "Notfalls die Stadt Besetzen"', *Novo*, no. 24, pp. 23–5.

Held, D. (1995) *Democracy and the Global Order: From the Modern State to Cosmopolitan Governance* (Cambridge: Polity Press).

Heraclides, A. (1992) 'The CSCE and Minorities: the Negotiations behind the Commitments, 1972–1992', *Helsinki Monitor*, vol. 3, no. 3, pp. 5–18.

Heraclides, A. (1993) *Helsinki II and its Aftermath: The Making of the CSCE into an International Organization* (London: Pinter Publishers).

Herman, E. and Hammond, P. (eds) (2000) *Degraded Capability: The Media and the Kosovo Crisis* (London: Pluto Press).

Hicks, B. (1992) *Bill Hicks: Relentless*, Columbia Tristar, VHS.

Hirst, P. and Thompson, G. (1996) *Globalization in Question: The International Economy and the Possibilities of Governance* (Cambridge: Polity Press).

Hockstader, L. (1997a) 'Troops Seize Bosnian TV Towers', *Washington Post*, 2 October.

Hockstader, L. (1997b) 'Hard-Line Bosnian Serbs' Power Eroding', *Washington Post*, 8 October.

Hockstader, L. (1998) 'A Bosnian Town in Limbo', *Washington Post*, 16 March.
Holbrooke, R. (1997) 'In Bosnia, Patience', *Washington Post*, 28 September.
Huber, K. J. (1993) 'The CSCE and Ethnic Conflict in the East', *RFE/RL Research Report*, vol. 2, no. 31, pp. 30–6.
Huntington, S. (1991a) *The Third Wave: Democratization in the Late Twentieth Century* (Oklahoma: University of Oklahoma Press).
Huntington, S. (1991b) 'Democracy's Third Wave', *Journal of Democracy*, vol. 2, no. 2, pp. 12–34.
Huntington, S. (1993) 'The Clash of Civilizations?', *Foreign Affairs*, vol. 72, no. 3, pp. 22–49.
Hutchison, K. B. (1997) 'The Bosnia Puzzle needs a new Solution', *New York Times*, 11 September.
Hutton, W. (1995) 'Why Britain must Fight in Bosnia', *Guardian*, 30 August.
HRW (1996a) *Bosnia-Herzegovina: the Continuing Influence of Bosnia's Warlords*, Human Rights Watch/Helsinki Report, vol. 8, no. 17(D), December.
HRW (1996b) *Bosnia-Herzegovina: the Continuing Influence of Bosnia's Warlords. Summary*, Human Rights Watch Publications. Available from: <http://www.hrw.org/summaries/s.bosnia96d.html> [Accessed 19 December 1996].
IAP (1999) *Interim Agreement for Peace and Self-Government in Kosovo*. Available from: <http://www.transnational.org> [Accessed 24 April 1999].
ICG (1996a) *Mostar Elections Political Analysis*, ICG Bosnia Report 12a. 13 July. International Crisis Group. Available from: <http://www.intl-crisis-group.org/projects/bosnia/report/bh12arep.htm> [Accessed 20 December 1996].
ICG (1996b) *Mostar Elections Technical Analysis*, ICG Bosnia Report 12b. 13 July. International Crisis Group. Available from: <http://www.intl-crisis-group.org/projects/bosnia/report/bh12brep.htm> [Accessed 14 January 1997].
ICG (1996c) *Aid and Accountability: Dayton Implementation*, ICG Bosnia Report 17, 24 November. Sarajevo: International Crisis Group.
ICG (1997a) *Media in Bosnia and Herzegovina: How International Support can be more Effective*, ICG Report, 7 March. Sarajevo: International Crisis Group.
ICG (1997b) *Going Nowhere Fast: Refugees and Internally Displaced Persons in Bosnia and Herzegovina*, ICG Report, 30 April. Sarajevo: International Crisis Group.
ICG (1997c) *Beyond Ballot Boxes: Municipal Elections in Bosnia and Herzegovina*, ICG Bosnia Project, 10 September International Crisis Group. Available from: <http://intl-crisis-

group.org/projects/bosnia/report/bh26rep.htm> [Accessed 28 November 1997].

ICG (1997d) *ICG Analysis of 1997 Municipal Election Results*, ICG Bosnia Project Press Release, 14 October International Crisis Group. Available from: <http://intl-crisis-group.org/projects/bosnia/report/bhxxpr10.htm> [Accessed 28 November 1997].

ICG (1997e) *Hollow Promise?: Return of Bosnian Serb Displaced Persons to Drvar, Bosansko Grahov and Glamoc*, ICG Bosnia Project, 15 December International Crisis Group. Available from: <http://www.intl-crisis-group.org/projects/bosnia/report/bh29rep.htm> [Accessed 4 February 1998].

ICG (1998a) *Changing the Logic of Bosnian Politics: ICG Discussion Paper on Electoral Reform*, ICG Bosnia Project, 10 March. Available from: <http://www.intl-crisis-group.org/projects/bosnia/report/bh32rep.htm> [Accessed 1 April 1998].

ICG (1998b) *Working Towards Security within a Political Framework*, International Crisis Group, April. Available from: <http://www.intl-crisis-group.org/projects/bosnia/reports/bhxx17.htm> [Accessed 21 May 1998].

ICG (1998c) *Minority Return or Mass Relocation*, International Crisis Group, 14 May. Available from: <http://www.intl-crisis-group.org/projects/bosnia/reports/bh33rep1.htm> [Accessed 21 May 1998].

ICG (1999a) *Is Dayton Failing?: Bosnia Four Years After The Peace Agreement*. International Crisis Group, 28 October. Available from: <http://www.intl-crisis-group.org/projects/bosnia/reports/bh51repa.htm> [Accessed 14 January 2000].

ICG (1999b) *Starting from Scratch in Kosovo: The Honeymoon is Over*. International Crisis Group, 10 December. Available from: <http://www.intl-crisis-group.org/projects/sbalkans/reports/kos31rep.htm> [Accessed 14 January 2000].

ICoB (1996) *Unfinished Peace: Report of the International Commission on the Balkans* (Washington: Carnegie Endowment for International Peace/Aspen Institute, Berlin).

ICTY (1998) *Outreach Symposium Marks the First Successful Step in Campaign for Better Understanding of the ICTY in the Former Yugoslavia*, Press Release, The Hague, 20 October.

Ignatieff, M. (1998) *The Warrior's Honor: Ethnic War and the Modern Conscience* (London: Chatto & Windus).

Jatras, G. (1997) 'Vilifying the Serbian Scapegoat?', *Washington Times*, 20 July.

Jenkins, S. (1997) 'Ulster of the Balkans: British Troops have been sent on a Mission Impossible in Bosnia', *The Times*, 17 December.

Johnson, A. R. (1997) 'Two Scenarios for Bosnia', *RFE/RL Newsline*, end note, vol. 1, no. 160, II, 14 November. Available from: <http://www.rferl.org/bosnia-report/archives.html>.

Johnstone, D. (1997) 'Selective Justice in The Hague: the War Crimes Tribunal on Former Yugoslavia is a mockery of Evidentiary Rule', *The Nation*, 22 September.

Joksimovich, V. (1997) 'What to do in Bosnia?', *Washington Post*, letters, 13 October.

Kaldor, M. (1997) 'One Year after Dayton', in *Dayton – Continued in Bosnia-Herzegovina* (Vol. 1) (The Hague: Helsinki Citizens' Assembly) pp. 28–30.

Kaldor, M. and Vejvoda, I. (1997) 'Democratization in Central and East European Countries', *International Affairs*, vol. 73, no. 1, pp. 59–82.

Kaminski, M. and Etz, W. (1999) 'Viceroy Petritsch Strives to Make Hobbled Bosnia Into 'Viable State', *Wall Street Journal*, 27 December.

Kaplan, R. D. (1997) 'Was Democracy just a Moment?', *Atlantic Monthly*, December, pp. 55–80.

Kasapovic, M. (1997) 1996 'Parliamentary Elections in Bosnia and Herzegovina', *Electoral Studies*, vol. 16, no. 1, pp. 117–21.

Keane, J. (1988) *Democracy and Civil Society: on the Predicaments of European Socialism, the Prospects of Democracy, and the Problem of Controlling Social and Political Power* (London: Verso).

Kebo, A. (1997) 'Interview with Carlos Westendorp', *Oslobodjenje*, 7 October. Available from: <http://www.ohr.int/press/i971007a.htm> [Accessed 29 May 1998].

Kelly, M. (1998) 'Step by Step, preventing destruction of Bosnia', *International Herald Tribune*, 22 January.

Kenney, G. (1997a) 'Take off the Blinders on Bosnia Policy', *Los Angeles Times*, 5 June.

Kenney, G. (1997b) 'Not solving Bosnia', *Washington Times*, 22 October.

Kenney, G. (1997c) '"New Imperialism" of Bosnia Mission', *The Times*, letters, 20 December.

King, N. Jr. (1998) '"Suits" such as Mr Klein push for an Anthem or a New Flag', *Wall Street Journal*, 26 August.

Kissinger, H. (1997) 'Limits to what the US can do in Bosnia', *Washington Post*, 22 September.

Klein, J. P. (1998a) 'Interview with Jacques Paul Klein', *Reporter Digest*, Banja Luka, no. 20, February. Posted on Tribunal Watch e-mail list 10 February 1998. Available from: <http://listserv.acsu.buffalo.edu/archives/twatch-l.html>.

Klein, J. P. (1998b) 'Interview with Principal Deputy High Representative Jacques Paul Klein', *Vercernji List*, 18 April. Available from: <http://www.ohr.int/press/i980418a.htm> [Accessed 29 May 1998].

Krauthammer, C. (1997) 'Pursue Bosnia's War Criminals? No', *Washington Post*, 12 December.

Kritz, N. J. (1993) 'The CSCE in the New Era', *Journal of Democracy*, vol. 4, no. 3, pp. 17–28.

Kroc, J. (1996) 'Untying Macedonia's Gordian Knot: Preventive Diplomacy in the Southern Balkans', in J. Letterman, W. Demars, P. Gallney and R. Vayryren (eds) *Preventive and Inventive Action in Intrastate Crisis* (Indiana: University of Notre Dame/Institute for International Peace Studies) pp. 258–329.

Krol, M. (1995) 'Where East meets West', *Journal of Democracy*, vol. 6, no. 1, pp. 37–43.

Kupchan, C. A. (1997) 'To prevail in Bosnia keep US Troops there', *Los Angeles Times*, 3 October.

Landcent (1998) *Landcent Joint Press Briefing*, Sarajevo, 8 May. Posted on Tribunal Watch e-mail newsgroup, 14 May 1998. Available from: <http://listserv.acsu.buffalo.edu/archives/twatch-l.html>.

Lange, Y. and Fuller, E. (1996) 'Media in the Trans-Caucasus: the Influence of Politics and Money', *OSCE ODIHR Bulletin*, vol. 4, no. 3, pp. 6–11.

Lewis, A. (1997) 'Abroad at Home', *New York Times*, 29 September.

McFarlane, B. (1988) *Yugoslavia: Politics, Economics and Society* (London: Pinter).

Maclay, M. (1997) 'Television Wars', *Prospect*, November, pp. 30–3.

McMahon, C. (1998) 'Georgia's Refugee problem worsens', *Chicago Tribune*, 27 May.

Maddox, B. (1997) 'Cook delivers Warning on Bosnia', *The Times*, 20 May.

Malcolm, N. (1994) *Bosnia: a Short History* (London: Papermac).

Marchlewski, W. (1997) 'Non-Governmental Organizations in Bosnia and Herzegovina: the Cultural and Political Context of the Present Situation in Bosnia and Herzegovina', in, Dialogue Development, *Survey of Bosnian Civil Society Organisations: Mapping, Characteristics, and Strategy* (Copenhagen: Dialogue Development).

Mayall, M. (1991) 'Non-intervention, Self-determination and the "New World Order"', *International Affairs*, vol. 67, no. 3, pp. 421–9.

Mayall, M. (1994) 'Sovereignty and Self-determination in the New Europe', in H. Miall (ed.) *Minority Rights in Europe: The Scope for a Transnational Regime* (London: Pinter Publishers) pp. 7–13.

Mearsheimer, J. (1997) 'The only Exit from Bosnia', *New York Times*, 7 October.

Mertus, J. (forthcoming) 'Prospects for National Minorities under the Dayton Accords – Lessons from History: the Inter-War Minorities Schemes and the "Yugoslav Nations"', draft chapter for book forthcoming by Kluwer Press on Minority Rights in Europe, edited by S. Wheatley.

Miller, W. L., White, S. and Heywood, P. (1998) *Values and Political Change in Postcommunist Europe* (London: Macmillan).

Mimica, J. (1995) 'Ethnically Mixed Marriages from the Perspective of the Universal Declaration of Human Rights', in I. Agger (ed.) *Mixed Marriages: Voices from a Psycho-Social Workshop held in Zagreb, Croatia* (European Community Humanitarian Office) pp. 19–22.

Morrison, F. L. (1996) 'The Constitution of Bosnia-Herzegovina', *Constitutional Commentary*, vol. 13, pp. 145–57.

Mullerson, R. (1993) 'Minorities in Eastern Europe and the Former USSR: Problems, Tendencies and Protection', *Modern Law Review*, vol. 56, no. 6, pp. 793–811.

Mullerson, R. (1997) *Human Rights Diplomacy* (London: Routledge).

Norton-Taylor, R. (1999) 'Allied Force: The Audit', *Guardian*, 11 June.

Norton-Taylor, R. (2000) 'Nato under fire for choice of targets in Kosovo', *Guardian*, 7 January.

Numanovic, S. (1998) 'Interview with the High Representative', *Dnevni Avaz*, 30 April. Available from: <http://www.ohr.int/press/i980430a.htm> [Accessed 29 May 1998].

NYT (1998) 'Creating professional Bosnian Media', *New York Times*, editorial, 30 April.

O'Connor, M. (1997) 'NATO says it shut Serb Radio to silence Propaganda', *New York Times*, 21 October.

O'Connor, M. (1998a) 'West sees Payoff from backing flexible Leaders in Bosnia', *New York Times*, 24 January.

O'Connor, M. (1998b) 'Decision Deferred on Control of key Bosnian Town', *New York Times*, 16 March.

O'Connor, M. (1998c) 'On local Level, Bosnians are learning to get along', *New York Times*, 4 May.

O'Donnell, G. (1996a) 'Illusions about Consolidation', *Journal of Democracy*, vol. 7, no. 2, pp. 34–51.

O'Donnell, G. (1996b) 'Debate: Democratic Consolidation: Illusions and Conceptual Flaws', *Journal of Democracy*, vol. 7, no. 4, pp. 160–8.

O'Donnell, G., Schmitter, P. C. and Whitehead, L. (eds) (1986) *Transitions from Authoritarian Rule* (Baltimore: Johns Hopkins University Press).

O'Hanlon, M. (1997) 'What to do in Bosnia?', *Washington Post*, letters, 13 October.

Observer (1999) 'There is no alternative to this war', *Observer*, editorial, 28 March.

Offe, C. (1996) *Varieties of Transition: the East European and East German Experience* (Cambridge: Polity Press).

OHRB (1996a) *Office of the High Representative Bulletin*, 1, 6 May. Available from: <http://www.ohr.int/bulletins/b9960506.htm> [Accessed 31 January 1997].

OHRB (1996b) *Office of the High Representative Bulletin*, 2, 13 May. Available from: <http://www.ohr.int/bulletins/b960513.htm> [Accessed 31 January 1997].

OHRB (1996c) *Office of the High Representative Bulletin*, 3, 20 May. Available from: <http://www.ohr.int/bulletins/b960520.htm> [Accessed 31 January 1997].

OHRB (1996d) *Office of the High Representative Bulletin*, 4, 27 May. Available from: <http://www.ohr.int/bulletins/b960527.htm> [Accessed 31 January 1997].

OHRB (1996e) *Office of the High Representative Bulletin*, 5, 4 June. Available from: <http://www.ohr.int/bulletins/b960604.htm> [Accessed 31 January 1997].

OHRB (1996f) *Office of the High Representative Bulletin*, 6, 11 June. Available from: <http://www.ohr.int/bulletins/b960611.htm> [Accessed 31 January 1997].

OHRB (1996g) *Office of the High Representative Bulletin*, 8, 23 June. Available from: <http://www.ohr.int/bulletins/b960623.htm> [Accessed 31 January 1997].

OHRB (1996h) *Office of the High Representative Bulletin*, 9, 5 July. Available from: <http://www.ohr.int/bulletins/b960705.htm> [Accessed 31 January 1997].

OHRB (1996i) *Office of the High Representative Bulletin*, 10, 16 July. Available from: <http://www.ohr.int/bulletins/b960716.htm> [Accessed 31 January 1997].

OHRB (1996j) *Office of the High Representative Bulletin*, 11, 22 July. Available from: <http://www.ohr.int/bulletins/b960722.htm> [Accessed 31 January 1997].

OHRB (1996k) *Office of the High Representative Bulletin*, 12, 29 July. Available from: <http://www.ohr.int/bulletins/b960729.htm> [Accessed 31 January 1997].

OHRB (1996l) *Office of the High Representative Bulletin*, 13, 6 August. Available from: <http://www.ohr.int/bulletins/b960806.htm> [Accessed 31 January 1997].

OHRB (1996m) *Office of the High Representative Bulletin*, 14, 13 August. Available from: <http://www.ohr.int/bulletins/b960813.htm> [Accessed 31 January 1997].

OHRB (1996n) *Office of the High Representative Bulletin*, 15, 20 August. Available from: <http://www.ohr.int/bulletins/b960820.htm> [Accessed 31 January 1997].

OHRB (1996o) *Office of the High Representative Bulletin*, 17, 3 September. Available from: <http://www.ohr.int/bulletins/b960903.htm> [Accessed 31 January 1997].

OHRB (1996p) *Office of the High Representative Bulletin*, 18, 11 September. Available from: <http://www.ohr.int/bulletins/b960911.htm> [Accessed 31 January 1997].

OHRB (1996q) *Office of the High Representative Bulletin*, 19, 29 September. Available from: <http://www.ohr.int/bulletins/b960929.htm> [Accessed 31 January 1997].

OHRB (1996r) *Office of the High Representative Bulletin*, 23, 31 October. Available from: <http://www.ohr.int/bulletins/b961031.htm> [Accessed 31 January 1997].

OHRB (1996s) *Office of the High Representative Bulletin*, 24, 8 November. Available from: <http://www.ohr.int/bulletins/b961108.htm> [Accessed 31 January 1997].

OHRB (1996t) *Office of the High Representative Bulletin*, 25, 15 November. Available from: <http://www.ohr.int/bulletins/b961115.htm> [Accessed 31 January 1997].

OHRB (1996u) *Office of the High Representative Bulletin*, 26, 22 November. Available from: <http://www.ohr.int/bulletins/b961122.htm> [Accessed 31 January 1997].

OHRB (1996v) *Office of the High Representative Bulletin*, 27, 2 December. Available from: <http://www.ohr.int/bulletins/b961202.htm> [Accessed 31 January 1997].

OHRB (1996w) *Office of the High Representative Bulletin*, 28, 9 December. Available from: <http://www.ohr.int/bulletins/b961209.htm> [Accessed 31 January 1997].

OHRB (1996x) *Office of the High Representative Bulletin*, 29, 17 December. Available from: <http://www.ohr.int/bulletins/b961217.htm> [Accessed 31 January 1997].

OHRB (1997a) *Office of the High Representative Bulletin*, 32, 10 January. Available from: <http://www.ohr.int/bulletins/b970110.htm> [Accessed 31 January 1997].

OHRB (1997b) *Office of the High Representative Bulletin*, 33, 17 January. Available from: <http://www.ohr.int/bulletins/b970117.htm> [Accessed 26 March 1997].

OHRB (1997c) *Office of the High Representative Bulletin*, 34, 26 January. Available from: <http://www.ohr.int/bulletins/b970126.htm> [Accessed 31 January 1997].

OHRB (1997d) *Office of the High Representative Bulletin*, 35, 4 February. Available from: <http://www.ohr.int/bulletins/b970204.htm> [Accessed 26 March 1997].

OHRB (1997e) *Office of the High Representative Bulletin*, 36, 11 February. Available from: <http://www.ohr.int/bulletins/b970211.htm.> [Accessed 26 March 1997].

OHRB (1997f) *Office of the High Representative Bulletin*, 37, 18 February. Available from: <http://www.ohr.int/bulletins/b970218.htm> [Accessed 26 March 1997].

OHRB (1997g) *Office of the High Representative Bulletin*, 38, 26 February. Available from: <http://www.ohr.int/bulletins/b970226.htm> [Accessed 26 March 1997].

OHRB (1997h) *Office of the High Representative Bulletin*, 39, 6 March. Available from: <http://www.ohr.int/bulletins/b970306.htm> [Accessed 26 March 1997].

OHRB (1997i) *Office of the High Representative Bulletin*, 40, 13 March. Available from: <http://www.ohr.int/bulletins/b970313.htm> [Accessed 26 March 1997].

OHRB (1997j) *Office of the High Representative Bulletin*, 41, 20 March. Available from: <http://www.ohr.int/bulletins/b970320.htm> [Accessed 26 March 1997].

OHRB (1997k) *Office of the High Representative Bulletin*, 42, 29 March. Available from: <http://www.ohr.int/bulletins/b970329.htm> [Accessed 29 August 1997].

OHRB (1997l) *Office of the High Representative Bulletin*, 44, 18 April. Available from: <http://www.ohr.int/bulletins/b970418.htm> [Accessed 29 August 1997].

OHRB (1997m) *Office of the High Representative Bulletin*, 45, 25 April. Available from: <http://www.ohr.int/bulletins/b970425.htm> [Accessed 19 August 1997].

OHRB (1997n) *Office of the High Representative Bulletin*, 46, 4 May. Available from: <http://www.ohr.int/bulletins/b970504.htm> [Accessed 19 August 1997].

OHRB (1997o) *Office of the High Representative Bulletin*, 47, 10 May. Available from: <http://www.ohr.int/bulletins/b970510.htm> [Accessed 19 August 1997].

OHRB (1997p) *Office of the High Representative Bulletin*, 48, 16 May. Available from: <http://www.ohr.int/bulletins/b970516.htm> [Accessed 19 August 1997].

OHRB (1997q) *Office of the High Representative Bulletin*, 49, 28 May. Available from: <http://www.ohr.int/bulletins/b970528.htm> [Accessed 19 August 1997].

OHRB (1997r) *Office of the High Representative Bulletin*, 50, 4 June. Available from: <http://www.ohr.int/bulletins/b970604.htm> [Accessed 19 August 1997].

OHRB (1997s) *Office of the High Representative Bulletin*, 51, 19 June. Available from: <http://www.ohr.int/bulletins/b970619.htm> [Accessed 19 August 1997].

OHRB (1997t) *Office of the High Representative Bulletin*, 52, 27 June. Available from: <http://www.ohr.int/bulletins/b970627.htm> [Accessed 19 August 1997].

OHRB (1997u) *Office of the High Representative Bulletin*, 54, 15 July. Available from: <http://www.ohr.int/bulletins/b970715.htm> [Accessed 19 August 1997].

OHRB (1997v) *Office of the High Representative Bulletin*, 55, 23 July. Available from: <http://www.ohr.int/bulletins/b970723.htm> [Accessed 19 August 1997].

OHRB (1997w) *Office of the High Representative Bulletin*, 56, 31 July. Available from: <http://www.ohr.int/bulletins/b970731.htm> [Accessed 19 August 1997].

OHRB (1997x) *Office of the High Representative Bulletin*, 57, 8 August. Available from: <http://www.ohr.int/bulletins/b970808.htm> [Accessed 29 August 1997].

OHRB (1997y) *Office of the High Representative Bulletin*, 59, 5 September. Available from: <http://www.ohr.int/bulletins/b970905.htm> [Accessed 6 November 1997].

OHRB (1997z) *Office of the High Representative Bulletin*, 60, 22 September. Available from: <http://www.ohr.int/bulletins/b970922.htm> [Accessed 3 November 1997].

OHRB (1997A) *Office of the High Representative Bulletin*, 61, 1 October. Available from: <http://www.ohr.int/bulletins/b971001.htm> [Accessed 3 November 1997].

OHRB (1997B) *Office of the High Representative Bulletin*, 62, 11 October. Available from: <http://www.ohr.int/bulletins/b971011.htm> [Accessed 3 November 1997].

OHRB (1997C) *Office of the High Representative Bulletin*, 63, 22 October. Available from: <http://www.ohr.int/bulletins/b971022.htm> [Accessed 3 November 1997].

OHRB (1998a) *Office of the High Representative Bulletin*, 65, 6 February. Available from: <http://www.ohr.int/bulletins/b980206> [Accessed 1 April 1998].

OHRB (1998b) *Office of the High Representative Bulletin*, 66, 23 February. Available from: <http://www.ohr.int/bulletins/b980223> [Accessed 1 April 1998].

OHR BiH (1997) *BiH TV News Summary*, 10 November. Office of the High Representative e-mail service.

OHR BiH (1998) *BiH TV News Summary*, 15 July. Office of the High Representative e-mail service.

OHR FBH (1996) *Agreement on the Establishment of the Federation Implementation Council*, Federation Forum Meeting, Washington, 14 May 1996. Office of the High Representative. Available from: <http://www.ohr.int/docu/d960514b.htm> [Accessed 19 August 1997].

OHR FBH (1997a) *Draft Amendment to Constitution of Sarajevo*, Sarajevo, 27 March. Office of the High Representative. Available from: <http://www.ohr.int/docu/d970327d.htm> [Accessed 19 August 1997].

OHR FBH (1997b) *Side Agreement on the Implementation of Sarajevo Protocol*, Sarajevo, 27 March. Office of the High

Representative. Available from: <http://www.ohr.int/docu/d970327b.htm> [Accessed 19 August 1997].

OHRPS (1997) *Press Statement*, Office of the High Representative, 24 December Office of the High Representative e-mail service, posted 24 December 1997.

OHRR (1996a) *Report of the High Representative for Implementation of the Bosnian Peace Agreement to the Secretary-General of the United Nations*, 14 March. Available from: <http://www.ohr.int/reports/r960714a.htm> [Accessed 29 October 1996].

OHRR (1996b) *Report of the High Representative for Implementation of the Bosnian Peace Agreement to the Secretary-General of the United Nations*, 10 July. Available from: <http://www.ohr.int/reports/r960710a.htm> [Accessed 29 October 1996].

OHRR (1996c) *Report of the High Representative for Implementation of the Bosnian Peace Agreement to the Secretary-General of the United Nations*, 1 October. Available from: <http://www.ohr.int/ reports/r961001a.htm> [Accessed 29 October 1996].

OHRR (1996d) *Report of the High Representative for Implementation of the Bosnian Peace Agreement to the Secretary-General of the United Nations*, 10 December. Available from: <http://www.ohr.int/ reports/r961210a.htm> [Accessed 31 January 1997].

OHRR (1997a) *Report of the High Representative for Implementation of the Bosnian Peace Agreement to the Secretary-General of the United Nations*, 14 April. Available from: <http://www.ohr.int/reports/r970416a.htm> [Accessed 12 May 1997].

OHRR (1997b) *Report of the High Representative for Implementation of the Bosnian Peace Agreement to the Secretary-General of the United Nations*, 11 July. Available from: <http://www.ohr.int/reports/r970711a.htm> [Accessed 19 August 1997].

OHRR (1999) *Report by the High Representative for Implementation of the Peace Agreement to the Secretary-General of the United Nations*, 1 November. Available from: <http://www.ohr.int/reports/r991101a.htm> [Accessed 14 January 2000].

OHRS (1997a) *Speech by the High Representative, Carlos Westendorp, to the Peace Implementation Council in Bonn, 9 December*. Office of the High Representative e-mail service, posted 9 December 1997.

OHRS (1997b) *Priority list for the RS Parliament and Government to be implemented in the forthcoming month based on the Dayton Peace Agreement, Annex to the Speech of Dr Hanns Schumacher, 27 December*. Office of the High Representative Speeches. Available from: <http://www.ohr.int/speeches/s971227b.htm> [Accessed 7 January 1998].

OHRS (1997c) *New Year Message by the High Representative, Mr Carlos Westendorp, 31 December*. Office of the High Representative e-mail service, posted 31 December 1997.

OHR SRT (1997a) *SRT Pale News Summary*, 11 August. Office of the High Representative e-mail service.
OHR SRT (1997b) *SRT Banja Luka News Summary*, 27 November. Office of the High Representative e-mail service.
OHR SRT (1997c) *SRT Banja Luka News Summary*, 10 December. Office of the High Representative e-mail service.
OHR SRT (1997d) *SRT Banja Luka News Summary*, 17 December. Office of the High Representative e-mail service.
OHR SRT (1998a) *SRT Banja Luka News Summary*, 5 January. Office of the High Representative e-mail service.
OHR SRT (1998b) *SRT Banja Luka News Summary*, 25 May. Office of the High Representative e-mail service.
OHR SRT (2000) *OHR: Summary Radio-Television Republika Srpska*, 4 January. Office of the High Representative e-mail service.
ONASA (1997) *ONASA Report*, 13 August. Private e-mail posting.
OSCE DB (1997a) *Democratisation Programme: Strategies and Activities for 1997*, OSCE Democratisation Branch, January.
OSCE DB (1997b) Untitled information document, OSCE Democratisation Branch, 26 February.
OSCE DB (1997c) 'Regional Centre Mostar priority and strategy paper: summary, planned activities, Head Office suggestions' (First Draft), unpublished paper. OSCE Democratisation Branch, no date.
OSCE DB (1997d) 'Regional Centre Sokolac priority and strategy paper: summary, planned activities, Head Office suggestions', unpublished paper. OSCE Democratisation Branch, no date.
OSCE DB (1997e) 'Regional Centre Tuzla priority and strategy paper: summary, planned activities, Head Office suggestions', unpublished paper. OSCE Democratisation Branch, no date.
OSCE DB (1997f) *OSCE's Mandate and the Role of NGOs in the Newly Emerging Civil Society of Bosnia and Herzegovina*, OSCE Democratisation Branch, no date.
OSCE DB (1997g) *Major Activities of the Rule of Law Programme*, OSCE Democratisation Branch, no date.
OSCE DB (1997h) *Rule Of Law Analysis Report*, OSCE Democratisation Branch, February.
OSCE DB (1997i) *Rule Of Law Analysis Report*, OSCE Democratisation Branch, March.
OSCE DB (1997j) *Monthly Report*, no. 1, OSCE Democratisation Branch, February.
OSCE DB (1997k) *Monthly Report*, no. 2, OSCE Democratisation Branch, March.
OSCE DB (1997l) *Monthly Report*, no. 3, OSCE Democratisation Branch, April.

OSCE DB (1997m) *Semi-Annual Report*, OSCE Democratisation Branch, no date.

OSCE EASC (1997a) *OSCE Election Appeals Sub-Commission Statement*, 26 May, Case Number ME-049. E-mail communication from OSCE Mission in Bosnia.

OSCE EASC (1997b) *OSCE Election Appeals Sub-Commission Statement*, 26 May, Case Number ME-050. E-mail communication from OSCE Mission in Bosnia.

OSCE EASC (1997c) *OSCE Election Appeals Sub-Commission Statement*, 17 July, Case Number ME–109. E-mail communication from OSCE Mission in Bosnia.

OSCE EASC (1997d) *OSCE Election Appeals Sub-Commission Statement*, 15 Aug, Case Number ME-073A. E-mail communication from OSCE Mission in Bosnia.

OSCE EASC (1998) *OSCE Election Appeals Sub-Commission Judgement*, Case Number IMP–48, 17 April. Available from: <http://www.oscebih.org/imp–48.htm> [Accessed 13 May 1998].

OSCE MBH (1998a) *1997 Election Results National Assembly of Republika Srpska*, OSCE Mission in Bosnia and Herzegovina. Available from: <http://www.oscebih.org/RSresults.htm> [Accessed 3 June 1998].

OSCE MBH (1998b) *Implementation '97*, OSCE Mission in Bosnia. Available from: <http://www.oscebih.org/implmnt.htm> [Accessed 13 May 1998].

OSCE MBH (1998c) *Final Election Results*, OSCE Mission in Bosnia. Available from: <http://www.oscebih.org/elect98res.htm> [Accessed 28 September 1998].

OSCE MBH (1998d) *Bosnia and Herzegovina Seat Allocation*, OSCE Mission in Bosnia. Available from: <http://www.oscebih.org/elect98–seatAll.htm> [Accessed 23 October 1998].

OSCE MDO (1997) *Media Development: Strategies and Activities for 1997*, Sarajevo: OSCE Media Development Office, 12 February.

OSCE ODIHR (1995) *CSCE/OSCE Provisions Concerning Persons Belonging to National Minorities* (Warsaw: Office for Democratic Institutions and Human Rights).

OSCE PEC (1996a) *Bilten*, 1. (Sarajevo: Provisional Election Commission) July.

OSCE PEC (1996b) *Bilten*, 3. (Sarajevo: Provisional Election Commission) October.

OSCE PEC (1997) *1997 Rules And Regulations as amended and recompiled from the 1996 rules*. (Sarajevo: Provisional Election Commission) May.

Owen, D. (1996) *Balkan Odyssey* (London: Indigo).

Park, W. and Rees, G. W. (eds) (1998) *Rethinking Security in Post-Cold War Europe* (London: Longman).

Parrott, B. (1997) 'Perspectives on Postcommunist Democratization', in K. Dawisha and B. Parrott (eds) *Politics, Power and the Struggle for Democracy in South-East Europe* (Cambridge: Cambridge University Press) pp. 1–39.

Pateman, C. (1996) 'Democracy and Democratization', *International Political Science Review*, vol. 17, no. 1, pp. 5–12.

Petras, J. and Vieux, S. (1996) 'Bosnia and the Revival of US Hegemony', *New Left Review*, no. 218, pp. 3–25.

Petritsch, W. (1999) 'The Future of Bosnia Lies with its People', *Wall Street Journal*, 17 September.

Pfaff, W. (1993) 'Invitation To War', *Foreign Affairs*, vol. 72, no. 3, pp. 97–109.

PIC (1995) *Conclusions of the Peace Implementation Conference held at Lancaster House*, London, 8–9 December 1995. Office of the High Representative Document. Available from: <http://www.ohr.int/docu/d951208a.htm> [Accessed 4 February 1997].

PIC (1996a) *Chairman's Conclusions of the Peace Implementation Council. Florence, 13–14 June*. Office of the High Representative. Available from: <http://www.ohr.int/docu/d960613.htm> [Accessed 4 February 1997].

PIC (1996b) *Implementation of the Human Rights Provisions of the Peace Agreement*. Office of the High Representative. Available from: <http://www.hr.int/docu/d960613.htm> [Accessed 4 February 1997].

PIC (1996c) *Conclusions: Guiding Principles of the Civilian Consolidation Plan. Ministerial Meeting of the Peace Implementation Council Steering Board, Paris, 14 November*. Office of the High Representative. Available from: <http://www.ohr.int/docu/d961114b.htm> [Accessed 4 February 1997].

PIC (1996d) *Ministerial Meeting of the Peace Implementation Council Steering Board, Paris, 14 November, Summary of Conclusions*. Office of the High Representative. Available from: <http://www.ohr.int/docu/d961114a.htm> [Accessed 4 February 1997].

PIC (1997a): *Communique: Political Declaration from Ministerial Meeting of the Steering Board of the Peace Implementation Council, Sintra, 30 May*. Office of the High Representative. Available from: <http://www.ohr.int/docu/d970530a.htm> [Accessed 19 August 1997].

PIC (1997b): *Bonn Peace Implementation Conference 1997: 'Bosnia and Herzegovina 1998: Self-Sustaining Structures'*, Bonn, 10 December. Office of the High Representative. Available from:

<http://www.ohr.int/docu/d971210a.htm> [Accessed 12 December 1997].

PIC (1997c) *Summary of Conclusions: Bonn Peace Implementation Conference 1997: 'Bosnia And Herzegovina 1998: Self-Sustaining Structures'*, Bonn, 10 December. Office of the High Representative. Available from: <http://www.ohr.int/docu/d971210b.htm> [Accessed 12 December 1997].

PIC (1998) *Declaration of the Ministerial Meeting of the Steering Board of the Peace Implementation Council, Luxembourg, 9 June.* Office of the High Representative. Available from: <http://www.ohr.int/docu/d980609a.htm> [Accessed 3 August 1998].

Plavsic, B. (1998) Interview: Biljana Plavsic: 'Our People will see the benefits of our Policy', *James Hill's Weekly*, 3 April. Posted on Tribunal Watch e-mail newsgroup, 3 April 1998. Available from: <http://listserv.acsu.buffalo.edu/archives/twatch-l.html>.

Prentice, E. (1999) 'Kosovo links with Belgrade "severed"', *The Times*, 5 July.

Price, N. (1999) 'Judges get to work in Kosovo', *Associated Press*, 3 July.

Pridham, G. and Lewis, P. (1996) 'Introduction', in G. Pridham and P. Lewis (eds) *Stabilising Fragile Democracies: Comparing New Party Systems in Southern and Eastern Europe* (London: Routledge) pp. 1–22.

Pridham, G. and Vanhanen, T. (1994) 'Introduction', in G. Pridham and T. Vanhanen (eds) *Democratization in Eastern Europe: Domestic and International Perspectives* (London: Routledge) pp. 1–14.

Rees, L. (1997) 'The Murderer's Tale', *Guardian*, 7 October.

RFE/RL BR (1997) 'Second Anniversary of the Dayton Agreement', *RFE/RL Bosnia Report*, vol. 1, no. 17, 19 November. Available from: <http://www.rferl.org/bosnia-report/archives.html>.

RFE/RL BR (1998a) 'Ethnic Clashes Rock Bosnia', *RFE/RL Bosnia Report*, vol. 2, no. 17, 29 April. Available from: <http://www.rferl.org/bosnia-report/archives. html>.

RFE/RL BR (1998b) 'Media Warning', *RFE/RL Bosnia Report*, vol. 2, no. 18, 6 May. Available from: <http://www.rferl.org/bosnia-report/archives.html>.

RFE/RL Newsline (1997a) '"Croatian Community of Herceg-Bosna" set up', *RFE/RL Newsline*, vol. 1, no. 38, II, 26 May. Available from: <http://www.rferl.org/newsline/search>.

RFE/RL Newsline (1997b) 'Plavsic wants U.S. help for Bosnian Serb Army', *RFE/RL Newsline*, vol. 1, no. 112, II, 8 September. Available from: <http://www.rferl.org/newsline/search/>.

RFE/RL Newsline (1997c) 'Westendorp threatens "Bye-Bye Mr Krajisnik"', *RFE/RL Newsline*, vol. 1, no. 150, II, 31 October. Available from: <http://www.rferl.org/newsline/search/>.

RFE/RL Newsline (1997d) 'Plavsic wants to join U.S. Military Programme', *RFE/RL Newsline*, vol. 1, no. 158, II, 12 November. Available from: <http://www.rferl.org/newsline/search/>.

RFE/RL Newsline (1997e) 'Muslims want Serbs in U.S. Programme', *RFE/RL Newsline*, vol. 1, no. 160, II, 14 November. Available from: <http://www.rferl.org/newsline/search/>.

RFE/RL Newsline (1997f) 'OSCE criticises Bosnian Serb Vote', *RFE/RL Newsline*, vol. 1, no. 168, II, 26 November. Available from: <http://www.rferl.org/newsline/search/>.

RFE/RL Newsline (1997g) 'Croats, Serbs do not want stronger Mandate', *RFE/RL Newsline*, vol. 1, no. 175, II, 9 December. Available from: <http://www.rferl.org/newsline/search/>.

RFE/RL Newsline (1997h) 'Westendorp imposes Law on Bosnian Citizenship', *RFE/RL Newsline*, vol. 1, no. 181, II, 17 December. Available from: <http://www.rferl.org/newsline/search/>.

RFE/RL Newsline (1997i) 'US President outlines definite Agenda...and gives Warning', *RFE/RL Newsline*, vol. 1, no. 183, II, 19 December. Available from: <http://www.rferl.org/newsline/search/>.

RFE/RL Newsline (1998a) 'Klein backs Plavsic's Prime Minister', *RFE/RL Newsline*, vol. 1, no. 192, II, 9 January. Available from: <http://www.rferl.org/newsline/ search/>.

RFE/RL Newsline (1998b) 'Plavsic says Dodik's Election "Saved" Republika Srpska', *RFE/RL Newsline*, vol. 2, no. 11, II, 19 January. Available from: <http://www.rferl.org/newsline/search/>.

RFE/RL Newsline (1998c) 'Deputy Mayor sacked after Death of Serbian Couple', *RFE/RL Newsline*, vol. 2, no. 75, II, 20 April. Available from: <http://www.rferl.org/newsline/search/>.

RFE/RL Newsline (1998d) 'Bosnian Croat informs Tudjman of Plan to set up Splinter Party', *RFE/RL Newsline*, vol. 2, no. 109, II, 9 June. Available from: <http://www.rferl.org/newsline/search/>.

RFE/RL Newsline (1998e) 'Plavsic says "Spirit of Dayton" biggest threat to Dayton', *RFE/RL Newsline*, vol. 2, no. 137, II, 20 July. Available from: <http://www.rferl.org/newsline/search/>.

RFE/RL Newsline (1998f) 'Albright urges Bosnian Serbs to back Dayton', *RFE/RL Newsline*, vol. 2, no. 167, II, 31 August. Available from: <http://www.rferl.org/newsline/search/>.

RFE/RL Newsline (1998g) 'International Community acts tough with Nationalists', *RFE/RL Newsline*, vol. 2, no. 169, II, 2 September. Available from: <http://www.rferl.org/newsline/search/>.

RFE/RL Newsline (1998h) 'New Bosnian Serb President Takes Office', *RFE/RL Newsline*, vol. 2, no. 214, II, 5 November. Available from: <http://www.rferl.org/newsline/search/>.

Rieff, D. (1995) *Slaughterhouse: Bosnia and the failure of the West* (London: Vintage).

Rodriguez, J. (1998) 'Our Man in Sarajevo', *El Pais*, 29 March. Translation available from: <http://www.ohr.int/articles/a980329a.htm> [Accessed 4 May 1998].

Rogers, M. (1998) 'NATO agrees Plans to extend Bosnian Force', *Jane's Defence Weekly*, vol. 29, no. 19, 13 May, p. 3.

Rose, G. (1998) 'The Exit Strategy Delusion', *Foreign Affairs*, vol. 77, no. 1, pp. 56–67.

Rose, R. (1997) 'Where are Postcommunist Countries Going?', *Journal of Democracy*, vol. 8, no. 3, pp. 92–108.

Rosenthal, A. M. (1997) 'On my Mind; Solution for Bosnia', *New York Times*, 26 September.

Rozen, L. (1999) 'Follow the leader', *Salon*, 2 July.

RRTF (1997a) *Return and Reconstruction Task Force Report*, April, Office of the High Representative. Available from: <http:www.ohr.int/rrtf/r9704.htm> [Accessed 1 April 1998].

RRTF (1997b) *Return and Reconstruction Task Force Report*, July, Office of the High Representative. Available from: <http:www.ohr.int/rrtf/r9707.htm> [Accessed 1 April 1998].

RRTF (1997c) *Return and Reconstruction Task Force Report*, December, Office of the High Representative. Available from: <http:www.ohr.int/rrtf/r9712.htm> [Accessed 1 April 1998].

Rubin, A. P. (1996) 'Dayton, Bosnia and the Limits of the Law', *The National Interest*, no. 46. Private e-mail posting.

SAFAX (1998a) 'Union of Social Democrats – from Inspiration to Failure', *BH Perspective*, 16 February. Sarajevo: Safax Agency. Available from e-mail list: <safax-mp@bih.net.ba>.

SAFAX (1998b) 'Media in Bosnia and Herzegovina: Spreading Democracy', *Media News*, no. 1, 9 March. Sarajevo: Safax Agency. Available from e-mail list: <safax-mp@bih.net.ba>.

SAFAX (1998c) 'What is the MSAG?', *Media News*, no. 1, 9 March. Sarajevo: Safax Agency. Available from e-mail list: <safax-mp@bih.net.ba>.

SAFAX (1998d) 'New Party despite all', *Our Chances*, vol. 2, no. 20, 11 July. Sarajevo: Safax Agency. Available from e-mail list: <safax-mp@bih.net.ba>.

Sammary, C. (1995) *Yugoslavia Dismembered* (New York: Monthly Review Press).

Schedler, A. (1998) 'What is Democratic Consolidation?', *Journal of Democracy*, vol. 9, no. 2, pp. 91–107.

Schmitter, P. C. (1994) 'Dangers and Dilemmas of Democracy', *Journal of Democracy*, vol. 5, no. 2, pp. 57–74.

Schmitter, P.C. and Karl, T. L. (1991) 'What Democracy is ... and is Not', *Journal of Democracy*, vol. 2, no. 3, pp. 4–17.

Schumpeter, J. (1943) *Capitalism, Socialism and Democracy* (London: George Allen and Unwin).

Seligman, A. B. (1992) *The Idea of Civil Society* (New York: Free Press).

Seroka, J. (1988) 'The Interdependence of Institutional Revitalisation and Intra-Party Reform in Yugoslavia', *Soviet Studies*, vol. XL, no. 1, pp. 84–99.

Seroka, J. (1989) 'Economic Stabilization and Communal Politics in Yugoslavia', *Journal of Communist Studies*, vol. 5, no. 2, pp. 125–47.

Shaw, M. (1994) *Global Society and International Relations: Sociological Concepts and Political Perspectives* (Cambridge: Polity Press).

Shenon, P. (1998) 'US and Allies plan to curb Bosnian Propaganda', *New York Times*, 24 April.

Silber, L. (1996) 'Bosnian Serb "War Crime Court": Karadzic Regime comes up with Alternative to the Hague Tribunal', *Financial Times*, 20 June.

Silber, L. and Clark, B. (1996) 'Pressure mounts over Bosnian Poll', *Financial Times*, 14 June.

Silber, L. and Little, A. (1996) *The Death of Yugoslavia* (revised edn) (London: Penguin Books/BBC Books).

Smillie, I. (1996) *Service Delivery or Civil Society?: Non-Governmental Organisations in Bosnia & Herzegovina* (CARE Canada).

Smith, C. (1998) 'Crime and Corruption in Bosnia's Deep South', *Reuters*, 4 March. Posted on Tribunal Watch e-mail list 4 March 1998. Available from: <http://listserv.acsu.buffalo.edu/archives/twatch-l.html>.

Smith, R. J. (1998a) 'Local Government hits Snag in Bosnia: Refusal to share Power with Minorities leads to Boycotts, Violence', *Washington Post*, 29 January.

Smith, R. J. (1998b) 'Bosnia Muslims won't Recall Serbs, Croats: US Official Assails setting of Conditions', *Washington Post*, 4 February.

Smith, R. J. (1999) 'US Officials Expect Kosovo Independence', *Washington Post*, 24 September.

Solana, J. (1997) 'Perspectives on Bosnia: Why NATO must Persevere', *Los Angeles Times*, 16 October.

Sorensen, J. S. (1997) 'Pluralism or Fragmentation', *War Report*, May, pp. 34–5.

Spencer, M. (1998) 'Rethinking Bosnian Democracy', *In These Times*, vol. 22, no. 6, 22 February, p. 10.

Stanton, K. (1993) 'Pitfalls of Intervention: Sovereignty as a Foundation for Human Rights', *Harvard International Review*, vol. 16, no. 1, pp. 14–16.

Steele, J. (1997a) 'Bosnia Polls Supremo prompts Fears', *Guardian*, 13 September.

Steele, J. (1997b) 'An out and out act of Betrayal in Bosnia', *Guardian*, 11 November.

Steele, J. (1999a) 'UN forces fight to make old foes work together', *Guardian*, 1 July.

Steele, J. (1999b) 'Russian troops arrive too late to raise Serb hopes', *Guardian*, 7 July.

Steele, J. (1999c) 'Reversals in workplace leave Albanians on top', *Guardian*, 8 July.

Stoel, M. van der (1994) 'Preventive Diplomacy', *Forum*, Council of Europe, December, pp. 35–7.

Storey, H. (1995) 'Human Rights and the New Europe: Experience and Experiment', *Political Studies*, XLIII, pp. 131–51.

Stubbs, P. (1996) 'Perspectives on NGO Development in Croatia, Slovenia and Bosnia-Herzegovina', in *Background Papers for 'Social Reconstruction and Social Development: An Agenda for Change'*, International Conference, Zagreb, Croatia, 21 May.

Stubbs, P. (1997) *Social Reconstruction and Social Development in Croatia and Slovenia: the role of the NGO sector*, Occasional Papers in Social Studies, no. 7, Leeds Metropolitan University International Social Policy Research Unit.

Suljagic, E. (1998) Interview with Senior Deputy High Representative Hanns Schumacher, *Dani*, 11 April. Available from: <http://www.ohr.int/press/i980411a.htm> [Accessed 29 May 1998].

Szasz, P. (1995a) 'Protecting Human and Minority Rights in Bosnia: A Documentary Survey of International Proposals', *California Western International Law Journal*, vol. 25, no. 2, pp. 237–310.

Szasz, P. (1995b) 'The Quest for a Bosnian Constitution: Legal Aspects of Constitutional Proposals Relating to Bosnia', *Fordham International Law Journal*, vol. 19, pp. 363–407.

Szasz, P. (1996) 'Current Developments: the Protection of Human Rights through the Dayton/Paris Peace Agreement on Bosnia', *American Journal of International Law*, vol. 90, pp. 301–16.

Sztompka, P. (1996) 'Looking Back: the Year 1989 as a Cultural and Civilizational Break', *Communist and Post-Communist Studies*, vol. 29, no. 2, pp. 115–29.

Talbott, S. (1996) 'Democracy and the National Interest', *Foreign Affairs*, vol. 75, no. 6, pp. 47–63.

Talbott, S. (1997) 'Globalization and Diplomacy: A Practitioner's Perspective', *Foreign Policy*, no. 108, pp. 69–83.

Thompson, M. (1992) *A Paper House: the Ending of Yugoslavia* (London: Vintage).

Thompson, M. (1994) *Forging War: the Media in Serbia, Croatia and Bosnia-Herzegovina* (The Bath Press/Article 19).

Thornberry, C. (1996) 'Saving the War Crimes Tribunal', *Foreign Policy*, no. 104, pp. 72–85.

Tocqueville, A. de (1945) *Democracy in America* (New York: Vintage Books).

UKHO (1997) *Rights Brought Home: the Human Rights Bill*, United Kingdom Home Office White Paper. Available from: <http://www.official-documents.co.uk/document/hoffice/rights/rights.htm> [Accessed 7 November 1997].

UN (1992) *An Agenda for Peace: Preventive Diplomacy, Peacemaking and Peace-keeping*, Report of the Secretary-General, 17 June. A/47/277–S/24111. Available from: <http://www.un.org> [Accessed 28 April 1998].

UN (1994) *An Agenda for Development*, Report of the Secretary-General, 6 May. A/48/935. Available from: <http://www.un.org> [Accessed 28 April 1998].

UN (1995a) *Supplement to an Agenda for Peace: Position Paper of the Secretary-General on the Occasion of the Fiftieth Anniversary of the United Nations*, 3 January A/50/60–S/1995/1. Available from: <http://www.un.org/Docs/SG/agsupp.html> [Accessed 24 April 1998].

UN (1995b) *Security Council Unanimously Authorises Multinational Military Implementation Force to Ensure Compliance with Peace Agreement for Bosnia and Herzegovina*, Press Release SC/6143, 15 December. Available from: <http://www.un.org.> [Accessed 24 April 1998].

UN (1996) *Agenda for Democratization: Supplement to Reports on Democratization*, A/51/761, 20 December. Available from: <http://www.un.org.> [Accessed 24 April 1998].

UN (1998) *Press Briefing by High Representative on Bosnia and Herzegovina*, UN Press Briefing, 27 July. Posted on Justwatch e-mail newsgroup, 29 July 1998. Available from: <http://listserv.acsu.buffalo.edu/archives/justwatch-l.html>.

UN (1999a) *Resolution 1244*, 10 June. Available from: <http://www.un.org/Docs/scres/1999/99sc1244.htm> [Accessed 20 July 1999].

UN (1999b) *Report of the Secretary-General Pursuant to Paragraph 10 of Security Council Resolution 1244*, 12 June. Available from: <http://www.un.org/Docs/sc/reports/1999/s1999672.htm> [Accessed 14 January 2000].

UN (1999c) *Report of the Secretary-General on the United Nations Interim Administration Mission in Kosovo*, 12 July. Available from: <http://un.org/Docs/sc/reports/1999/s1999779.htm> [Accessed 20 July 1999].

UN (1999d) *UNMIK Convenes First Meeting of Kosovo Transitional Council*, UN Press Release, 16 July. Available from: <http://www.un.org/peace/kosovo/unmikpr12.htm> [Accessed 20 July 1999].

UN (1999e) *UNMIK: The First Six Months*, December. Available from: <www.un.org/peace/kosovo/pages/six_months/> [Accessed 14 January 2000].

USDoS (1995) *US Leadership and the Balkan Challenge. Deputy Secretary of State Strobe Talbott, remarks at the National Press Club, Washington DC, 9 November*, released by the Office of the Spokesman. US Department of State. Available from: <http://www.state.gov/ www/current/bosnia/bostal2.htm> [Accessed 12 November 1996].

USDoS (1996a) *Prospects of Peace with Justice in Bosnia. Testimony of John Schattuck, Assistant Secretary of State, Bureau of Democracy, Human Rights and Labour before the Committee on International Relations, US House of Representatives, 1 February*, U.S. Department of State. Available from: <http://www.state.gov/www/current/bosnia/feb1_bosnia_justice.html>. [Accessed 12 November 1996].

USDoS (1996b) *Statement by Secretary of State Warren Christopher on the Bosnian Elections*, released by the Office of the Spokesman 18 September. U.S. Department of State. Available from: <http://www.state.gov> [Accessed 2 February 1998].

USDoS (1997) *Bosnia and Herzegovina Country Report on Human Rights Practices for 1996*, released by the Bureau of Democracy, Human Rights, and Labour, 30 January. U.S. Department of State. Available from: <http://www.state.gov/www/issues /human_rights/1996_hrp_report/bosniahe.html> [Accessed 5 February 1997].

USDoS (1998a) *Address to the Pacific Council on International Policy, Ambassador Robert S. Gelbard, Special Representative of the President and Secretary of State for the Implementation of the Dayton Peace Agreement, Los Angeles, California, 27 January*. Available from: <http://www.state.gov/www/policy_r...s/1998/ 980127_gelbard_bosnia.html> [Accessed 21 May 1998].

USDoS (1998b) *Bosnia and Herzegovina Country Report on Human Rights Practices for 1997*, released by the Bureau of

Democracy, Human Rights, and Labour, 30 January. U.S. Department of State. Available from: <http://www.state.gov/www/global/human_rights/1997_hrp_reprt/bosniahe.html> [Accessed 2 February 1998].

USDoS (1998c) *Statement on Bosnia before the House National Security Committee, Secretary of State Madeleine K. Albright, Washington, DC, 18 March*, released by the Office of the Spokesman, U.S. Department of State. Available from: <http://secretary.state.gov/www/statements/1998/980318.html> [Accessed 21 May 1998].

USDoS (1998d) *Testimony before the Senate Foreign Relations Committee, Robert S. Gelbard, Special Representative of the President and Secretary of State for the Implementation of the Dayton Peace Accords, Washington, DC, 6 May*. Available from: <http://www.state.gov/www/policy_remarks/1998/980506_gelbard_sfrc.html> [Accessed 21 May 1998].

Vejvoda, I. (1996) 'By way of Conclusion: to avoid the Extremes of Suffering ...', in D. A. Dyker and I. Vejvoda (eds) *Yugoslavia and After: A Study in Fragmentation, Despair and Rebirth* (London: Longman) pp. 248–63.

Verdery, K. (1996) 'Nationalism, Postsocialism, and Space in Eastern Europe, *Social Research*, vol. 63, no. 1, pp. 77–96.

Vulliamy, E. (1997) 'UK aid to Bosnia under fire', *Guardian*, 24 January.

Walker, M. (1997) 'Summit draws Europe's Big 4', *Guardian*, 10 October.

Walker, M. (1998a) 'Karadzic's Days of Freedom are numbered, says Envoy to Bosnia', *Guardian*, 30 January.

Walker, M. (1998b) 'EU gets tough with Entrants', *Guardian*, 28 March.

Walker, T. (1997a) 'British Troops rescue Karadzic Men from Siege', *The Times*, 10 September.

Walker, T. (1997b) 'Poll gives Serbs chance to come in from Cold', *The Times*, 24 November.

Washington Post (1997) 'Clearing the Bosnian Air', *Washington Post*, editorial, 6 October.

Washington Post (1998) 'The Muslims' Turn', *Washington Post*, editorial, 22 February.

Westendorp, C. (1997a) Interview with Carlos Westendorp, *Slobodna Bosna*, 30 November. Available from: <http://www.ohr.int/press/i971130a.htm> [Accessed 29 May 1998].

Westendorp, C. (1997b) Interview with Carlos Westendorp, *Vercernje Novine*, 31 December. Available from: <http://www.ohr.int/press/i971231a.htm> [Accessed 29 May 1998].

Westendorp, C. (1999) 'Lessons Bosnia Taught Us', *Wall Street Journal*, 19 May.

Wilkinson, T. (1997a) 'Cracking down on stacking the Deck in Bosnia', *Los Angeles Times*, 8 August.

Wilkinson, T. (1997b) 'Trying to extract War from Journalism', *Los Angeles Times*, 26 October.

Wilkinson, T. (1998) 'In a twist, Serbs serve as Model', *Los Angeles Times*, 1 February.

Williams, M. (1996) 'Polling for Partition', *Index on Censorship*, vol. 25, no. 4, pp. 12–17.

Wilson, G. (1998) 'The Dayton Accords reshape Europe', in, International Action Center (ed.) *NATO in the Balkans* (New York: International Action Center) pp. 141–62.

Woodger,W. (1997) 'The Letter of Democracy and the Spirit of Censorship: The West Runs the Media in Bosnia', unpublished document, October.

Woodward, S. L. (1995) *Balkan Tragedy: Chaos and Dissolution after the Cold War* (Washington DC: The Brookings Institution).

Woodward, S. L. (1996a) 'Implementing Peace in Bosnia and Herzegovina: a Post-Dayton Primer and Memorandum of Warning', *Brookings Discussion Papers* (Washington DC: The Brookings Institution) May.

Woodward, S. L. (1996b) 'The West and the International Organisations', in D. A. Dyker and I. Vejvoda (eds) *Yugoslavia and After: A Study in Fragmentation, Despair and Rebirth* (London: Longman) pp. 155–76.

Woodward, S. L. (1998) 'Avoiding another Cyprus or Israel: a Debate about the Future of Bosnia', *The Brookings Review*, vol. 16, no. 1, pp. 45–8.

Woollacott, M. (1996) 'Bosnian's choice: it's Vote or Die', *Guardian*, 14 September.

Woollacott, M. (1997a) 'NATO puts Future on the Line in Bosnia', *Guardian*, 12 July.

Woollacott, M. (1997b) 'There's no Fighting in Bosnia but it's a pretty lousy Peace', *Guardian*, 27 December.

Zakaria, F. (1997) 'The Rise of Illiberal Democracy', *Foreign Affairs*, vol. 76, no. 6, pp. 22–43.

Index